Human Rights in a Changing World

Human Rights
in a Changing World

Antonio Cassese

Temple University Press
Philadelphia

Temple University Press, Philadelphia 19122

Published 1990

Printed in Great Britain

Library of Congress Cataloging-in-Publication Data

Cassese, Antonio.
[Diritti umani nel mondo contemporaneo. English]
Human rights in a changing world/Antonio Cassese.
p. cm.
Translation of: I diritti umani nel mondo contemporaneo.
Includes bibliographical references and index.
ISBN 0–87722–746–2
1. Human rights.   I. Title.
K3240.4.C36813   1990
342′.085—dc20
[342.285]
                 90–42112 CIP

Contents

vi *Contents*

Introduction

There is much talk today of human rights. They are discussed in international organizations such as the UN, in national parliaments, in the press, to emphasize their importance or to denounce governments that disregard them. President Carter regarded the protection of human rights in the world as the fulcrum of international action by the United States. Other countries are less ambitious and more modestly confine themselves to listing promotion of respect for human rights among the pillars of their foreign policy.

Almost every day newspapers are filled with accounts of discrimination, massacres, torture or forced disappearances of political opponents. Horrors and tyranny are certainly not new in human history. The difference is that today there is a new parameter for assessing them: *breach of this or that human right*. This is an indubitable advance. The international community can look anew at what is happening and make judgments that formerly applied only at a national level. It can condemn, denounce or commend. Before 1948, the citizenry of a state might protest at violations committed by the authorities of that state or by a foreign state, using as the standard of evaluation the values of the West, and specifically the constitutions of Western Europe or the United States. For instance, there were protests against Fascist Italy's suppression of freedom of expression and association; against the discrimination against blacks in the United States; against the subjection of native populations in British colonies to inhuman exploitation; and against the Soviet Union where rights and freedoms were being increasingly infringed.

Since 1948 – that is after the adoption of the Universal Declaration of Human Rights – all countries in the world, including those that had not gone through the long historical process of formation of the modern liberal-democratic state, have at their disposal an *international code*, to decide how to conduct themselves and how to judge others. This is a code that not only has the virtue of *universal application*, but also includes valuable principles in areas previously neglected by the constitutions of Western states. Previously, a state was accused of massacring an entire population: today, international norms talk of genocide, using this term with full awareness of its scope. Previously, it could be said that a state was torturing its citizens: today, in addition to torture, international norms forbid any 'inhuman or degrading treatment or punishment'. Previously, all one could do was denounce certain governments for neglecting the interests of their population: today, they can be accused of breaking the international rules providing for the right to food, the right to decent housing, the right to a healthy environment, and so on. Looked at properly, this does not mean merely that new definitions and a new 'labelling' system are available, but something much more important. We now have *parameters for action*, available to states and individuals: the international rules on human rights impose modes of behaviour by requiring governments to act in a certain way, and at the same time legitimize the complaints of individuals if those rights and freedoms are not respected.

The area of human rights protected at world level has become quite broad. Firstly, it includes *civil liberties*. These consist primarily of the 'free space' that every government must guarantee the individual by not interfering in a certain private sphere: the right to life and security, to privacy, to 'family life', to private property; the possibility of expressing one's opinion freely, of practising a religion, of peaceful assembly. Civil liberties also cover the state's obligation to articulate its structures in such a way as to guarantee a minimum of respect for the human person, as well as full justice in cases of abuse: the right not to be subjected to arbitrary measures by governmental authorities, access to justice and the right to a fair trial. The international community further enforces *political rights* (the possibility for the individual to contribute, alone or in association with others, to the life and action of government: the right to associate, to form political parties, to take part in elections, to be elected to the various state offices, and so on). Also recognized at international level are *economic and social rights*. These are entitlements that the individual has *vis-à-vis* the state, in order to obviate social inequalities and economic imbalances, and to limit disadvantages caused by nature, age, and so on. By contrast to the other rights, the state is not bound to meet these entitlements all at once, but may see to them gradually, taking account of the economic and structural problems it has to face. In addition to the rights belonging to individuals, international norms also cover those of *minorities* and of *peoples*. Peoples in particular have, on certain conditions, the fundamental right to self-determination, that is, the right both freely to choose their own international status and to adopt the type of government most suited to popular aspirations.

If, then, every day some state is denouncing violations committed by other countries, if the media lend their support to this denunciation (or more often draw attention to facts and events that have frequently taken place in silence), all this is due *also* to the existence of this broad set of international principles, which function like a kind of decalogue – to be observed, and enforced. All the inhabitants of the world benefit from the same principles, and can voice their protest when they see them violated. Human rights are an ideological and normative 'galaxy' in rapid expansion, with a specific goal: to increase safeguards for the dignity of the person. Human rights represent an ambitious (and in part, perhaps, illusory) attempt to bring rationality into the political institutions and the societies of all states. However, this is not the abstract rationality the dangers of which were brought home to us by T. W. Adorno and M. Horkheimer many years ago, but a rationality tinged with Christian values and with a number of great 'secular' concepts of the Enlightenment tradition, which alone can awaken us from the oppressive nightmare of inhumanity.

This last point deserves some emphasis. It is an important feature of this new ideology, and of the 'teaching' to which it has given rise, that there is a continuity with certain earlier currents of thought. These currents of thought are known to all: the Christian concept of man as a unique, unrepeatable microcosm whose need to be realized in full must be recognized; the principle, likewise proclaimed by Christian doctrine, of the equality of human beings (recall the admirable words of St Paul's epistle to the Galatians: 'There is neither Jew nor Greek, there is neither bond nor free, there is neither male nor female: for ye are all one in Christ Jesus': 3,28); the conception of 'natural rights'; the Enlightenment; pacifism; the ecumenism of the Second Vatican Council (1962–5). The names of the thinkers who did so much to help to free man from the yoke of despotism are equally well known: Locke, Voltaire, Montesquieu, Rousseau, Kant.

The issue of human rights, so important politically and in terms of the ideologies, customs and, above all, civil progress of modern states, is one that has inspired not only politicians, religious organizations, and trade unions, but also private individuals and non-governmental organizations (such as Amnesty International), that strive to secure conformity with the international standards set up to protect those rights. It has also been explored by scholars, but often they only cover one sector. It has been dealt with by constitutional lawyers, international lawyers (often as if it were a field on its own, detached from and unrelated to the broader theme of the evolution of the contemporary international community), political scientists, political and general philosophers. But I feel that each of them has ended acting like the scientist referred to by Anatole France in his autobiography: he recounts how as a boy he visited the *Jardin des Plantes* museum in Paris; approaching a paleontologist for information about a mammoth tooth, he was told that as the tooth was not in one of his glass cases, the man was unable to say anything about it. I believe that it is important to start to take a look at the various 'glass cases' to see whether it is possible to secure a more articulated view than the one supplied by each individual specialist.

This is what I have sought to do in this book. It has deliberately not been conceived as a systematic, ordered exposition of the wide-ranging material. I have consciously chosen an inquiring approach: by taking 'samples' in a few major areas, I have sought to throw light, at least in flashes, on the whole topic.

As for the content, I did not wish to confine myself to the rights of individuals, but have also considered those of peoples, in particular the right not to be the victim of genocide and the right to self-determination.

Let me come to the arrangement of the book. I have tried in the first three chapters to supply some general reference points. I have sought to set the material against its historical background, clarifying the origins of human rights and the reasons for their current importance by examining the birth and impact of the major international text (the 1948 Universal Declaration), while also showing the limits to the claimed 'universality' of those rights.

In the chapters contained in Part II I have considered – once again not systematically but, as it were, transversally – what I feel to be the great scandals of our epoch: genocide, apartheid, the forced disappearance of political opponents, torture, hunger in underdeveloped countries. Occasionally (I am referring in particular to the chapter on hunger) I have chosen to look at an individual but emblematic 'case', rather than deal generally with the whole theme. I have done this both in the hope that this way of approaching the problem may make the account livelier and more interesting, and because through the prism of that 'case' it may be possible to throw light on the whole phenomenon of which it is specific evidence.

The book ends with three chapters where I again take a general look at the underlying issues and seek to erect some signposts within the maze of problems. Is there agreement on how human rights are to be understood and how they are to be realized? What point have we reached in the international protection of those rights, and what directions are states taking now? Are we advancing, albeit gradually, or are we assuaging our consciences with rhetoric while individuals are suffering in prisons, at work, on the streets, in the ghettos, because they are starving, are maltreated, tortured or discriminated against? Above all, what can we, as ordinary citizens of sovereign states, do if we do not wish to remain deaf to the demands of those individuals? These are very serious questions, and hard to answer, but it is necessary for us to consider them.

Finally, I have included two appendices to the book. The first is the Universal Declaration of Human Rights (1948), and the second comprises brief outlines of those international organizations (intergovernmental or private) which seem to me to be among the most active in the field of human rights. I felt that some brief information on their action might be useful for a general picture of how the international organizations that are making the greatest efforts to promote the protection of those rights actually operate.

Though the various chapters are linked and constitute a fabric that I hope is closely woven, I have nevertheless endeavoured to make each of them independent, and readable in itself. I have sought to bear in mind the reader who has only a little time or prefers to concentrate on only one or two themes.

For some time various friends or colleagues have reproached me for often taking off my professorial hat and replacing it with another, that of the popularizer. But how can I do otherwise, since I am now firmly convinced that the standards of behaviour of the international community, however effective in certain areas (for instance, inter-state trade or diplomatic relations) remain much too fragile at several crucial points (in particular on how armed violence is to be limited and how respect for human dignity is to be ensured). In these areas, the lack of international sanctions must be supplemented by other methods of 'enforcement', foremost among them, in my view, public opinion. Obviously I do not mean the hasty, short-memoried opinion formed by newspapers or television – everyone knows the limits of that even if he or she may not have read Habermas – but the opinion shaped by those who ponder, read, discuss, protest, denounce and do not forget. That is the public opinion at which these pages are specifically aimed. In 1904 a great novelist wrote to a friend that what were needed were books that would be 'like an ice-axe for the frozen seas within us'.[1] Without wishing to aim so high, I should be perfectly content if this volume could at least arouse some unease in all those who sit inert in front of the tragic events we live through, bestirring themselves only to 'cultivate their garden'.

In the pages that follow I have endeavoured to take advantage of the experience I have been acquiring since 1967 in the diplomatic and political spheres. The immediate stimulus to taking up these themes came, however, from the need to hold a series of seminars in 1985–6 at the Institut Universitaire de Hautes Etudes Internationales (IUHEI) in Geneva, and in 1987–8 at the European University Institute (EUI) in Florence. I am particularly grateful to the EUI for having given me the chance to complete the necessary research and to write the final version of the book. It would be truly hard to find an institution more favourable to research (as well as to teaching). I dedicate the book to the students and researchers of Geneva and Florence, for the enthusiasm and patience they have shown. As everyone knows who has had the good fortune to teach, speaking to young people eager to understand is always the best way of prodding oneself to look further.

This English edition is largely based on the Italian original text, which however has been extensively revised, updated and improved. The original version was written before the momentous changes that took place in the structure and political outlook of Central and Eastern European countries. These changes are of course having a great deal of impact on the attitude which those countries take towards the philosophy and practice of respect for human rights. It is now too early to assess the scope and dimension of this impact; it is also too early to appraise the extent to which the recent internal upheavals will influence the international attitude of Socialist countries and their approach to international rules and supervisory machinery. Nevertheless, I have endeavoured to take these new developments into account as much as possible, by revising and bringing up to date the relevant parts of the manuscript. I am grateful to Ms J. Greenleaves and Mr I. Fraser for translating a large portion of the Italian text. I am greatly indebted to Ms S. Marks for ably revising the translation from a legal viewpoint and to Mr A. Clapham for efficaciously and painstakingly helping to overhaul, redraft, bring up to date and supplement the English version. Finally I owe a debt of gratitude to Ms E. Zaccardelli, for typing and retyping the text with her usual skill and forbearance.

Part I

A Decalogue for Five Billion Persons

1

The Emergence of Human Rights on to the World Stage

The traditional pattern of the international community

If in order to understand the international situation of the last couple of centuries – let us say from the peace of Westphalia (1648) until the end of the nineteenth century – you open one of those books professing to present that situation in concepts, outlines and general formulas, you will immediately realize that individuals and peoples played no part at all. Take, for instance, some classics of international law: Vattel (Swiss, writing in 1758), or G. F. De Martens (German, writing in 1788) or Wheaton (American, writing in 1836), or A. G. Heffter (also German, writing in 1844). As you peruse their most famous books, you will hardly find any place for bodies other than sovereign, independent states. If occasionally individuals are mentioned, it is only to say that every state is bound to treat citizens of other European countries or of the United States in a civil fashion. There is still less talk of individuals in the work of the great thinkers who studied the political reality of their time: Hobbes, Locke, Spinoza, Montesquieu, Kant, Rousseau. Each of these, though very alert to the function of man within society, when it comes to discussing international relationships concludes – whether bitterly or resignedly – that in this field states alone dominate.

Indeed, between the seventeenth and early twentieth century international relations were essentially relations between government entities, each of them sovereign over a more or less vast territory and over a population living on that territory. There are three chief characteristics of the international community in this period.

Firstly, states live in a state of nature. This is not the one described by Hobbes and Spinoza, that is, the 'state' in which there are no laws or common political institutions dictating conduct to be followed, whereas friction, conflict, and above all war, hold sway with minimum human contact between state communities. In such a system, war has absolute primacy, constituting an essential, indispensable element (to such a point that in 1731 Giambattista Vico, in giving a definition of the 'natural *jus gentium*' wrote that it is the 'law whereby the victors regulate the blind fury of arms and the unrestrained insolence of victory, and the conquered console themselves for the damage of war and the subjection of conquest').[1] The international community constituted a 'state of nature' more in the sense described by Locke: as a condition in which there are laws, albeit few (and reduced to freely concluded agreements, and the right to punish offences caused by others and to demand adequate reparation), while there are no judges, policemen or parliaments (institutions created only with the transition to the 'state of society', within the various state communities). This 'state of nature' can, however, for Locke too, easily degenerate into a 'state of war', in which the laws no longer count and there is no possibility of appointing a judge common to the contending parties, but force alone reigns (or as Locke says, 'enmity, malice, violence and mutual destruction').[2]

In this general setting, particular weight attached to a principle that constituted the necessary consequence of the individualistic relationships among members of this anarchic society: reciprocity. By virtue of this principle, relations among subjects obeyed a rigid logic of *quid pro quo*. This logic permeated all relationships. Rules governing social relations were principally bilateral agreements, or in some cases multilateral ones: all, however, based on mutual benefit for the contracting parties. When the benefit for one party came to be lacking, that party was entitled to mark this change by denouncing the treaty or invoking the famous *clausola rebus sic stantibus* (on the strength of which, should a major change occur in the circumstances on which the agreement was based, it may cease to exist). Reciprocity had implications also for the consequences of breach of the treaty. The injured party could respond to the breach by demanding reparations or imposing a sanction, if it had the political and military capacity. No other state had the power or the right to intervene. The relationship of responsibility was set up only between the one committing the wrongful act and the victim. Even the few general international rules (those on the sea, on diplomatic and consular immunity, on respect for territorial sovereignty) were not created to protect general interests, i.e. interests going beyond the individual parties, but only the interest of each party, or of all parties combined. And any breach of these rules did not give rise to a right in all other legal subjects in order that sanctions might be applied, or the responsible state might be asked to compensate the damage done to the victim. Only the state damaged by the wrongful act (the state prevented from using the high seas, whose territory was violated, or whose diplomatic emissaries had their liberty infringed) could in practice act on the violation. The international community was truly a juxtaposition of subjects, each concerned only with its own well-being and its freedom of manoeuvre, each pursuing only its own economic, political and military interests, each bent more on consolidating and if possible expanding its power and authority than on protecting any general interests.

The third peculiar feature of the international community of this period is that *peoples* and *individuals* do not count. It seems almost as if they do not exist, being absorbed and overshadowed by the 'princes': the sovereign states, the only real actors on the world stage. The peoples are nothing but objects dominated by the various sovereigns. Frequently they pass from one sovereign to another, depending on the fortunes, failures and successes of the various rulers. Individuals are less overshadowed; but only insofar as they constitute emanations of their sovereigns. The citizens of a state who travel abroad to settle, trade, set up industries or simply visit the country, remain under the protection and aegis of the nation state: to it the state of residence has to account if its authorities infringe the foreigners' rights, take away their goods or treat them in an arbitrary fashion. Individuals thus become beneficiaries of a series of international legal standards – those on protection of foreigners – which of course regulate only relationships among sovereign entities, but end up safeguarding interests and the property of citizens of each one of them. These individuals, however, remain, I repeat, mere beneficiaries of those standards: as is shown by the fact that if their rights and interests are injured by a foreign state and their own state decides not to intervene through diplomatic channels or not to start legal proceedings before international arbitrators (set up before the controversy), they can do nothing against their authorities' failure to act. In this case too they remain pawns in the game among the powers, advanced or sacrificed according to momentary whims, or at any rate, the political inclinations of the various sovereigns.

This situation is exactly reflected in the various treatises and textbooks on international law of the period – books used by diplomats and politicians as well as by scholars, judges and professors, which therefore had considerable influence on the thinking of generations of people. In those books (by Vattel, Wheaton, de Martens, Heffter and the others I mentioned earlier), peoples are considered only in order to rule out the possibility of 'savage' (or 'barbarian' or 'semi-barbarian', as others, such as Lorimer,[3] call them) peoples being regarded as subjects of international relations. There is still less mention of the peoples of the various sovereign states, which, for those authors, constitute a whole with the respective governments, in the sense that they disappear behind those governments – even if it is assumed, in rather theoretical terms, that it is for their benefit and advantage that the government authorities carry out their sovereign functions. As for the individuals, they are mentioned only when they become 'aliens', thus within the conditions and limits that I have just mentioned. The only category of individuals that acquires some independent weight is that of pirates, regarded as dangerous enemies of the whole human race and hence liable to the severest penalties from any state in the world. Individuals thus appear in very clear shape (as passive subjects of international law, or holders of international obligations, as Hans Kelsen was to put it in the 1920s, in a formalist concept that poorly respects reality). They appear only as a negative factor, as a manifestation of evil, against which every sovereign can and must fight with all his might. The condition of peoples and individuals in this period was well characterized as long ago as 1937 by the great Italian jurist Roberto Ago, who defined them as 'negative subjects' of the international community[4] – while various other scholars between the 1930s and 1950s were to treat them as 'mere objects' of intergovernmental norms.

The ideologies that began to change things on the international stage

The conditions I have briefly described remained essentially unchanged for several centuries. Only a few marginal modifications were brought about towards the middle of the nineteenth century by the theory of nationalities, passionately advocated by Pasquale Stanislao Mancini.[5] Mancini's conception put the stress on the importance of the various *nations*: human groups united by a common language and culture, common traditions and customs. Mancini saw some European states as governing several nationalities, whereas other nationalities were broken up among several states. Examples were the Austrian Empire on the one hand, and Italy and Germany on the other. He went on to maintain that every sovereign state should contain one nation, and one only, within its boundaries. Accordingly, the nations rather than the states ought to be the real subjects of the international community. Mancini was speaking only for those European nations I have mentioned (the colonial peoples did not count for him, as shown among other things by a speech he gave to the Chamber of Deputies in 1885; for him, non-white peoples were manifestly outside the scope of civilization).[6] This doctrine, which embodied the ideals of the ruling classes of a number of European countries – it is indeed no coincidence that it was taken up by the leading German jurist J. C. Bluntschli[7] – had some following at metalegal level as an ideal of political action. It was to a certain extent due to it that some nation states (Italy, Germany) were formed, and that later, the boundaries of some large states were redrawn at the end of the First World War, so as to take account of the various nationalities. As a scientific doctrine however, it ended in failure, for it sought to mix heterogeneous concepts, and above all, it confused the level of political struggle with the level of scientific enquiry.

The real turn-around came first in 1917, and then in 1945: towards the end of the First World War and after the end of the Second. This was perhaps no coincidence: people need to be shaken up by deep, radical upheavals in order to rethink social structures and patterns of life, to decide to renew the framework of human coexistence, in an effort to adapt to new developments in reality.

Towards the end of the First World War, two great political leaders, Lenin and Wilson, launched a new slogan: the right of peoples to decide their destiny. However the viewpoints of the two statesmen were very different. Lenin proposed to redistribute international power along new lines: by giving the colonial peoples the right to become independent and hence to form states; and by allowing national peoples subject to central authorities belonging to other nationalities to acquire independence. What Lenin advocated was, then, on the one hand the creation of new states on the international scene (the colonial peoples) and on the other, the reshaping of some existing states so as to bring them more into line with the aspirations of peoples. Wilson's view was very different, being moderate and respecting the colonial empires. The President of the United States proposed that existing borders be reconsidered at the end of the First World War, allowing peoples to opt for the sovereignty of their choice. The object was, thus, to create new state structures or redistribute authority within the framework of the existing empires. As for the colonial peoples, Wilson maintained the need to take their aspirations into account by putting them on the same plane as the demands of the colonial powers. In essence, his idea was to grant these peoples forms of self-government – though of course within the framework of existing colonial control.

As we know, at the end of the First World War the principle of self-determination was realized only where the political ideas of the two statesmen overlapped. Some multinational states were dismantled (especially the Austro-Hungarian and Ottoman Empires); for the colonial peoples, the system of mandates was brought in. This was a form of bland neo-colonialism: the colonial powers retained their authority in Africa, Asia and the South Pacific, but it was toned down and somewhat moderated in favour of the indigenous populations. All the same, however modest its initial implementation may have been, the principle of self-determination had sown the seeds of subversion in the constitutional order. These seeds were to bear fruit after the Second World War, when Lenin's anti-colonialist version finally became a reality, overthrowing the social foundations of the international community and radically cutting into the political and territorial (though not the economic) power of the Western industrial countries.

After the Second World War the second great revolutionary phenomenon took place in the international community: the launching of a *natural-law doctrine of human rights*, directly impinging upon the relationships between each state and its citizens. However, the attempt to introduce some of the great principles proclaimed in a number of Western countries (France, Britain, the United States) to the world community as a whole had had some cautious precedents. Let us pause to consider them.

Two illuminating episodes in the period following the First World War

After the First World War, two attempts had been made, both failures, to proclaim the principle at international level of equality among individuals – one of the bastions of human rights. It will be instructive to consider these two attempts briefly, in order to understand the forces that were operating against them.

The first came in 1919. When the League of Nations Covenant was being drawn up – the international treaty that was to lay the foundations for a new international community after the disasters of the First World War – the Japanese delegation formally proposed that the Covenant contain a provision stating that: 'The equality of nations being a basic principle of the League of Nations, the High Contracting Parties agree to accord, as soon as possible, to all alien nationals of states members of the League, equal and just treatment in every respect, making no distinction, either in law or in fact, on account of their race and nationality'.[8] Explaining this text on 13 February 1919 to the Commission on the League of Nations, the Japanese Delegate, Baron Makino, made an eloquent speech, noting that race discrimination still existed in law and in fact and that the clause he proposed was to be 'regarded as an invitation to the Governments and peoples concerned to examine the question more closely and seriously, and to devise some acceptable means to meet a deadlock which at present confronts different peoples'.[9] What were the implications of the Japanese proposal? An international rule incorporated in a fundamental treaty was to proclaim that all *aliens* should 'as soon as possible' be placed on an equal footing. This did not of course mean proclaiming equality among the nationals of each contracting state, or among these and all foreigners; but only non-discrimination against citizens of other League member states, and only these, on the basis of race or nationality. In short, any member state, say Great Britain, would have to refrain from discriminating on grounds of race or nationality between, say, Italians, French and Japanese; similarly, it would have to refrain from discriminating on grounds of race between, say, Poles of different stock (e.g. between Jewish and non-Jewish Poles). We are, then, quite remote from the consecration at *universal* level of the principle of equality. The provision proposed by the Japanese, in addition to aiming only at a *future* solution of the problem, was still conceived from the traditional angle from which individuals were at the time considered: that of the treatment of aliens. From that viewpoint, the advance being proposed consisted in striving for the abolition of discrimination by race or nationality.

Despite the relatively limited scope of the proposal, it was sharply rejected, particularly because of opposition from Britain, Australia and Greece.[10] A much milder, watered-down proposal[11] presented later by the Japanese was likewise thrown out for it marshalled a majority of votes but fell short of the unanimity which was required, according to the Chair, President Wilson.[12] I shall not dwell on the arguments put forward by Japan's opponents (Britain, Poland and the United States), since most of them are essentially specious – but the British delegate, Lord Robert Cecil also pointed out that the 'solution of the racial question could not be attempted by the Commission [on the League of Nations] without encroaching upon the sovereignty of states members of the League',[13] adding that the Japanese proposal 'opened the door to serious controversy and to interference in the domestic affairs of states members of the League'.[14] The truth is that the Western great powers neither would nor could accept a principle that would have encroached heavily on their discriminatory practices against citizens of other areas of the world, and would have ended up threatening even the similar practices they still tolerated within their own national systems (I have in mind above all, of course, racial discrimination in the United States).[15] In 1919, then, the proposal from one of the few non-white powers attending Geneva – a proposal that would certainly have acted as a powerful leaven if introduced to the international community – was rejected mainly by the efforts of the Western powers among whom human rights had been conceived. The international community was not yet ripe for adopting those values.

Another attempt to proclaim the rejection of racial discrimination at international level was made in 1933. This time, however, the clash was among white states, among Western powers, some of which were now less insensitive to the principle of equality of the human person. Moreover, this time the viewpoint from which the question was considered was no longer the *traditional* one of treatment of aliens but the *modern* one of respect for the values of the human person as such.

As we know, the treaties concluded after the First World War protected the linguistic, ethnic and religious minorities of some countries of Central and Eastern Europe. Protection of these minorities was essentially a response to political requirements. One significant episode is emblematic of the crisis of the endeavour to move from the strictly political dimension to a broader viewpoint inspired by respect for human rights.

In 1933, a German citizen of Jewish origin, Franz Bernheim, complained to the Council of the League of Nations about the breaches by Germany of the German-Polish Treaty of 1922.[16] In particular, he relied on the section protecting minorities in Upper Silesia (which then belonged to Germany). Bernheim, who had lived in Upper Silesia from 1931 to 1933, had been sacked by a German firm in April 1933, like all Jewish employees. In his passionate appeal, he recalled the various laws and ordinances against Jews promulgated in April 1933 by the German government, insisting that they had introduced serious racial discrimination into the whole of Germany; he then dwelt in particular on the effects of that legislation in Upper Silesia, asserting that they ran

contrary to the Treaty I have just cited. The German delegate to
the Council of the League immediately raised various objections.
He pointed out that Bernheim had no link with Upper Silesia either
by origin or by family. Bernheim thus had no 'right whatever to
submit a petition on general questions and on the application of the
German laws in Upper Silesia, seeing that these laws did not in any
way affect him';[17] nor was Bernheim entitled from either 'the point
of view of birth or his condition of life to be regarded as the
qualified representative of the general interests of the Upper
Silesian population'.[18] Such formal arguments are typical examples
of the kind of objections of which diplomats are so fond.

   In the ensuing debate, various delegates sought, more or less
skilfully, to run with the hare and hunt with the hounds. The Polish
representative, however, in a vigorous speech, touched a raw nerve.
Having rejected the German objections, he pointed out that while
from a formal point of view the Council could admittedly deal only
with the fate of the Jewish minorities in Upper Silesia, nevertheless
'All Members of the Council had, however, at least a moral right to
make a pressing appeal to the German Government to ensure equal
treatment for the Jews in Germany'.[19] This 'moral right' followed
in his opinion from a series of declarations made by German
delegates, in 1919, 1930 and 1932, as well as from German
acceptance of a Council Resolution of 1922. In any case, the Polish
delegate went on, the case the Council was considering seemed
highly instructive: 'The striking example of the Jewish minority in
Germany, which had legal protection only in a small portion of
German territory, must doubtless lead to the conclusion that the
present system for protecting minorities has all the defects of an
inadequate system.'[20] He concluded by noting that 'A minimum of
rights must be guaranteed to every human being, whatever his
race, religion or mother tongue.'[21] These words may today seem
obvious, but at the time they caused a sensation.

   As often happens, the German objections and the vacillations by
other states led to the appointment of a Committee of Jurists with
instructions to verify formally the well-foundedness of the points
raised by the German delegate. That Committee met, and found
Germany in the wrong. The Council then decided to take note of an
assertion made previously by the German delegate: if some blame
had to be assigned to Germany, confined obviously to Upper
Silesia, it could derive only from 'errors due to misconstructions of
internal [German] laws by subordinate authorities; these errors
would be corrected'.[22] On the strength of this affirmation (marked,
note, by a truly unique 'diplomatic' hypocrisy), the Council

decided to adopt a report inviting Germany to bring the violations to an end. The report was passed, with Germany and Italy abstaining: the latter, while sharing the opinion of the Committee of Jurists, abstained because 'certain general considerations which perhaps exceeded the Council's competence had been put forward' in the Council[23] (a sibylline phrase whereby Italy set up a smoke-screen of legal argument to conceal its political approval of what the Germans were doing).

But the question of discrimination against Jews did not rest there. A few months later, Germany asked the Assembly of the League of Nations to bring the section of the League's annual report relating to minorities before a committee of the Assembly itself. The question of minorities thus came up again in the Assembly's VIth Committee. That Committee had a very lively debate on a question of principle: whether in every modern civil state all citizens ought to enjoy equal treatment both in law and in fact. Most states replied in the affirmative; only one delegation (the German one) stated instead that a sovereign state had the right to regard such an issue as a domestic matter. Among the more advanced states, a leading position was taken by France, which made two proposals: firstly, to reaffirm the principle that all states not bound by treaties on minorities had to treat their minorities according to 'at least as high a standard of justice and toleration' as required by those treaties. Secondly, France proposed to declare that if a state had concluded a treaty on minorities, the clauses of that treaty should not be interpreted in the sense of excluding some categories of citizens from the benefits of those clauses; in other words, minorities within a state were protected even if they were not on the territory designated specifically in the treaties.[24] The reference to the Bernheim case was clear and was indeed purposely spelled out by the French delegate: on the French proposal, Germany had to treat German Jews without discrimination even outside Upper Silesia, i.e. in the whole of Germany. It is hardly surprising, then, that the German delegate came out against the proposal, stating that 'the Jewish problem in Germany [was] a special problem *sui generis* and [could] not possibly be treated [. . .] simply like an ordinary minority question'.[25] Even though improved by the Greek delegate, Politis, the French proposal was thus rejected by Germany, as far as the part we are talking about is concerned. By Article 5 of the League's Covenant (whereby decisions of the Assembly could be adopted only with 'the agreement of all the Members of the League represented at the meeting'), the French proposal was rejected.

What lesson can we draw from this episode? That in 1933, national sovereignty was still opposed to full respect for human rights for all. The principle of equality – the very basis of all rights and fundamental freedoms – was not yet regarded as one of the indispensable cornerstones of human coexistence. It was no coincidence that Germany's vote against the French proposal was given on 11 October 1933 and that only three days later, on 14 October, Hitler broadcast his famous speech announcing Germany's withdrawal from the League (because other states were unprepared to grant 'true equality of rights to Germany', and were leaving it in an 'undignified' position). Hitler was thus protesting against discrimination in the international sphere that was undoubtedly less severe than what he was practising in Germany against certain groups of German citizens.

Germany's isolation on the question of the Jewish minority was certainly not the cause of its withdrawal from the League, especially since the League's own rules had allowed her to block a resolution which *de facto* condemned her. But the simultaneity of Germany's break with the essential postulates of civilized existence – even though these were still purely ethical norms – and its departure from the body that was supposed to bring together all 'civil' states is significant. This sombre coincidence at the same time highlighted the close link between Nazi barbarism and the total denial of human rights.

Respect for human dignity thus came up against its first stumbling-block in Germany's firm stance that national sovereignty could not tolerate any international interference in internal affairs. The break, on this and other no less significant points, between Germany and the rest of the international community was later to lead to the outbreak of war, which thus ended up being a bloody conflict between aggressive, racist states on the one hand, and states loyal to the great postulates of human rights, or at any rate opposed to aggressive war, on the other.

Self-determination of peoples and human rights

The nature of that great conflict and the reasons for it were clearly perceived by various statesmen, above all Franklin D. Roosevelt and Winston Churchill. It was on the former's initiative that acceptance by the world of certain great freedoms, at the level of international relations, was proposed. This great and generous programme was taken up by other politicians and gradually ended up being translated into international norms and institutions. *Three great ideals* – the right of peoples to self-determination, human rights, and pacifism (not the 'ingenuous' pacifism of the Enlightenment, but an 'armed' pacifism) – were thus consecrated in the United Nations Charter. The Charter incorporated no less than seven references to human rights, and in essence sketched out an action programme for the future, though without placing firm commitments on states in either the field of human rights or that of the right of peoples to self-determination.

It was the historical and political developments following adoption of the Charter that gave flesh and blood to the ideology of human rights and the ideology of self-determination. In 1948 came the proclamation of the Universal Declaration of Human Rights, followed in 1966 by the two UN Covenants on the subject. In 1960 the famous Resolution 1514 (XV) was adopted, on the independence of colonial peoples, explicitly enunciating the self-determination of peoples in connection with those colonies;[26] in 1966 the two Covenants elevated the right of self-determination to the level of fundamental premise and prerequisite of human rights; in 1970 came the UN General Assembly's conferment on that right of the rank of one of the six fundamental principles governing friendly relations among states.[27] In the course of a couple of decades, the two great doctrines (along with 'armed pacifism') thus ended up solidly implanted among the great normative precepts of the international community, at the same level as other basic principles (like that of state sovereignty and that of non-interference in internal affairs) that had governed relations between states since the seventeenth century.

These two great doctrines (like pacifism, which I shall not deal with here) have had an extremely important role in international life. They have subverted the very foundations of the world community, by introducing changes, adjustments and realignments to many political and legal institutions. Though coming from different ideological backgrounds (with the principle of self-determination having a mainly Socialist stamp and that of human rights a Western one), both doctrines have had the same function: they have powerfully contributed to the *democratization* of international relations. From this viewpoint they have had the same role as did some of the great ideas of the eighteenth and nineteenth centuries for the development of the modern state: the concepts of natural rights, of the social contract or of the separation of powers. Like these ideas, the two doctrines in question have displayed their explosive force in various areas of the international social fabric, though over a very broad space of time. To be sure, they have not changed the actual structure of that community or the main rules of the game. Sovereign states have remained the true holders of power; authority continues to be distributed among various powers; there are still no centralized agencies charged with stating, ascertaining and enforcing the law; each powerful state continues in the main to deal with national interests, with little weight being attributed to collective needs going beyond the requirement to harmonize aspirations and necessities of several states. Nevertheless, the two doctrines have introduced seeds of subversion into this framework, destined sooner or later to undermine and erode the traditional structures and institutions, and gradually – over a very broad space of time, the course of which cannot yet be foreseen – to revolutionize those structures and institutions. They have acted like a powerful corrosive agent which, though it may not have succeeded in immediately destroying the pillars of traditional power, is nevertheless gradually eating away parts of them, fragmenting the most fragile parts and gradually weakening the supporting structures of the institutions, so that we can already hear them creak.

2

The Universal Declaration of Human Rights Forty Years On

The great texts of the past

If one looks at the political documents where bold imaginative men wrote down what they demanded of governmental authority, and sketched out their 'project' for society, one is struck by a number of features.

First of all, these texts — I am thinking not so much of the English incunabula of human rights, the 1215 Magna Charta and the 1689 Bill of Rights, but of the American Declarations of 1776–89 and the French Declaration of 1789 — emphatically proclaim a particular *conception of man and of society*. One finds not only the ideas of eighteenth-century men, but above all a projection of their *model* of man and society. For those Declarations, 'man' (I take the word from the Declarations themselves) is worthy of being called 'man' only if he fulfils these conditions: to be free, equal, to have undisturbed enjoyment of his property, not to be oppressed by a tyrannous government and to be able freely to realize himself. As the Virginia Declaration (1776) puts it, all men should be able freely to 'obtain happiness and safety', or as the Massachusetts Declaration (1780) proclaims, to 'enjoy, in security and tranquillity, their natural rights and the blessings of life'.

The model is above all one of *society*. Society must be made up of free individuals equal with each other (except, as the French Declaration puts it, for 'social distinctions . . . based only upon general usefulness', justified by diversity of 'virtues and talents') and subject only to the law, which in turn is and must be an expression of the general will; political institutions should exist only as a means of realizing the freedom of the individuals and their common good. As Article 12 of the French Declaration vividly puts it: 'the guarantee of the rights of man and the citizen necessitates a public force; such a force, therefore, is instituted for the advantage of all and not for the particular benefit of those to whom it is entrusted'. Still more general is the statement in the Pennsylvania Declaration (1776); according to Article V, 'the government is, or ought to be, instituted for the common benefit, protection and security of the people, nation or community; and not for the particular emolument or advantage of any single man, family or set of men, who are a part only of that community'. Wherever authority degenerates, and oppresses individuals, the latter have the right to oppose it. Article IV of the Maryland Declaration (1776) states that 'the doctrine of non-resistance against arbitrary power, and oppression, is absurd, slavish and destructive of the good and happiness of mankind'.

The second striking aspect is the *peremptory and absolute* character of the Declarations (especially the French one). They lay down that man and society must be as they proclaim; no alternative is admitted. For judging man and society, the *sole evaluative yardstick* offered is respect for the rights of man. These are regarded as the alpha and omega of the social universe, the litmus paper with which one can test whether a human community should be approved or condemned, the basic criteria of any modern vision of society. The preamble to the French Declaration asserts, in the most categorical way, that 'ignorance, forgetfulness or contempt of the rights of man are the sole causes of public misfortunes and of the corruption of governments'. Even more forthright is Article 16: 'every society in which the guarantee of rights is not assured or the separation of powers not determined has no constitution at all'. In this context 'constitution' is clearly intended to mean an organized, modern society, that is more than just a barbarous juxtaposition of individuals struggling against one another.

A third striking feature of the Declarations is the large number of *political myths* woven into them — and by myths I mean vivid, ideological constructs that social groups more or less consciously develop in order both to seek to understand social relationships, and to give themselves a justification for their own actions and to guide their own impulses. Even the existence of the 'natural, inalienable and sacred rights of man' is a myth, based as it is on the concept that man, before entering into society, is already a bearer of 'innate' rights. In this we find the myth of the 'state of nature', which is followed by the 'state of society' following the conclusion of a 'social contract'. The preamble to the Massachusetts Declaration (1780) states that 'the body-politic is formed by a voluntary association of individuals; it is a social compact by which the whole people covenants with each citizen and each citizen with the whole people that all shall be governed by certain laws for the common good'. And Article III of the New Hampshire Declaration (1783) states that 'when men enter into a state of society, they surrender up some of their natural rights to that society, in order to insure the protection of others; and without such an equivalent, the surrender is void'.

Another myth is that of the sovereignty of the Nation. Article 3 of the French Declaration proclaims that 'the source of all sovereignty resides essentially in the nation; no group, no individual may exercise authority not emanating expressly therefrom'; similarly Article II of the Virginia Declaration (1776) earlier stated that 'all power is vested in, and consequently derived from, the people'. No account is taken of social groups, of the economically powerful, of companies and other commercial entities that in various ways condition the inclinations and decisions of individuals. All the various intervening factors are cancelled out with a stroke of the pen: the people are the source of power and authority; whoever does not derive legitimacy from the people cannot and should not wield power. This magnificent illusion ambitiously sought to 'wipe out' all the influences of the aristocracies, of social castes, of the medieval guilds and of various other hierarchies of many kinds.

But the most powerful myth of all is that of the *Law*. Article 6 of the French Declaration announces that law is 'the expression of the general will': a concept obviously derived from Rousseau, and embraced in the Declaration with all the equivocations and mystifications that he espoused. The Law, being the expression of the people and being general, cannot err. Accordingly, it is for the Law to define the limits of the freedom of each individual *vis-à-vis* the others: to identify 'actions . . . injurious to society' (Article 5 of the French Declaration); to determine the cases in which a man may be accused, arrested and detained; to specify the penalties that may be inflicted on the guilty; to establish what is to be meant by 'public order', and so on. The Law is omnipotent, and at the same time exempt from all criticism, as long as it is the expression of the general will ('la volonté générale n'erre jamais', the *Encyclopédie* had proclaimed).[1]

In speaking of the Law, we have touched on another characteristic of the Declarations. If one asks how they can function in practice, one realizes immediately that they are *highly manipulable texts*, since they offer a series of loopholes and escape routes to the organs of political power. The latter are entitled to determine the limits of freedom, lay down what may be 'harmful to society', when 'public order' may legitimately restrict the exercise of liberty, and so on. The sole restriction on possible abuses of political power is the Law. The fact that all such decisions are taken not by the executive authority but by the legislative assembly is supposed to be protection against arbitrariness. And yet, if we look closely, we realize that the Declarations do not indicate how the Law is to be made: although they insist that all citizens should take part in making laws, directly or through their representatives, they fail to specify the minimum conditions which must be fulfilled in order for the Law to be a genuine expression of the people. To be sure, the English 'Bill of Rights' (1688–9) laid down that elections had to be free; and the concept was echoed by Article IX of the Massachusetts Constitution (1780), which added that everyone had an equal right to vote and to stand for election. But apart from these few indications, nothing is really said about preventing abuses by the Law. It is mythically conceived as free from original sin, immaculate and unassailable.

In short, looking back, the Declarations certainly remain documents of enormous ideological and political importance, but they are also a source of dangerous equivocations and a legitimation of many abuses.

Let us now look at the *genealogy* of the Declarations. Their 'ancestors' are well known and can be reduced essentially to two. The first is to be found in the political institutions of the time and in the imperative necessity of eliminating them. To this extent one source of the Declarations was absolutism, with all its arbitrariness, and the desire of emergent groups to free themselves, both from the unnecessary burdens laid on individuals by those state structures, and from the corporate-type social fragmentation inherited from the feudal system. This explains why the Declarations, like the other great political documents that accompanied them, were obsessed by the idea that authority — by definition oppressive – had to be circumscribed as far as possible: powerful defences had to be erected around the freedom of the individual which would be unassailable by the state. Freedom meant the individual's power to act without being disturbed by the state, as Benjamin Constant argued forcefully in 1819.[2]

The other great source of the Declarations is the thought of certain philosophers who developed a number of essential concepts: those of the state of nature and the state of society; of the social contract; of 'human nature' conceived of as something immutable and coterminous with man (accordingly radically different from animals: 'les animaux sont séparés de nous par des barrières invariables et éternelles' says the *Encyclopédie*);[3] of inalienable rights possessed by man from the fact of his being human, irrespective of the social context in which he lives; of the separation of powers (the need to deprive the monarch of the excessive power he still enjoyed in the eighteenth century); and of human dignity. The names of the philosophers who stated or developed these concepts are just as familiar: Locke in England, Montesquieu, Voltaire and Rousseau in France, Thomas Paine in the United States, Kant in Germany.

Whole libraries on the one hand, and the desire for liberation from obsolete political and social structures on the other then came together in the short texts of the Declarations with which we are here concerned. By themselves, they have exercised greater force and had more earth-shaking effects than all their ideal progenitors put together, greater force too than all the barricades later erected in their name.

The great political documents to which I have referred so far are the forebears of the Universal Declaration of Human Rights. Those documents, along with others, mark the beginning of the modern era and set forth a new vision of man and society — or to be more precise, they bring to maturation the new concept of man and society that had been fermenting since the Renaissance – since the discourse on 'De hominis dignitate' by Pico della Mirandola.[4] Those 'sacred' texts were, of course, doomed from the outset to be disregarded thousands and thousands of times. Nevertheless, their primary significance remains that they are *unshakeable decalogues*, indicating the road which states must follow if they are to combine respect for the individual personality of their citizens with full development of the potentialities of society as a whole.

Those texts acquired their value as guides for action from the fact that they became *constitutional* law in many modern states: that is, sets of norms that are legally binding and are reinforced with the sanctions under the laws of those states. In this way the thought of a few great philosophers was given flesh and blood, and transformed into legally binding 'codes'. As we shall see, this has not happened in the case of the Universal Declaration.

The world scene in the early 1940s

To understand the Universal Declaration, we have to start from far away and approach it slowly, in order to discover gradually all its hidden nooks and crannies.

Let us first of all ask what the international scene was like in the first half of the 1940s, before the Declaration was produced. I shall first consider – very briefly – international relations (obviously, from the viewpoint we are interested in) and then the internal situation, both constitutionally and ideologically, in a number of major states.

How did the world scene look? Since 1939 a terrible war had been raging, involving a great part of the international community, with the Axis Powers on the one side and the Allies on the other. With the passage of the years there came an awareness that the war had become, in effect, a radical conflict between, on the one hand, states pursuing a racist policy of aggressive imperialistic expansion, and, on the other hand, states increasingly presenting themselves as defenders of peace and the freedom of peoples and of individuals. Even states with imperialist tendencies like the United States, Great Britain and France opposed the brutal, aggressive hegemonism of the Axis Powers; similarly, authoritarian states like the Soviet Union opposed Germany's racism and contempt for humanity. The idea thus began to emerge that one significant cause of the war lay in Hitler's contempt for human rights and freedoms. If, then, a repetition of such a catastrophe were to be avoided, there would have to be an awareness of the importance of the interdependence of peace and human rights, and action after the war would be needed to ensure that the attainment of these dual objectives would become an essential priority for all states and for the international community as a whole. As Winston Churchill stated in 1946 when he re-launched the idea of an 'iron curtain' in his famous speech at Fulton, Missouri: 'To give security to these countless homes, they must be shielded from the two giant marauders, war and tyranny'.[5]

In this context, little by little, a *renewed natural-law doctrine* began to gain currency: the idea that respect for human rights (along with the maintenance of peace) ought to constitute the *point of no return* for the new world community that would emerge after the defeat of the Axis powers. Various voices proclaimed this new outlook. I shall mention only two, both of them in high places.

The first, from the United States, was that of its great leader Franklin D. Roosevelt. This was not by chance, since Roosevelt had been the President of the 'New Deal', that is, of the moral revolt against a society ridden with social and economic inequalities. The President, a champion of what we today would call equal 'economic and social rights' for all Americans, delivered a message to Congress on 6 January 1941 *sketching out the new world society* that was to arise from the ruins of the war.[6] This great project had as its fixed point respect 'by the whole world' for four freedoms: freedom of speech and expression; freedom to worship God; freedom from want (a phrase that Roosevelt picked up from a reporter in a press conference given at Hyde Park on 5 July 1940, and to which – as has been pointed out by some leading scholars[7] – he then gave the meaning of 'the removal of certain barriers between nations, cultural in the first place and commercial in the second place', whereas we would today take 'freedom from want' to mean 'economic and social rights'); and freedom from fear (with attendant reductions in armaments aimed at preventing armed aggression). This was not just a programme outlined by the leader of one of the Great Powers for its future action on the world scene; it was also posited as a point of reference for action by other states. A few months later, in August 1941, the programme was included in the Atlantic Charter (drawn up by Roosevelt and Churchill but open to accession by all other states, and in fact signed by many of the Allies).

Roosevelt's message constitutes, as we shall see, the driving force that was, on a world scale, to lead to the proclamation of human rights and subsequently the drawing-up of the Universal Declaration.

There were other developments at the same time at various levels, specifically at the level of civil society, but in the same direction. This fermentation was taking place among several groups and in several states – for instance, among Jewish associations: as the details of the Nazi misdeeds gradually emerged, they sought to translate their indignation and horror into codes of conduct and operational structures that would be able to prevent a relapse into such barbarism. I shall mention here the spokesman of another stream of ideas: the Frenchman Jacques Maritain, who had a vast influence both in Europe and in the United States.

Maritain, a political philosopher with a strong Catholic background, contributed, in speeches and in writing during the first half of the 1940s, to the development of the study of human rights. The essence of his main book of those years, *Human Rights and Natural Law* (translated into English in 1943),[8] is briefly as follows. The social conception on the basis of which post-war society ought to be constructed should have four essential characteristics: it should be *personalist* (society is a whole made up of persons whose dignity is anterior to it); *communal* (the person tends naturally to a community in which the common good is superior to that of individuals, subject to the proviso that this cannot justify infringements of the rights of each person); *pluralist* (the dignity of the human person can unfold only in a plurality of autonomous communities); and finally *theist* or *Christian* (not in the sense that every member of the society has to believe in God and be a Christian, but 'in the sense that in the reality of things, God, principle and end of the human person and prime source of natural law, is by the same token the prime source of political society and authority among men').[9]

The ultimate aim of this conception was the 'establishment of a brotherly city',[10] in which 'man shall be free from misery and bondage'. Maritain wrote that these characteristics were denied by 'old bourgeois individualism' and 'the totalitarianisms of today, whose worst form is Nazi racism'.[11] In more concrete terms, this meant implementing the four great freedoms identified by Roosevelt, as positive law and then introducing them into the 'economic and political organizations of the civilized world'.[12] This meant abandoning the classical notions of absolute state sovereignty, not only in the international sphere but also in the national order:[13] at the level of inter-state relations the repudiation of sovereignty would imply the establishment of a 'federation of free peoples'; at the national level, renunciation of the privileges of absolute sovereignty would mean that the state would have to reduce itself to the simple function of a co-ordination and control agency, especially in the economic sphere.

Let us now take a look at the geopolitical context in which these natural law ideas developed. On the one hand there were the great Western democracies: the United States, Great Britain, and France. Despite their imperialistic tendencies and the discrimination they applied in their colonial empires, and despite persisting inequalities on home territory, they nevertheless took a common line on fundamental respect for certain major principles of democratic parliamentary systems. Alongside these states were those of Central and Latin America, which in various ways, and often without putting them into practice, had adopted the Western models of government and administration of society. All these countries were in principle open to possible *projections of human rights onto the international scene.* Ultimately this meant proclaiming on a world scale what was already stated in their national constitutions.

On the other hand there were the Soviet Union and the large Asian countries. The Soviet Union was hostile to human rights not only because the Stalinist system of government was profoundly and radically authoritarian, but also because of the legacy of Marxist thought. L. Kolakowski must be credited with having clearly demonstrated the total contradiction between the thought of Marx (and Lenin and Trotsky) and the fundamental concepts of human rights.[14] The theory of human rights as conceived in the natural law tradition is based on three main pillars: firstly, that those rights are inherent in human nature and do not require any positive recognition (in other words, they 'subsist' even when specifically denied by states); secondly, the natural order on which those rights are based is universal and immutable, irrespective of the particular social context; and thirdly, those rights belong to individuals as such, not social groups. Marx repudiates all three of these principles. When he speaks of capitalist society, he notes that human rights are in reality a mere expression of a class – the bourgeoisie – and express in universal and abstract, and hence mystificatory, terms the needs of that class. They do not descend from on high, but are specifically posited by men in quite definite societies and epochs: they are therefore profoundly 'historical' and reflect quite definite social aspirations of certain groups. While it is important to gain their recognition within capitalist societies, this is only because freedoms and rights may be useful for subverting the existing order more quickly. Accordingly, freedoms and rights have a purely instrumental value. In communist society, conversely, those rights are no longer of any use, since the complete integration of individual and community has been achieved: class conflict has been eliminated, and every individual becomes a participant in the whole, without there being any further obstacles or interruptions to the realization of the freedoms and aspirations of the individual. In communist society human rights therefore become superfluous.

To a very large extent, then, the doctrine of human rights was in conflict with ideology and practice in the Soviet Union (although of course one should not underestimate the great emphasis laid by Marxist thought on social and economic rights and social equality, nor should one neglect that important contribution to the theory of human rights by Marxist 'revisionism', to which S. Lukes[15] has appropriately drawn attention).

In addition to being at variance with ideology and practice in the Soviet Union, the doctrine of human rights was not in conformity with the great traditions of thought of Asia. I shall refer to this point in the next chapter.

The debate at the United Nations (1946–8)

Let us now ask what the situation was in the United Nations in the years 1946–8, when the Universal Declaration was drawn up.

The membership of the World Organization was at the time 58. Of these, fourteen were Western countries in a political, if not 'geographical', sense (including such countries as New Zealand and Australia); twenty were Latin-American; six were Socialist,

from Central or Eastern Europe (the Soviet Union, Czechoslovakia, Poland, Ukraine, Byelorussia, as well as Yugoslavia,
which, at least in this context, sided with the Socialist bloc); four
were African (Egypt, Ethiopia, Liberia, the South African Union);
fourteen were Asiatic in a geographical and political sense (Burma,
China, India, Iran, Iraq, Lebanon, Pakistan, the Philippines, Siam
[now Thailand], Syria, Turkey, Yemen, Afghanistan, Saudi
Arabia).

One should not, however, assume that the world was already
divided into the three groupings that exist today – the Western
countries, the Socialist nations, and the Third World. Those states
which we now call 'developing countries' were then largely
pro-Western. They had not yet become fully aware of their different
political and cultural background. They still looked to the West
with the respect of those who had only just shaken off colonial ties,
and did not yet dare to proclaim the sense of rebellion seething
inside them. Alternatively (as in the case of countries that had not
undergone the humiliation of colonization, like Siam, China,
Afghanistan and Saudi Arabia), they unconsciously imitated
Western modes of thought and lifestyles. Accordingly, when we
come to look at the positions taken by those countries in the big
debate on the Declaration, we will immediately note that the
essential differences were not between the Western world and the
Orient, or between the industrialized world (liberal in tradition
and capitalist in structure) and what we now call the Third World.
The clashes and the conflict were instead between the great
Western democracies and the countries of Socialist Europe.

If we bring the debates into sharper focus we discover four broad
alignments. Firstly, there was a group of Western countries that
took the lead from the start, and in a certain sense set the tone of
the debates: the United States, France and Great Britain, followed
by the other states of the political West (prominent among them
Australia). A second group that acted with considerable vigour and
cohesiveness was Latin America: those countries not only valiantly
supported the cause of human rights, but were sometimes bolder
than the industrialized countries of the West in suggesting solutions
or defending wording that even the West hesitated to accept.
Confronting these two groupings was the unified, intransigent
group from Socialist Europe, the only alignment capable of
opposing the Western theses with tenacity and insistence. Fourthly
there were the Asian countries which had little weight, except for
the Moslem ones led by Saudi Arabia and Pakistan, which neither
opposed the West's proposals nor shared the Socialist objections;

instead they expressed reservations dictated by Moslem cultural tradition regarding religion and family life.

As I have already suggested, although it is possible to identify these four alignments, the essential confrontation was between the West and Socialist Europe. This emerges clearly from the debates that took place over the two years concerned, and is confirmed by one important fact: the 'Drafting Committee' was made up entirely of delegates from the West – in the political and cultural sense – and Socialists – the members were Australia, Chile, France, Lebanon, the Soviet Union, Great Britain and the United States.

Let us, then, take a look at the East-West confrontation. Before indicating the main theses of the two antagonists, I wish to highlight one point that I consider essential: the discussion that unfolded in the United Nations on the Declaration was all in all *an aspect of the 'cold war'*. The West stoutly defended the parliamentary democratic gospel of their tradition, endeavouring constantly to project it onto the world stage. According to a biographer of Eleanor Roosevelt, who played a decisive role in the drafting of the Universal Declaration, one of her advisers, J. P. Hendrick, a representative of the State Department, stated that the US policy should be 'to make a Declaration that [is] the carbon copy of the American Declaration of Independence and [the US] Bill of Rights'.[16] The Socialists interpreted this action as an attempt to export Western values internationally, above all to use them against the Eastern bloc; they reacted by instrumentalizing human rights and reducing them to a means of political and ideological struggle. That the topic had been turned into an element in the cold war can be seen not only from the content of the delegate's speeches, but also from the context: I am thinking chiefly of the acrimony with which the delegates of the Ukraine, Czechoslovakia and Poland attacked the West at the General Assembly,[17] and the no less irate replies of the British representative.[18] I am also thinking of the insistence with which the various representatives of the Socialist countries (especially the representative of the Soviet Union)[19] emphasized the importance of the right to rebel against government authorities or, as he termed it, 'the right to resist acts of tyranny and oppression' – a right which was rejected by others, including the United States, as a source of sedition and subversion.[20] On the other hand, that the confrontation was primarily ideological, was later emphasized by Secretary of State J. F. Dulles in a letter sent in 1949 to the American Bar Association: among other things he pointed out that the Universal Declaration, just like 'the French Declaration of the Rights of Man, is a major element in the great ideological struggle that is now going on in the world, and in this respect Mrs Roosevelt has made a distinctive contribution in defense of American ideals'.[21]

The *Western theses* can be summarized quite briefly. They were aimed at extending on a world scale the solemn principles of the three big democracies in which human rights originated and flourished: Great Britain, the United States and France. Essentially, it was those countries (largely followed by those from different geographical areas that were ideologically close to them) which proposed the proclamation at intergovernmental level of the natural-law conceptions that had inspired their great domestic political texts. But there is one important point to stress. Undoubtedly, the Declaration was conceived under the stimulus of Roosevelt's great message of 1941, as was stated at the General Assembly by the delegates of Haiti, the Lebanon, Chile, France and Paraguay;[22] on 9 December 1948 the Chilean delegate even went so far as to state that the Declaration 'was to a certain extent the moral testament' of the United States President.[23] Nevertheless, the West proposed proclaiming at the world level *only the civil and political rights*, and only in the *essentially individualistic conception* they had had in the eighteenth and nineteenth centuries. It was only in a second stage, given the hostility of the Socialist countries and under strong pressure from the Latin-Americans (who played a most important part in this connection) that the West agreed to incorporate into the Universal Declaration a number of economic and social rights as well – entirely unknown to the 'sacred' texts of the Western tradition.

What was the position of the *Socialists*? After considerable diffidence and much scepticism, they agreed to collaborate in drafting the Declaration once they had seen that the West was prepared to accept a number of economic and social rights in the text. Accordingly, they participated in the drafting of the Declaration, formulating proposals and amendments, which were, however, in part rejected. For that reason, they ultimately abstained from the vote on the Declaration as a whole (as did South Africa and Saudi Arabia, for different reasons).

In what spirit did the Socialists co-operate in drafting the Declaration? They started from the position that in any case all the rights it protected were fully recognized and practised in their countries (as was stated in black and white by, among others, the Soviet delegate Mr Vyshinsky at the session of 10 December 1948).[24] Accordingly, the Declaration was regarded as a goal relevant only to the Western countries and to the Third World ones still oppressed by the colonial powers. As one illustration of other similar statements, I shall cite what the Ukrainian delegate said on 9 December 1948: 'It was, of course possible to draft a declaration containing great humanitarian principles, but those principles should bear some sort of relation to the every-day facts of contemporary life in capitalist countries . . . In capitalist countries there was and always would be a flagrant contradiction between what was said in the Declaration on Human Rights and reality'.[25] As a decalogue applicable to the non-Socialist countries (particularly the Western ones, to which the Socialists' attention continually turned, almost as if they were their sole interlocutors and opponents), the Declaration had, so far as the Eastern European countries were concerned, to be rigorous, exacting and effective, it also had to incorporate rights which the West persistently refused to recognize and apply.

A first line of action by the Socialists therefore consisted of proposing the insertion in the Declaration of a number of important rights: the principle of equality (that is, the ban on discrimination based on race, sex, colour, language, religion, political opinion, national origin, property, birth or other status); the right to rebel against oppressive authorities; the right to participate in street demonstrations as an aspect of the freedom of association; the right of national minorities to have their collective rights recognized and respected; the right to self-determination of colonial peoples; the right of workers to have at their disposal newspapers and other publications to disseminate their ideas.

Another important policy line, likewise aimed at using the Declaration as a weapon to criticize the Western countries, consisted of asking that mechanisms be provided for implementing the rights sanctioned in the Declaration. As can clearly be seen from various speeches by Socialist delegates, these mechanisms were to accompany the economic and social rights. The Eastern European countries' argument was simple: these rights, which are fully respected in the Socialist bloc, are daily trampled underfoot in the West; accordingly, what sense is there in proclaiming them unless methods of supervision are provided that are capable of inducing the Western countries to respect them?

A summary of the Socialist assessment of the Declaration from the two viewpoints just mentioned is conveniently provided in a speech by the Ukrainian delegate at the session of 9 December 1948. He stated that 'A study of the Universal Declaration of Human Rights consequently showed a series of rights which could not be exercised in view to the present conditions and the economic structure of a great number of countries, whereas several elementary democratic rights, which could be realized in a capitalist society, had been deliberately omitted'.[26]

The Socialist countries then put forward a third fundamental concept, this time of more ideological than political derivation. This was the concept that human rights should be respected and permitted as long as they remained within the 'democratic' context, that is, as long as they did not furnish grist to the mill of fascism. In other words, if those rights could be utilized to promote, defend or revive fascism, there were no longer grounds for recognizing them. It followed that the rights of association, free expression of thought, freedom of the press and participation in the cultural life of the community found their impassable limit in the need to save democratic societies from fascism, to promote 'progress' and to struggle against 'war'. The Western conception that everyone should enjoy freedom in equal measure, even those who intended to destroy freedom, was seen as misguided. For the Socialists this was simply an absurdity or a heresy. The Eastern European countries present at the United Nations in 1946–8 therefore submitted a number of amendments aimed at *limiting* civil rights and freedoms, in the way I have just mentioned. All of these amendments were rejected. Clearly, the concept of the struggle against fascism served for Eastern Europe to show that in the West an excess of freedom led to the revival of fascism.

The Socialist strategy was not, however, confined to proposing changes aimed at strengthening the potential watchdog character of the Declaration. The Socialists also put forward an argument *with another aim* – an argument that was quite probably dictated not by the intention of instrumentalizing human rights in a cold-war context, but by exclusively ideological assumptions. The Socialists maintained that human rights ought to be conceived in such a way as to make them compatible with state sovereignty, or, as the Soviet delegate put it at the meeting of 10 December 1948, with 'the sovereign rights of democratic Governments'.[27] It was a consequence of this general conception that human rights were to be realized *by each state in the context of its national system*. In other words, the parameters laid down at world level were to be utilized and implemented in practice in the context of each sovereign state: the community of states was, as it were, to hand the baton to each individual state. It was incumbent on the authorities of that state alone to implement the rights in question. As can be seen, this thesis – which subsequently became one of the fundamental tenets of the Soviet conception – ended up contradicting the demands addressed to the West to practise economic and social rights *effectively*, and hence to permit international interference in this connection. Clearly, the concept was not only broadly dangerous to human rights, but ultimately scarcely compatible with the Socialists' other strategy: to turn human rights into a political tool in order to 'subvert' the Western countries as far as possible. Logically, the Socialists ought to have toned down their rigid conception of state sovereignty.

The content of the Declaration

What was the outcome of the confrontation, and the rather limited convergences, between East and West?

Looking closely, one sees that the Declaration largely reflects the approach of the Western liberal democracies. Suffice it to point out that the preamble states that 'the highest aspiration of the common people' is the advent of a world in which four freedoms are recognized – the same four freedoms proclaimed by Franklin D. Roosevelt in 1941. The Declaration does not however imitate the great texts of the past. Firstly, it does not have the doctrinaire, dogmatic character of the French Declaration, but rather adopts the pragmatic approach of the British and United States Declarations. And in addition to enunciating rights, the Declaration provides in some cases an indication of the procedures whereby they can be made operational at the national level. For instance, Article 8 proclaims the right to effective remedies against violations of human rights; Article 10 provides for the right to a fair trial.

But let us look at the content more closely. For this purpose, it is best to allow oneself to be guided, at least some of the way, by one of the fathers of the Declaration, the Frenchman René Cassin, who described its scope as follows.[28] He rightly pointed out that the Declaration is founded on four fundamental pillars. First come the *personal* rights (the right of equality; the right to life, liberty and security, etc.: Articles 3 to 11). Then come the *rights that belong to the individual in his relationships with the social groups in which he participates* (the rights to privacy of family life and to marry; to freedom of movement within the national state, or outside it; to have a nationality; to asylum in case of persecution; rights to property and to practise a religion: Articles 12 to 17). The third group is that of *civil liberties and political rights* exercised in order to contribute to the formation of government organs or to take part in the decision-making process (freedom of conscience, thought and expression;

freedom of association and assembly, the right to vote and to stand for election; the right of access to the government and public administration: Articles 18 to 21). The fourth category is that of *rights exercised in the economic and social area* (i.e., those rights which operate in the sphere of labour and production relationships and in that of education, rights to work and social security and to free choice of employment, to just conditions of work, to equal pay for equal work, the right to form and join trade unions, to rest and leisure, to health care, to education and the right to participate freely in the cultural life of the community: Articles 22 to 27).

A fifth section – which Cassin calls the 'pediment of the temple' erected on the four 'pillars' I have mentioned – covers some fairly *disparate* provisions (Articles 28 to 30). Firstly, there is the right to a 'social and international order in which the rights and freedom set forth in the Declaration can be fully realized' (Article 28). This provision was first proposed by the Lebanon, above all to meet Western objections to economic and social rights and to the fact that they are different in nature from civil and political rights because they call for 'positive' efforts by states. Article 28 is aimed at emphasizing that these rights can be implemented only if a favourable social structure is set up that allows them to take root, and if the general international context encourages economic development on the part of poor countries, or more redistribution of wealth on the part of the advanced countries. Article 29(1) provides for *duties* owed to the community. Other provisions cover the possible 'limitations' on rights, which are of three orders: firstly, the need to ensure due respect for the rights of others and to meet the just requirements of morality, public order and general welfare in democratic societies Article 29(2); secondly, the need to exercise the rights and freedoms in ways that do not conflict with the aims and principles of the UN: Article 29(3) (essentially, in conformity with the overriding goal of safeguarding peace; for instance, one may not disseminate war propaganda); thirdly, the need for the rights not to be neutralized or undermined by the exercise of other rights and freedoms enunciated in the Declaration (for instance, the freedom of expression and thought does not cover the carrying out of activities aimed at setting up a dictatorship: Article 30). Clearly, the second and third of these limitations were provided at the instance of the Socialists, or more exactly to take account of their theses and demands.

The ambiguities and lacunae in the Declaration

I now wish to draw attention to one of the chief shortcomings of this text – one that I hasten to say was probably inevitable.

At many crucial points the Declaration contains gaps, by merely leaving areas to the (unspecified, uncontrolled) 'law' of each state. Let me simply mention Article 29 – a provision of fundamental importance because it indicates what are the admissible limitations on human rights. It states that the relevant limitations are those 'determined by law', and goes on to list 'morality', 'public order', 'the general welfare in a democratic society' and so on. Clearly, these are rather vague concepts that can be defined in concrete terms only by national laws: so everything is left up to legislators in the individual states.

Reading Article 29 and other provisions of the Declaration, one is reminded of what I said earlier about the myth of the law which we found in the great Declarations of the past, especially the French one (where the myth came directly from the writings of Rousseau). In 1946–8 it was also maintained that the law was a useful bulwark against arbitrariness by the executive. Reference to the law was seen as a panacea for preventing abuses and high-handedness. Indeed, this was spelt out to the General Assembly on 10 December 1948 by the delegate from Uruguay, who warmly approved the norm on the possible limitations of human rights, noting that 'the general character of the law and the fact that it was usually formulated by representative organs were guarantees against arbitrary action'.[29] But does this 'panacea' not lend itself to manipulation? Experience in modern states shows that all too often the law can be 'manipulated' at the executive's whim, either because there is a continuum between the executive and the parliamentary majority, or because the parliamentary assemblies are facades that do not express needs different from those of the executive.

Even more dangerous than the Declaration's ambiguities are its *generalities*. For instance, as I have noted Article 28 provides for the right to 'a social and international order in which the rights and freedoms set forth in the Declaration can be fully realized'. What does such a 'social order' look like? And what is meant by 'international order'? Above all, which conditions favour the promotion and observance of human rights?

No less sibylline is the statement in Article 29(1) that 'everyone has duties to the community, in which alone the free and full development of his personality is possible'. What is the content and scope of these duties? The only clear aspect of the provision is a metalegal concept: the development of the human person can take place only in the context of the community (family, society, state, and so on); the individual can therefore realize himself not in some 'splendid isolation', but only through contact with other human beings and within social groups. This is, then, a political-philosophical concept. But at a normative level, we remain in the dark as to what precisely are the duties that we are bound to respect in those communities.

The Declaration's ideological roots

It is more illuminating in seeking to understand the Declaration, to hold it up, as it were, to the light, so as to identify its conceptual progenitors. These were essentially three: the natural-law framework (much diluted, as we shall see); the influence of the Socialist countries' statism; the nationalistic principle of sovereignty, introduced by almost all states in a final effort to curb the supranational, indeed progressive and even futuristic, thrust of the Declaration. Let us pause for a moment and look at each of these three components in detail.

The *natural-law framework*, inspired particularly by the West, already appears in the preamble, which talks of the 'inherent dignity' of human beings and their 'equal and inalienable rights'. Article 1 goes on to state that 'all human beings are born free and equal in dignity and rights'. Here we again find Rousseau's great concept, of the equality of all at birth and of human rights as pre-existing the state (one is reminded of the famous opening to the *Contrat social*: 'Man is born free, and yet we see him everywhere in chains'. This is one of the most revolutionary assertions of the eighteenth century, one of those that have most changed history, demolishing caste and class privileges, and introducing the fundamental idea that people *ought* to be distinguished only by their natural endowments. This affirmation, already made in the French Declaration, can be seen again in the Universal Declaration. Here, though, it is attenuated in many ways. Above all, the right to rebel against tyranny, essential to any natural-law conception (when the state fails to recognize the rights that pre-exist it, the individual is entitled to rise up against it), has been much blunted. In fact, it appears only in the preamble and in indirect fashion: 'it is essential, if man is not to be compelled to have recourse, as a last resort, to rebellion against tyranny and oppression, that human rights should be protected by the rule of law'. As I indicated earlier, while the Socialist countries wanted this right spelt out, the Westerners opposed it for fear of legitimizing insurrection. The compromise solution consisted in the watered-down acknowledgement I have just cited. The other fundamental right that is part of any natural-law decalogue – the right of petition against abuses – fared even worse. The Socialists and France wanted it recognized; indeed, France proposed the recognition of a right to petition both government authorities and the United Nations.[30] However, the proposal was rejected by the majority, once again, for fear of entrenching human rights that would be dangerous to national sovereignty.

Another attenuation of the natural-law vision consisted in recognizing not only the individual as bearer of rights, but also *social groups* as *loci* for the realization of his 'personality'. The *family* (Article 16(3): 'the family is the natural and fundamental group unit of society and is entitled to protection by society and by the state'); the *national community* (Article 22, Article 27(1), Article 29(1)) and the *international community* (Article 28).

Let us now consider the impact of the *Socialist* ideological framework. This influenced the Declaration in four main ways. First of all, it influenced it through the concept that the individual does not live isolated in a metahistorical universe (as the authors of the French Declaration appeared to believe), but rather lives *hic and nunc*, in a particular social milieu that determines or conditions life and practical potential, and puts specific obstacles in the way of the exercise of fundamental rights. This concept was primarily embodied in Article 22, which forms the preamble to a set of economic and social rights by enunciating their underlying political philosophy, that 'everyone, as a member of society, has the right to social security' and so on. Secondly, the Socialist influence can be noted in the inclusion of the economic, social and cultural rights (Articles 22–27). Thirdly, the countries of Eastern Europe managed to gain acceptance for their idea of the individual's *duties* towards the community (Article 29(1)). Fourthly, the idea prevailed that rights are acceptable only if exercised in such a way as not to clash with the objectives and principles of the United Nations (Article 29(3)), or the exercise of rights by other individuals or groups (Article 30) – an attenuated version of the Socialist demand to fight the rebirth of fascism.

The framework I have called *nationalistic*, as being inspired by the need to safeguard national sovereignty as much as possible, took shape above all in the elimination of the right to petition, in the emasculation of the right to rebellion and in the non-inclusion of the rights of national minorities. These measures, as I said above, were initiatives of the Western states, who were fearful of seeing a Declaration that would in some way stimulate centrifugal forces within them, or even legitimize subversive groups. Another way of taking precautions against possible 'humanitarian excesses' and of protecting state sovereignty to the maximum extent was the decision not to endow the Declaration with binding legal force. It was adopted as merely a mutual, solemn promise, binding at the ethical and political levels but it did not impose actual legal obligations on states. The Socialists were against this devaluation, believing that a legally binding act would have been a better weapon in their campaign against the rottenness of the West (on the questionable assumption that the values upheld in the Declaration were at any rate fully implemented in their countries and consequently they had nothing to fear from a legally binding document).

It is interesting to note, then, that the nationalistic conception that ended up permeating the Declaration was not the one advanced by the Socialists, but the one maintained – from a position that was, all in all, defensive – by the Western countries.

Who won and who lost in 1948?

Re-reading the Declaration forty years on – with hindsight – we can confirm that at least at first sight the Declaration represented a great victory for the West. It marked the achievement of Franklin D. Roosevelt's great dream: to see projected onto the world scene some of the noble ideals of the liberal democratic tradition of the West. Henceforth these ideals would be valid not only for the Western democracies, but they would also constitute the reference point and the goal for quite different types of state – different in civilization, historical tradition, social structure, economic development and political organization – from the industrialized countries of the North. The natural-law ideals of respect for human dignity were thus extended to the whole world: not only to UN member states, but to all states of the world community. And this was why, on a suggestion from France, the title of the Declaration was changed from 'international' to 'universal'.[31]

It may be objected that this was a Pyrrhic victory, for several reasons. Firstly, the Socialist countries, as I said earlier, did not see the Declaration as a solemn decalogue valid for all, but merely as a weapon in the cold war, a weapon to attack the West. Secondly, they conspicuously dissociated themselves from the final Declaration, abstaining in the final vote of the text. Thirdly, two other important states, South Africa and Saudi Arabia, likewise abstained, demonstrating that they were not prepared to yield to the demands of the Declaration (a further two states, Honduras and Yemen, did not participate in the vote, but their reasons remain unknown). Fourthly, the Declaration merely expressed a set of ethical and political ideals, with no legally binding effect.

However, on closer inspection, it seems clear that the Declaration need not be considered a Pyrrhic victory. It was a real victory for the West certainly, but it was also a victory for other countries as well; above all, it was a victory – though certainly not an unmitigated one – for humanity as a whole. I shall now say why.

The West succeeded in securing acceptance not only for the idea of a world decalogue based on fundamental concepts from its classical tradition, but also for some specific demands (e.g. the right to property, and exclusion of the right to self-determination of peoples). But it is also true that the Socialists, as I said above, considerably reduced the impact of the Western ideas by securing approval for some fundamental postulates of the Marxist ideology (see the section on the debate at the United Nations above). More importantly, the debate on the Declaration gave the Socialist countries the impetus to begin their *slow march towards human rights*. They started off by openly distrusting the whole concept of human rights, regarding it as futile Western propaganda; subsequently, when they saw that economic and social rights had been accepted, they began to participate and make proposals, a number of which were accepted. After approval of the Declaration, they graudally came to conceive the text not as a propaganda instrument, but as an ideal point of reference that should be respected – though for many years they merely paid lip service to it.

However, above all it was for the Third World that the Declaration – despite its narrow, Western mould – had the most important *educational effect*. In the 1950s and 1960s, when the various ex-colonial countries began to acquire independence, the Declaration acted as a lodestar, as a pointer to a state structure that is consistent with human dignity (indeed a number of these countries inserted at least part of the Declaration in their national constitutions, thus transforming it into a legally binding text within their domestic settings). Admittedly, a few of these states saw the

Declaration as providing merely broad guidelines, to be sacrificed whenever political or military needs or the demands of economic development seemed more imperative than the demands of human dignity. The fact remains, however, that – except for Iran[32] – none of these newly independent states has ever formally rejected or contested the Declaration; each has maintained it as an inspiration, even when 'special circumstances' have been seen as preventing its application.

The Declaration, despite all its weaknesses, has thus had the power of the great political or religious texts. It has gradually worn down the various resistances of the states that initially refused to uphold it, gradually involving them at the ethical and political level. If, then, approval of the Declaration initially marked a victory for the West, in the long term the victor has been the world community, since it has won a 'code of conduct' valid for all.

The present value of the Declaration

The Universal Declaration does not exhibit the serious moral and religious tension underlying the American political documents, nor is it underpinned by the doctrinaire dogmatism and unquestioned faith in a few supreme values (natural rights, reason, the individual) that so strongly permeated the French Declaration of 1789, constituting not only the limitations, but also the charm, of that vibrant, peremptory document. It is neither couched in the solemn and lofty language of the American Declarations, nor does it use the hard-hitting words of the French Declaration. In comparison with the great texts of the past, the 1948 Declaration seems dull, almost grey, devoid as it is of the solemn rhetoric in which its 'forebears' are worded, and of the emotive impetus which animates them. It is distinctly down to earth, without magniloquent appeals.

This should not surprise us. The American and French texts bore the imprint of highly cohesive and forceful ideologies specific to their age. Those texts reflected the ideas and demands of a particular society circumscribed in space and time. The American Declaration invoked *God*; the French one appealed to *Nature* and to *Reason*. The 1948 Declaration was unable to invoke either: a fact regretted by a number of the General Assembly delegates. The Lebanese delegate hoped that it would be said that the family 'is endowed by the Creator' with inalienable rights;[33] the delegates of Brazil and the Netherlands advocated reference to the divine origin of man;[34] but the Soviet Union opposed these proposals[35] and the Indian delegate insisted that the Declaration should remain outside any particular philosophical position.[36]

   The Universal Declaration is the *fruit of several ideologies: the meeting point of diverse conceptions of man and society.* As was rightly pointed out by P. Imbert,[37] it does not constitute the 'blow-up', at world level, of national texts, but their 'adjustment' to a multicultural world that is deeply heterogeneous and divided. To some extent, it has fulfilled the hope expressed in 1947 by the Chinese delegate to the UN Commission on Human Rights, that the Declaration should reconcile Confucius and Thomas Aquinas.[38] It follows that it could not be other than a compromise, and had to 'fly low'. Accordingly, we do not find in the Declaration either the peremptory assertion of a view as to the origin of man and society, nor the ill-concealed intrusion of any powerful political myths (as I noted above, the only such myth embraced in 1948 was that of the 'law', but not in the absolute terms of the texts of the past).

   The Universal Declaration's abstention from rhetoric is, however, also due to the need to speak to billions of people, with different religions, cultures, social traditions and political institutions. Only simple language, free from religious and philosophical resonances, could manage to address such different, often opposing, peoples. The 'greyness' of the Declaration is the necessary consequence of its composite origin, but was also largely desired by its 'fathers', in view of its diverse audience.

   What counts, over and above the Declaration's language, is that it is a *decalogue for five thousand million individuals.* Let us look at it from this point of view: we can then see that, despite all its lacunae and shortcomings, it has had the enormous merit of constituting *one of the factors for unifying humanity.* It has proclaimed a series of precepts that all of humanity is to observe – Eleanor Roosevelt was therefore right when, on 9 December 1948, she said that 'it might well become the Magna Charta of all mankind'.[39] Lord Acton's comment about the 1789 Declaration – that those two pages weighed more than whole libraries and than all of Napoleon's armies – may thus also be applied to the Universal Declaration, despite the contrary opinion of a great British international lawyer.[40]

   Ultimately, then, what was the Declaration's *real weight?* I have sought above to show that the Declaration has, almost imperceptibly, produced many practical effects – most of these visible only in the long term. The most important is an effect that I shall define in essentially negative terms: the Declaration is one of the fundamental parameters with which the international community *delegitimizes* states. A state that systematically tramples the Declaration under foot is not regarded as worthy of approval by the world community. For centuries, there was no single criterion in international society for approving or blaming its members. Now we have available the one supplied by the Declaration, along with Article 2(4) of the United Nations Charter (a state that breaks the peace is to be condemned) and Article 1 of the two 1966 Covenants on human rights (a state that denies the right of self-determination must be exposed). For a primitive, anarchic community such as the world community, this is already considerable progress.

One last question which needs our attention is whether, all these years after its proclamation, the Declaration is now *outdated*. In many respects, it is outdated; in others, it remains valid. The Declaration does not express contemporary values and practices in that it fails to sanction the right of peoples to self-determination (proclaimed in 1960, 1966 and 1970 in solemn acts of the General Assembly); it also fails to accord the 'right of petition' to victims of breaches of human rights (a right to some extent recognized, albeit with many qualifications and the greatest caution, in the Optional Protocol to the Covenant on Civil and Political Rights of 1966); and finally, it fails – except in a very indirect and convoluted fashion – to recognize the right of oppressed groups and peoples to take up arms against a despotic regime when there is no peaceful way to secure their human rights.

Thus there are grey areas; however, these have been partially clarified and fleshed out by subsequent declarations, covenants or conventions. On the whole, the Declaration remains a lodestar, which has guided the community of states as they gradually emerged from the dark age when the possession of armies, guns and warships was the sole factor for judging the conduct of states, and there were no general principles, accepted and approved by all, for distinguishing good from evil in the world community.

3

Are Human Rights Truly Universal?

The problem

As I said in chapter 2, mankind today has a number of great normative texts setting out the fundamental rights and freedoms that ought to be enjoyed by every individual on earth, and correlatively the self-limitations that states should adopt in order to guarantee these rights and liberties. It is no coincidence that these texts were drawn up under the aegis of the organization that brings together almost all states in the international community: the United Nations. The texts are known, if not to all, at least to many: the 1948 Universal Declaration of Human Rights, the 1966 Covenant on Civil and Political Rights, with its accompanying Optional Protocol (which provides for the right of individuals to make complaints concerning violations of the Covenant by governments), and the Covenant on Economic, Social and Cultural Rights, also of 1966.

The first document in this trilogy binds all states in the world; but not with those relatively heavy bonds deriving from true legal norms. It binds them through its moral and political weight, and through the authority derived from the fact that it constitutes a set of natural-law principles to which the states of the world are invited to adhere. The Covenants have different advantages. Precisely because they are actual treaties, they bind only those countries that have explicitly accepted them through the formal procedure of ratification or accession. They are therefore stronger in that they lay down binding legal imperatives, but at the same time they are also weaker in that they involve only those states that have agreed to observe them, some 90 out of 171 states.

The three documents seek to address the whole of mankind with a single voice. And they do indeed provide the same broad parameters of behaviour for all states. But it would have been unrealistic for them to set forth rigidly the same scheme of relationships between governments and individuals for all countries in the world; they could not, in other words, have projected onto the world stage the same *model of society* and the same *model of state*. Suffice it to note that the documents were drawn up by states of vastly diverse kinds: some industrialized, others developing; some with market economies, others with planned economies; pluralist states and one-party states; states with official national religions and others that were secular; military regimes and civilian regimes; monarchies and republics; autocratic governments and parliamentary democracies. It would have been unlikely that any of the 'fathers' of those great treaties would have agreed to the adoption by the world community of a system of government or model of society that was the radical negation of their own domestic regime. It is unrealistic to imagine a state collaborating in the setting up of an international normative framework destined to be used by others to deny the legitimacy of its own domestic political system.

Accordingly, the decalogues set up at the international level in no way 'favour' any of the various political or governmental systems I have just mentioned. They quite rightly do not attempt to make the internal political situation in the various countries fit some absurd Procrustean bed. Each country is left free to adopt the institutional arrangements and political system most congenial to it, those which best reflect its people's needs and its national traditions. All that the texts demand is respect for certain *minimum standards* concerning relations between the citizen and the state: respect for certain essential human rights, certain essential freedoms and the right to self-government. Each country is free to decide how to bring about this self-government (through a multi-party system or a single party; by proportional or first-past-the-post electoral systems, or on the basis of the 'blocked single slate'). Each country also has the right to decide how it will organize the periodic consultations necessary to appoint its ruling bodies, just as each state may decide how it will allow for citizen participation in government. Equally, each state may place restrictions on the fundamental rights and freedoms of its citizens for reasons dictated by requirements of public order or national security, morality or health. Finally, each state has the right to choose its own economic and social system − whether this be capitalist, socialist or of some other kind − so long as it respects and promotes certain rights enjoyed by individuals in the sphere of economic and social relations.

As can be seen, then, the international decalogues are very flexible. This flexibility is accentuated by the well-recognized limitations inherent in the supervisory mechanisms provided for at the international level. The states bound by the Covenants thus enjoy a large measure of manoeuvre.

Despite all this, the fact remains that the Declaration and the two Covenants set forth rules of universal scope, which are supposed, at least so far as their general thrust is concerned, to be valid for all states in the world, and which have as their beneficiaries the five thousand million inhabitants of the earth. But is this relative universality *real*? Are these rules, these universal precepts, perceived and implemented in the same way throughout the world, or do greater differences and divergences exist than those already allowed by the rules themselves?

One could easily reply that this search for universality is vain or otiose: not even within the most homogeneous group of states – the members of the Council of Europe – can one discern identical views on many crucial problems. Dissimilar views have even been taken by the two international organs responsible for ensuring the proper implementation of the European Convention on Human Rights: the European Commission and Court of Human Rights. By way of illustration, I shall mention the infamous 'five techniques to help interrogation' used by the British Security Forces in Northern Ireland in 1971: while the European Commission held in 1976 that the techniques amounted to torture proper,[1] the European Court found in 1978 that they did not cause a suffering so intense as to constitute torture, and rather amounted to 'inhuman or degrading treatment'.[2] Similarly, the refusal of British authorities to remove from the birth certificate of a male transsexual a reference to his being a female at birth – a reference that produced a good deal of adverse consequences for the social and working life of the person concerned – was unanimously regarded by the European Commission in 1984 as a breach of the 'right to respect for one's private life', whereas the European Court, by a majority vote, took the opposite view in 1986.[3] Plainly, such differences of opinion cannot be eliminated, nor indeed are they to be deprecated: human rights make up such a complex, multifaceted and intricate matter that divergences are inevitable, when it comes to the implementation of those rights.

The questions I have raised do not aim at establishing whether there exists complete uniformity in the interpretation and application of human rights standards. By raising those questions I intended rather to look at the *basic approaches and perceptions* taken by states in the area of human rights, in order to see to what extent they diverge or converge.

Before addressing these questions, I shall briefly dwell on two possible answers that would constitute easy ways out.

First, the questions raised above could be dismissed outright by those who still believe in the famous proposition by Joseph de Maistre: 'I have met in my life French, Italians, Russians, etc.; I even know, thanks to Montesquieu, that one can be Persian; but nowhere have I met in my life the man; if he does exist, this is without my knowing'.[4] It follows logically from this proposition that, as individuals and groups are different – by definition – there cannot exist any similarity of application or even perception of human rights standards in the various nations of the world. And yet, close analysis of the present condition shows, as I shall point out below, that convergences do indeed exist and that many states tend to take the same basic view of human rights.

Another answer to the above questions might be found in the work of the French philosopher Jean Hyppolite. In 1964 Hyppolite wrote of the paradox whereby our epoch is at the same time the one in which the 'existential sense of universality' is strongest, partly because 'all regions of the earth have now been discovered and have come into relationship with each other', and also the one in which there has been the clearest 'decline in universal foundations and standards'.[5] And yet, this answer, right in itself, is not enough: there are specific reasons, *peculiar to human rights*, that militate against this universality.

Divergences in philosophical conceptions and cultural traditions

Let me say immediately that universality is, at least for the present, a myth. Not only are human rights observed differently – certainly to differing degrees – in different countries; but they are also *conceived of* differently. I shall seek to identify the principal points on which the various countries of the world still seem far apart: in other words, the points at which the effort at *world unification*, pursued in developing the three great documents, has still not been accomplished.

Firstly, there are profound divergences in the *philosophical conception* of human rights. The Western countries continue tenaciously to defend their 'natural-law' view of human rights – the one they put forward when the three great texts were being drafted. For them, human rights are innate in individuals, are an intrinsic factor in the 'quality of the human person', and hence precede any state structure and must be absolutely respected by governments. A state that violates them in its laws and its actions breaches one of the very prerequisites of civil coexistence between states and may legitimately be brought to account.

For the Socialist countries, by contrast, human rights exist only in society and in the state, and only to the extent that they are specifically recognized. They do not pre-exist the state, but rather are accorded by it. The state may therefore limit them when circumstances so require.

Another important divergence concerns different *cultural and religious conceptions*. For the West, proclaiming human rights means above all protecting the sphere of individual freedom against the overweening power of an invasive state. This concept – which, as is well known, goes back to Locke – was very effectively brought out by Benjamin Constant in his famous essay on *Freedom ancient and modern* (1819)[6] – an essay in which many see a moderate reduction of the lofty principles proclaimed in 1789. 'For the ancients', wrote Constant, 'freedom was constituted by active, constant participation in the commonwealth. Our freedom ought to consist in the peaceful enjoyment of private independence . . .'[7] [I]ndividual autonomy is the foremost modern need'.[8] For the ancients, freedom 'consisted in the collective, but direct exercise of various parts of the whole sovereignty; in discussing in the public forum war and peace, in concluding treaties of alliance with foreigners, voting on laws, in pronouncing judgments, in examining accounts,' and so on; the ancients, though, 'accepted as compatible with this collective freedom the individual's complete subjection to the authority of the whole'.[9] It is precisely this subjection that man today forcibly rejects. Today, the individual delegates to others the exercise of political power: what concerns him is 'safety in private enjoyment' ('la sécurité dans les jouissances privées');[10] Constant characterized freedom as 'the guarantees accorded by the institutions for that enjoyment'.[11]

This is, broadly speaking, the Western conception of liberty. There is a markedly different view in the Socialist countries and again in the Third World. For the former, the individual's freedom can be realized only in a society in which classes, bound up with the capitalist system of production, have ceased to exist, so that the individual can fully participate without hindrance or inequalities in the life of the community. Taking up concepts that were first put forward by J. J. Rousseau, socialist thinkers and politicians argue that freedom does not necessarily mean putting restraints on an oppressive central power: the central power is an expression of the community and identifies itself with it. Freedom means rather the creation of mechanisms that promote and enhance integration between individual and community. The stress is no longer on the dialectic between liberty and authority, but on the dialectic between individual and community.

A still more radical difference in conception is the one between the Western and the Asian great cultural traditions. In the Buddhist conception, society is patterned on the family: the political leader – the emperor, in the past – is like the father of a family, with all the powers, authority and responsibilities of the *pater familias*. Freedom therefore consists not in guaranteeing a space free from possible invasion or oppression by the authorities, but in harmonizing as far as possible the individual's action with the leader's, in view of the duty of obedience owed to the latter.

Even more inclined to subject individuals to the political leader is the Hindu tradition, which has impregnated the social life, and especially the ideology, of India, right up to its Declaration of Independence, and beyond. In Hindu tradition, division into castes – though legally abolished – still involves an obligation on each member of a caste to accept their social status without rebellion. It is the task of all individuals to strive to act positively within their own caste, in order to pass to a superior caste in the next life, or at least not worsen their social standing after death. There is no question of any struggle against authority or of safeguarding a sphere of freedom against an external power.

Similar considerations hold true for Confucianism, a religion (and also a vision of society and of relations between individuals) that developed first in China and subsequently spread to Japan. In Confucian tradition the fundamental nucleus of society is the family; within this miniature social structure, the primary position goes to the head of the household, who is owed unconditional respect by the other members. This patriarchal vision is extended to the state: the Emperor is seen as the head of a family to whom absolute deference is owed. This leaves little room for human rights. The same is also true in the Islamic tradition, or at least in practice in the Islamic countries, which have in some respects steadily moved away from the principles of the Koran. In particular, although there is no radical incompatibility between Islam and the essential principles of human rights, there is a conflict as regards the relationship between man and woman: in Islam these are placed squarely in a relation of subordination, the latter to the former.

In the African tradition, which is to a large extent a tradition of tribal practices and customs, the individual's self-realization is through the community, which is headed by a leader, to whose authority all must bow. There is no reason to fight against the leader, since he does not oppress the members of the community, but rather guides them by acting in such a way as to allow them to integrate fully into the whole: what he does is thus beneficial to the interests of the collectivity.

It will be objected that all these Asian or African traditions have been, as it were, diluted or enfeebled by contact with the modern state: as soon as that characteristic construct of Western Europe has taken root in Africa or Asia, all its characteristic ambiguities and concerns have surfaced, including the dialectic between authority and liberty. This also explains why modern state structures have such difficulty functioning in so many African or Asian countries. It is a plant that puts down roots only slowly, and all too often finds itself there in inhospitable, if not indeed sterile, soil.

Divergences in treatment of the problem of international protection of human rights

Looking more closely at the attitude of states, one finds still further divergences and conflicts as regards a number of fundamental issues bound up with human rights.

Firstly, there is a difference between the Socialist 'statist' conception of human rights, and the current Western *international*, or rather 'metanational', view. I shall attempt to explain in what this divergence consists.

In the Socialist view, it is the task of the international community to agree on a series of broad rules or standards as to the categories or types of human rights to be recognized, that is, as to the restrictions that sovereign states have to accept in order to give sufficient 'space' to individuals within the internal system of each country. Once this step has been taken, it is for each state to lend greater specificity to these broad rules or standards. This is done through domestic legislation laying down the scope of the rights, the powers of the governmental authorities and the procedures open to individuals to seek redress should the rights be breached. At this point, the international community no longer has anything to say on the matter: only sovereign states can decide – though of course within the framework set by the international rules how human rights are to be observed and implemented. The international community 'passes the baton', as it were, to national systems, particularly as regards checks on observance of the rights in question. This means that so far as the Socialist countries are concerned, it is not for other states, or the organized international community, to inquire into the observance of human rights. This would contravene a fundamental principle of international law, namely the prohibition of interference in internal affairs – a principle that has the essential objective of protecting state sovereignty and keeping every country in the condition of self-sufficient, well-armoured monads. The sole exception to this rule of absolute non-interference in the affairs of other states is where breaches of human rights become so grave and systematic as to constitute a threat to peace. Only in this case is the organized international community entitled to intervene by discussing the situation, making recommendations and, if necessary, going further, even to the point of recommending or, if possible, ordering sanctions (the cases of South Africa, Chile and Israel – the latter for violations in the occupied Arab Territories – being, for the Socialist countries, examples of such exceptions to the rule of absolute non-interference).

The position of Western states, particularly Scandinavian countries and some other countries in Western Europe, is radically different. They hold that the modern state ought to become a sort of 'glass house', so that anyone can look in and establish whether what goes on there conforms to international standards. According to the West, this right to outside inspection may be exercised through the creation of international monitoring mechanisms, whose aim is to ascertain whether a state is in fact observing the international obligations it has assumed. In the view of these states it is absurd to make a sharp distinction between accepting obligations concerning human rights at the international level, and implementing those obligations at the national level. There must be a continuum, an uninterrupted chain between international and national actions. Why? For one very simple reason: the state agencies all too often fail to observe international obligations which come from 'outside'; or else national authorities charged with translating international obligations into domestic rules of conduct 'manipulate' these obligations and adapt them to the needs of national sovereignty – all the more so because normally the beneficiaries of the international rules are citizens of the state being called on to apply those rules, that is, the very individuals over whom the government authorities are seeking to maintain their power in other ways. Only the vigilant eye of the international community can ensure the proper observance of international standards, in the interest not of one state or another but of the individuals themselves.

A second difference between East and West, closely follows the first: it concerns the main features that international supervisory mechanisms ought to present. After long drawn-out debates, talks and negotiations, the Socialist countries have ended up accepting the Western idea that international instruments are needed to ensure, or at least encourage, national respect for international standards on human rights. This conversion to the West's idea was, however, a painful process, which carried with it the dilution of international supervisory procedures and the attachment of so many qualifications as practically to make them a blunt weapon. In the eyes of the West, the most effective form of international scrutiny is for the individual who is denied a right to which he or she is entitled, to 'activate' some form of international guarantee. And yet not even the West shows much enthusiasm for advocating international *judicial* guarantees: that is, international courts before which individuals could bring actions against states, accusing the latter of infringing upon human rights. The boldest Western countries (once again, the Western European states, plus some Scandinavian countries and Canada) do however assert the need at least to set up international monitoring agencies. An individual whose rights have been breached could then seek the moral and political 'condemnation' of the state responsible. Such a condemnation would not be an actual judgment, but rather a non-binding verdict. Besides, as is well known, the quasi-judicial procedures existing within the Council of Europe (procedures hinging on two bodies, the European Commission and Court of Human Rights) are quite exceptional, for attempts made in Latin America to establish similar mechanisms have not yet yielded significant results.

For the West the reasons behind this conception of international scrutiny are obvious. Firstly, only a monitoring system activated by those directly affected by breaches can prove truly effective, for if it is the case, which it usually is, that breaches have been committed by a state against its own citizens, no other international subject or agency has an interest in setting in motion a guarantee mechanism. Secondly, if the supervisory procedures are at least quasi-judicial, there is an assurance that the findings of fact will be something approaching the truth. Clearly, only adversarial proceedings, where both parties (the individual complainant and the accused government) have a chance to state their cases and an assessment is arrived at by a group of people truly independent of the parties, can provide the guarantees of equity and justice required in such a delicate area. The Western states (or at least many of them) have gradually come to embrace the concept of 'right of petition to an international body' which France, supported by the Eastern European countries, had proposed in 1946–8.[12] So the situation is now reversed with Eastern Europe steadfast against any right of international petition and the West its staunch supporter. It is too early to say whether the demise of control by Communist parties in Eastern Europe will affect any charge in this area of international relations.

Let us look at the limits within which the Socialist countries have come cautiously to approach the Western position on international supervision. For most states of Eastern Europe, the sole form of acceptable international supervision consisted in *periodic considera-tion* – by intergovernmental bodies – of reports on observance of international rules drawn up bv the individual states concerned. For most Eastern European states, this type of monitoring respects the concept of national sovereignty, while making some cautious concession to the need for international openness. National sovereignty is fully guaranteed since the subject of verification is the periodic report drawn up by the individual state itself: accordingly, everything is in full conformity with the notion that it is for each state to ensure application of the international norms within its own domestic order in accordance with the modalities it prefers. It is for the individual state to report to the international bodies on the way in which it has applied the international rules. The international body may make observations and comments, but never go so far as to make specific criticisms, let alone condemna-tions. From this point of view too, then, state sovereignty remains intact. It is easy to imagine how this kind of control is implemented in practice: every state tends to depict its own domestic system as a paradise, or something like it, and international bodies must confine themselves to articulating cautious doubts or setting forth considerations of a general nature. State sovereignty emerges victorious; individuals disappear from the international scene, and the violations they have suffered remain unexposed.

Another sharp differentiation, again chiefly between East and West, concerns the conception of the *link between human rights and the maintenance of peace*. For the Socialist countries, protection of human rights is one of the ways of promoting the maintenance of peaceful relationships among states. They start from the arguments put forward at the end of the Second World War and 'codified' in the United Nations Charter. The great conflagration that had shaken the world had largely been due to the racist, totalitarian policy of Nazism. Accordingly, if political systems that respected human rights were gradually to be furthered throughout the world, this would help to ward off the threat of another world conflict. This argument, correct in itself, can, however, lead to a fallacious conclusion: peace being the supreme goal, everything else takes *second place*; accordingly, if in some particular circumstance the need to respect human rights is liable to cause friction and conflict, thereby threatening peace, it must be swept under the carpet. Between the two goals, the one that must prevail is that of peace. Understood properly, this view is a logical extension of the idea that everything should turn around the essential pivot of state sovereignty, with its corollary of the prohibition on interference in the domestic affairs of other states. In fact, continually advocating the maintenance of friendly relationships among states as the ultimate goal leads to the perception that requiring some country to respect human rights may be a dangerous source of far-reaching disagreement, and accordingly such action should be rejected, indeed forbidden by the international community. (On this issue see however the qualifications I set out in the last section of this chapter.)

The West's view is radically different. For the Western countries, the need to ensure respect for human dignity is always pre-eminent. It is therefore acceptable for a state or group of states to take initiatives and make *demarches* towards another state to encourage, or even attempt to force it to show greater respect for human rights, even if this goes against 'good neighbourliness', or friendly relations in general. For the West, the proper balance between the need to respect the domestic affairs of foreign states and the countervailing requirement to do everything possible to promote respect for human rights is as follows. In cases where violations perpetrated in another state become serious, systematic and massive, intervention by other states or by international organs becomes acceptable, even if it necessarily gives rise to disagreements, tensions, or even conflict.

A fourth area, where there is a wide gap between Western countries on the one hand and Third World and Socialist states on the other, concerns the role and weight to be given to the 'international context' in the event of breaches of human rights. In the view of developing countries – joined here by Eastern European states – it is illogical and inappropriate to seek out violations committed in other states and then accuse the governments concerned of trampling on human rights. Breaches of those rights – not only civil and political rights but also, and even more so, economic, social and cultural ones – should instead be considered in the general context of the internal situation of the state being challenged, and also as regards the position of that state *vis-à-vis* other countries. According to this view, if account is not taken of the overall picture, two risks arise. Firstly, one fails to identify, and come to grips with, the *causes* of the breaches of human rights. These causes normally lie in underdevelopment; in the need to cope adequately with economic and social problems; and in international conditions, in the main economic ones, but also political ones (which are believed to explain why countries are, on occasions, compelled to suspend or restrict certain rights, such as trade union freedom, rights to private property or freedom of movement, in order to meet international economic pressures – for instance, the need to pay debts to foreign banks or cope with a fall in the price of raw materials). The second danger which lies in a 'narrow view' of breaches of human rights is that these breaches can be *instrumentalized* in order to criticize certain countries in which underdevelopment, transitory historical circumstances and so on, may make some restriction of freedom necessary. This instrumentalization is, according to those states, most often practised by Western countries, in order to point the finger at developing or Socialist countries and condition their actions at home and abroad.

The West's reply to this thesis is that all too often these arguments act merely as a 'rationalization' of domestic failings: facile excuses, to justify serious departures from international standards. These departures very often originate from authoritarian forms of government, particularly from military regimes. For the West there is very little foundation in the two theses mentioned, which amount to nothing more than 'ideology'.

As we can see, in this area too there is a considerable split between two groups, which seem to end up inevitably accusing each other of instrumentalization for propaganda purposes.

A fifth area where the confrontation seems no less bitter concerns the *relationship between two classes of human rights*: civil and political rights on the one hand, and economic, social and cultural ones on the other. According to the developing and many Socialist countries, the second group is the one that ought to be favoured in international action. There are two reasons. Firstly, these rights are intrinsically more important. What sense is there in talking of freedom of expression when one is hungry, jobless or homeless? Economic and social rights have absolute priority, for it is only when they are fully realized that it is possible to create the *de facto* equality that makes civil and political rights fully realizable. The second reason is that, especially in developing countries, it is in the economic and social fabric that the most painful shortcomings exist, so that this is where intervention is most needed. In those countries, economic and social backwardness means that not only are roads, hospitals, and infrastructures generally lacking, but so are elementary and higher education. This, then, is the area where intervention is needed, to narrow the gap which separates these countries from the industrialized ones. Accordingly, progressive recognition of economic, social and cultural rights must be insisted on, at the international level.

The Western states, by contrast, tend to put the emphasis on civil and political rights. This is firstly because these rights are a 'highlight' in their history, virtually symbolizing the progress of the modern state, having been wrested from despotic power following bitter struggle, rebellion or revolution. A second reason is that for Western countries respect for these rights continues to be of great significance. The major human rights issue in Western industrialized states remains: to what extent is the central apparatus to be limited so as to prevent it excessively invading the individual's sphere? The economic structure of these countries, with a market economy (so that individual initiative and enterprise still have an extremely important role), along with the excessive growth of the state, which tends to penetrate every area of private life, even the most intimate ones, mean that civil and political rights remain crucial. There is nothing more obvious for these states than to *project outwards* their own problems and concerns, and hence, internationally too, to favour this category of rights and freedom. Apart from that, though, there are also less 'ideological' motives. The Western countries stress that full enjoyment of material prosperity is worth little unless one is free to express one's ideas, elect the people one prefers to lead the state, or travel and move freely both at home and abroad. Civil and political rights thus remain indispensable, even if the state's effort has to concentrate primarily on raising the population's standard of living. It follows that it is meaningless to set up a hierarchy among categories of rights; above all, for the states in question, it is meaningless to relegate civil and political freedoms to second place, as if they were a luxury.

As we can see, in this case too the divergences among the various alignments of states are profound, and the diplomatic formulas that have been used to make the twain meet on paper are rather meaningless. One of these formulas speaks about the 'interdependence of civil and political rights with economic, social and cultural ones'. This convenient catchphrase serves to dampen the debate while leaving everything the way it was. The diplomats who thrash out these verbal solutions at international meetings go back home satisfied, each thinking their own interpretation of the (conveniently ambiguous) phrase agreed upon is the right one. In fact, the problems remain, and the political and ideological clashes are postponed, only to emerge even more pointedly at the next opportunity.

Divergences regarding particular human rights

Turning now to a consideration of specific rights and freedoms, here too we come up against considerable differentiation in the way states see these rights. Clearly, divergences can be noted in the way states apply the 'escape clauses' in order to allow themselves room for manoeuvre. These clauses allow for 'suspension of obligations' for reasons of public order, national security, morals, public health and so on. Admittedly, the various international supervisory bodies have managed to secure acceptance for the principle that these concepts ought not to be interpreted solely and exclusively in the light of corresponding national concepts. This has barred the way to utter fragmentation of those clauses and to total anarchy in the application of the rights that those clauses restrict and constrain. Nevertheless the fact remains that every state, though it cannot simply hide behind its own domestic law, retains considerable discretion, for it is impossible at the international level to furnish a uniform interpretation of the clauses, and the supervisory bodies have no judicial powers that would enable them to lay down binding interpretations. In the last instance, the scope of the escape clauses remains in the hands of the state concerned.

Furthermore, significant differences can be identified in the very conception of some specific human rights. I shall give only a few examples, starting with freedom of movement. For the Western countries, this is one of the most important forms of manifestation of the personality. How can an individual develop and achieve self-realization without being free to move about the national territory, freely choose residence and workplace, in a word, decide the 'area' most in line with individual interests and activities? This freedom also includes the possibility of going abroad, whether for leisure, self-improvement, or just to live in a country where one's qualities are better appreciated or better paid. For the West, freedom of movement is not only part of the concept of freedom of the individual and free enterprise, but also derives from an essential postulate: the human person has potential, and must be free to develop and enrich it. In other words, the basis for that freedom is not only the capitalistic-individualistic conception of the world, but also the conception of man that came to maturity with the Renaissance: the human person is seen as a microcosm containing a number of potential areas for development, all of which deserve an environment which will allow them to grow.

This view is bound to fall on deaf ears in the Third World and in the Socialist countries. In the former, the need for economic take-off necessitates drastic limitations on the 'brain-drain'. However much it may be the fault of colonialism, it is a fact that at independence those countries found themselves with very few graduates or other qualified people, and therefore had quickly to train new leaders and managers. It would therefore be illogical from their viewpoint to permit the expatriation of young people attracted abroad by easy gain or by the facilities of modern, well-equipped research centres. Similarly, within those countries there is a need to restrict movement: the rapid formation of a few urban centres, densely populated and with abundant service industries, dangerously impoverishes the countryside – where leaders and managers (technicians, doctors, engineers and so on) are also needed. Somewhat similar considerations have applied so far to many Socialist countries; however, there, in addition to economic reasons, there were more strictly political or ideological ones for restricting freedom of movement. All this has made the Third World and Socialist concept of freedom of movement diametrically opposite to that prevailing in the West.

Similar differences can be found, as regards the effect of science and technology on the enjoyment of human rights. Debate on this topic was initiated by France at the United Nations in the 1970s. For France and other Western countries, there was a need to identify and restrain the dangerous outcomes that modern technology might have for the privacy of individuals and groups. Not surprisingly, the problem was not seen in the same terms in non-industrial countries where the development of technology was welcomed. Far from seeking restrictions on the possible uses of computers, those countries instead pressed for the introduction of scientific and technological progress to their communities.

A third example concerns the right to development. The Third World, supported by the Socialists, latched onto this right as early as the 1970s. For them it was a fundamental right belonging both to individuals and to peoples and states. It was a multivalent right, referring both to improvement in economic conditions, and to social, political and cultural development. The entities on which the obligation to fulfil the right was incumbent were states, above all the industrialized ones. So far as the Western countries were concerned, by contrast, this right was a mere slogan; a subterfuge used to include as a human rights issue a demand that the Third World had long and loudly been proclaiming, namely, a demand for major economic assistance from the industrialized countries. As has been pointed out, utilization of human rights rhetoric for this demand had one clear aim: *to dramatize* it, by transforming it into a 'right' so that its bearers could exact its realization from those who, accordingly, had a 'duty' to respect and realize it. (See, however, the qualifications set out in the next section.)

Are there points of convergence?

After what I have written so far, it might be thought the international community was irremediably divided with no meeting point, even on this broad topic of human rights. Every state or group of states, while paying lip-service to a number of commonly accepted precepts, would in fact be serving national needs and interests which are not congruent with those precepts. The 'universality' of human rights standards would be merely a convenient cover, aimed at concealing underlying disputes and differences. That is undoubtedly true. However, there are elements that somewhat moderate and mitigate the ideological and political splits. I shall bring out three essential factors.

Firstly, it is a fact that the Universal Declaration and the various covenants, treaties and declarations that followed ended up involving and, as it were, 'ensnaring' states which were opposed or indifferent to certain aspects of human rights, either due to their historical and cultural traditions or due to different ideologies. Thus, as I have shown in the second chapter, the Socialist countries, having first shown perplexity over, and indeed hostility towards, the Universal Declaration, ended up collaborating in drafting it. Admittedly, they began by thinking of using it as a weapon in the Cold War. But they gradually came to believe in the Declaration as a great ethical and political decalogue that should inspire their actions. More or less the same thing happened to many Third World countries, which ended up energetically participating in producing, if not the Declaration (many of them were not yet independent in 1946–8), at least the 1966 Covenants. This involved them in a process of debate and negotiation in which, while they put forward their needs and asserted their demands, they also accepted many Western or Socialist conceptions. Thus, gradually, the various parameters included in the three international documents in question finished by offering the prospect of common lines of action. Admittedly, this process of unification remains at the moment mainly at a 'rhetorical' level, that is, a normative and to some extent ideological one. But in a world as divided, and fragmented, as the international community today, the existence of a *set of general standards*, however diversely understood and applied, in itself constitutes an important factor for unification.

I wish to stress a second point: despite the differences I have sought to illustrate, a *restricted core* of values and criteria universally accepted by all the states is gradually emerging.

Firstly, one has the impression that some consensus is coming about as to the *relative order of importance* of the various rights; in other words, an understanding in principle as to their 'hierarchy' (although of course any human right is important and indispensable *per se*, one may however establish an order of priority, subject to the caveat that this is tentative, historically relative and primarily operates as a sort of working hypothesis). This understanding is to some extent reflected in a speech delivered in 1977 by the then US Secretary of State Cyrus Vance.[13] In his view, the fundamental core of human rights is made up of the right to life and security: the right not to be tortured or killed illegally. There then follow rights relating to the fundamental needs of the human person: the rights to work, to decent housing, to nourishment, to protection of health. Thirdly, still in some sort of order of importance, are some civil and political rights like freedom of expression and of association, the right to choose a government and hold public office, and so on. I feel that this grading departs considerably from traditional Western conceptions and goes some way to meet the aspirations and ideological conceptions of the Third World and the Socialist countries. It might therefore be regarded as a point of *rapprochement* between the opposing views (the fact that subsequent US Administrations have not consistently upheld Vance's view in no way detracts from its intrinsic importance).

There has also been another convergence. Practically all states in the world seem to share the idea that some of the gravest breaches of human rights are : genocide, racial discrimination (in particular, *apartheid*), the practice of torture, and refusal to recognize the right of peoples to self-determination. This means that agreement in principle has developed, at least as regards an essential core of human values among almost all states in the world. It is foreseeable that this agreement in principle will gradually come to embrace an increasingly wide range of rights.

Furthermore, some convergence has come about in other important areas. For example, recently Eastern European states seem less unresponsive to the Western view of the *relationship between peace and respect for human rights* (reference to this view was made in the third section of this chapter). They now tend to take a somewhat looser view than before, as is evidenced by their voting in favour of General Assembly Resolution 37/200 of 18 December 1982, where it is stated that the absence of peace can in no way relieve a state from its obligation to ensure respect for the human rights of all those under its jurisdiction. Similarly, most Eastern European countries are in the process of changing their minds as far as *international monitoring* is concerned. They now seem less hostile to outside scrutiny of national implementation of international standards in a number of fields including human rights. Behind this shift in the attitude of Eastern European countries one can discern a change in their approach to the principle of non-interference in domestic affairs. Previously, those countries consistently insisted on the rule that states should neither inquire nor make representations about alleged breaches of human rights in other states, as such action ran counter to the long standing principle of non-interference. The only permissible exception was where the breaches were so serious, large-scale and systematic as to amount to a threat to international peace. Recently this approach has been relaxed, as is borne out by the final document adopted at Vienna, on 19 January 1989 by the CSCE (Conference on Security and Co-operation in Europe). All but one of the 35 states adopted the text on the 'Human Dimension of the CSCE' which is of striking importance (Romania entered a reservation). This text provides that each participating state is entitled to *request* from other states, through diplomatic channels, *information* about cases (including specific cases) which raise questions of human rights. In addition, each state may make *observations* to which responses must be given. Furthermore, each state can bring up those cases in *bilateral* meetings. Once a state has received the requested information or response, it may raise the whole question with other participating states in the CSCE. This shift from a *bilateral* to a *multilateral framework* can take place in two ways: a state can simply pass on the received information or response together with its own comments (if any) to the other participating states; or, it may raise the question at one of the meetings of the CSCE. Although of course the CSCE is primarily a European exercise, to a large extent it reflects emerging trends at the universal level.

Yet another area where *rapprochement* is taking place is the right to development. The cleavage between industrialized Western countries and developing nations, to which I drew attention in the preceding section, is now narrowing. This is borne out by the fact that on 4 December 1986 a number of Western countries (including France, Canada and Italy) voted in favour of a General Assembly Resolution on this matter (Resolution 41/128) (however, the United States cast a negative vote, while other Western states including the United Kingdom, the Federal Republic of Germany, Japan and Sweden abstained). This Resolution to a large extent amalgamated the approach of developing countries and that of the West, by diluting the former and incorporating a great number of Western demands relating to the need for developing countries to respect human rights, if they wish to benefit from economic co-operation with industrialized countries.

The third factor I consider important concerns the value of the Declaration and the two Covenants. Despite differences on their interpretation and application, no state (except perhaps for South Africa and Iran)[14] today casts doubt on the significance of these documents as 'targets to aim at' (*standards of achievement*, to use the words of the Universal Declaration). That is, states continue to see in these three documents a set of values that one should strive to realize. This implies that the various countries may gradually harmonize their respective conceptions and visions, drawing impetus, ideas and guidance from these three documents, even if retaining at the same time a divergent set of views and conceptions.

This seems to me to be demonstrated by a number of documents recently adopted by groups of states where traditionally human rights issues have been, if not alien, at least remote. I am referring in particular to the African Charter on Human and Peoples' Rights, approved in 1981,[15] and the two Islamic Declarations on Human Rights, approved in 1981[16] and 1986.[17] Reading these documents, one is immediately struck by the appearance of new rights, or by changes in the emphasis or character of rights already proclaimed in the three great international normative texts (for instance, the rights of peoples are stressed). This is not to say that these documents in any way contradict the underlying values internationally agreed upon. On the contrary, if anything, the recent documents reaffirm these values. Equally, it may be noted that some rights (for instance, that of equality between men and women, already consecrated in the Universal Declaration and the Covenants but in practice applied restrictively in some Arab countries) are vigorously asserted in the two inter-Arab documents. It is almost as if, despite awareness of the gap between what is and what ought to be, there was a desire to restate faith in an important international value, as being applicable at 'regional' level.

The three factors I have sought to bring out together with the new trends emerging in socialist countries[18] perhaps constitute pointers to an effort at gradual unification which, however slow and difficult, gives one hope that states' positions may come closer together, in the human rights field, as in others.

Part II

The Great Outrages against Humanity

4

How Does the International Community React to Genocide?

Genocide in the past

Though the term 'genocide' was coined by Raphael Lemkin in 1944[1] to designate the atrocities being committed by the Nazis in Europe, the phenomenon is, as we know, not new. From the most ancient times the extermination of entire human groups with common ethnic, racial or religious characteristics has been a widespread practice, linked from time to time with one of three factors.

Firstly, genocide has been linked with *wars of conquest*. The recurrent outcome of these has been a massacre of the population of the conquered countries. Secondly, *religion* has often justified the extermination of entire groups of religious opponents. The medieval crusades and the mass killing of Arabs, but also of Jews, well illustrate the extremes to which religious conflict and hatred of those who have embraced another faith can lead. Thirdly, and until very recent times, *colonial domination* by European powers in Latin America, Asia and Africa has been the occasion or cause of the destruction of whole indigenous peoples or populations. The most notorious example is that of the peoples of Latin America decimated by the Spanish Conquistadores.

But it is in our century that the worst and most systematic exterminations have been committed: that of the Armenians in 1915–16 by the Turks, and that of Jews and gypsies in 1939–45 by the Nazis. Let us pause to consider the main historical reasons for these two genocides and the characteristics that distinguish them.

The two genocides in 1915–16 and 1939–45 have a number of aspects in common. Firstly, their immense proportions were made possible by the modern state with its enormous bureaucratic apparatus, centralization of power and monopoly of economic and military resources. Indeed, in both cases, the policy of genocide, invented and planned by the central authorities of the state, was carried out through the use of modern means of communication (for instance, trains for the deportations) and the use of modern techniques in the most perverse forms. The historian Dadrian[2] has recently ascertained that in the case of the Armenians medical experiments were carried out on the victims and gas was used to eliminate them. Both atrocities were also perpetrated against the Jews and gypsies by the Nazis in groups. Another common feature is that the groups being exterminated had a different religion from the exterminators and a well-defined social status in society; both Armenians and Jews were normally in the mercantile professions or were active in industry and trade, as well as in the liberal professions. Those who killed them claimed that the members of the races to be eliminated had taken over a large share of power in civil society and in the state. A third common feature is that both Armenians and Jews were perceived and represented as disloyal to the state, as bearers of subversive ideologies. The Armenians 'rebelled' against the central government during the war in which Turkey was involved and in which the leadership of the Ottoman Empire increasingly felt itself fighting for the defence of Islam. According to the Ottoman authorities it was therefore necessary to prevent the Armenians from compromising the Empire's attempt to defend itself against the overbearing forces of the enemy. In the case of the Jews, they were normally portrayed as dangerous 'plutocrats' or 'marxists', enemies of the majority of the population. The suppression of Armenians and Jews thus also served to strengthen and consolidate dominant groups which were thereby fortified through various centrifugal forces inside them, which united them in a common hatred of the 'others', and in the desire physically to destroy them. As I. L. Horowitz has aptly pointed out: 'genocide is a fundamental mechanism for the unification of the national state'.[3] A further common feature is that the perpetrators of the genocide drew economic benefit from their massacres by taking over the victims' goods, businesses, and other activities. One further thing makes the two genocides similar: the basic ideology underlying them, an ideology aimed at regarding the other, the member of a different group, as a 'non-human being', as something to despise for not participating in the community of values of the dominant group.

For all their similarities, the two genocides were different in other respects. Firstly, the massacre of the Armenians resulted in the mass killing of an ethnic group belonging to the same state as that which was carrying out the massacre: the Armenians who died in 1915–16 were citizens of the Ottoman Empire. The war was only one of the 'factors' which unleashed the hatred that had been brewing for some time. (As is well-known, at the outbreak of war there were about two million Armenians on Turkish territory and about one million seven hundred thousand in Russia; the Turkish rulers had asked Turkish Armenians to carry out subversive activities among Russian Armenians and received a flat refusal; additionally, Armenian battalions were formed in Russia to support the Russian army in the fight against the Ottoman Empire; and the subsequent defeat of the Turks in Transcaucasia, in Russian-Armenian territory, as well as the intervention by Russian Armenians in the Turkish district of Van – to save Armenians living there from the first Turkish 'vendettas' – convinced the 'Young Turks' of the Armenians' 'betrayal', and induced them to start the deportation and subsequent extermination.) In the Nazi genocide, not only citizens of the German Empire but also Jews of every other state occupied by the Nazi army were massacred. Thus in this case, the war supplied the occasion for completing a 'comprehensive' programme of extermination, a programme which by its very nature had no limits of space.

Secondly, while the 'ideological' factor underlying the genocide committed by the Nazis was anti-Semitic racism, the ideology underlying and largely motivating the genocide of the Armenians was the nationalism of the 'Young Turks', their effort to unify and homogenize a state that was showing all too many symptoms of disintegration and fragmentation.

There is a third difference, relating to the international response to the two massacres. Although both the states responsible for the genocide emerged on the losing side of the war in which they had committed it, in the case of Turkey international condemnation was rather lukewarm. It is true that on 24 May 1915 Turkey's enemies (France, Britain and Russia) had stigmatized the massacre of the Armenians as 'crimes against humanity'; it is also true that after the defeat Turkey was compelled to institute proceedings against those responsible, and some leaders were sentenced to death (albeit in their absence). But the trials had little relevance so far as actual punishment of those guilty of the massacres went. Moreover, the Peace Treaty with Turkey (the Treaty of Sèvres of 11 August 1920), providing for the creation of an independent Armenian state, was extensively amended by the subsequent Treaty of Lausanne of 24 July 1923 which confined itself to an imposition on Turkey not to discriminate against Armenians, letting all the commitments to the creation of an independent Armenia fall, and above all containing an 'amnesty declaration' for all those guilty of genocide. On the other hand, in the case of Germany, the international community's response was, as we know, quite severe. The worst Nazi criminals were tried and punished, the German state was largely dismantled, and above all it was decided to put an end to such massacres by adopting an international treaty aimed at preventing the repetition of such horrific acts: the Genocide Convention approved in 1948 by the General Assembly of the United Nations,[4] with which I shall deal shortly.

I must however add that I share the opinion of the majority of those who have perused these sad pages of the history of humanity: even in comparison with the massacres committed after the Second World War, the genocide of the Jews constitutes, in both quantitative and qualitative terms, an *unicum*. This is not only because it had an underlying particularly elaborate, ancient and widespread ideology (anti-Semitism), but also because of the tragic proportions it assumed. The massacre of the Jews was the rigorous, consistent, implacable elimination of all those who belonged to another 'group' – an insane manifestation of a merciless desire physically to annihilate a part of the human race, almost as if its disappearance could regenerate and revive the rest of mankind. The 'exceptionality' of the extermination of the Jews is attested by an important circumstance rightly stressed by I. L. Horowitz:[5] the Nazis went so far as to let the persecution take precedence over economic considerations. That is, as long as they could kill Jews, they even committed 'economically disadvantageous' acts: for instance, trains transporting Jews to death camps had priority over trains transporting men and munitions to battlefields; dozens and dozens of Jewish scientists were expelled or compelled to flee Germany, thereby weakening the German cultural heritage and considerably damaging the Nazi war effort.

Another peculiarity of the genocide perpetrated by Nazis is its *maximum* utilization of the resources of modern technology for inhuman ends. One example is the solution to the 'logistical problem' always posed by genocide: destroying the bodies of the thousands of people killed. As L. Kuper notes,[6] this problem was solved with relative ease in Turkey (and, in the years following the Second World War, in Rwanda, Burundi and in Bangladesh) thanks to the existence of great rivers. The Nazis made a sinister 'invention': the cremation ovens – one of the most repugnant manifestations of the possible perversion of science and technology.

The Convention on Genocide: good news and bad news

The Convention, conceived in 1946–8 under pressure from Jewish groups in response to the horror aroused by the disclosure of the gas chambers, was drawn up with the full agreement of the Great Powers of the time. It was understood as a decisive instrument in the fight against genocide; it therefore seemed to its 'fathers' that in drawing it up they had made a major breakthrough in the history of humanity. That was not the case. In fact, this normative text, on which the hopes of so many people in so many states rested, ended up in almost complete failure. Why? Let us first of all look at the main content of the Convention, in order then to ask why it has not had any real impact in today's international community.

Briefly, the Convention lays down that genocide is an international crime punishable whether committed in wartime or peacetime; genocide specifies who may be punished for acts of genocide, and finally indicates who is to carry out that punishment.

Let us start with the definition. The Convention states that genocide means the killing or other acts of destruction of members of 'national, ethnic, racial or religious' groups. One requirement is always *dolus*, or 'the intent to destroy'.

It emerges from this definition that the Convention does not regard as genocide either the extermination of *political groups*, or *cultural* genocide (that is the destruction of the culture of a human group). The exclusion of political groups was desired essentially by the Soviet Union, which put forward various arguments. The principal ones were that political groups do not display stable, permanent characteristics, are not homogeneous as being based on the will, ideas and conceptions of their members (and thus on heterogeneous, changeable factors) and not on objective factors; moreover, extending the Convention's interdictions to political groups might have had a dangerous consequence: the United Nations and third countries would have felt it was legitimate to intervene in political struggle taking place within states, thereby prejudicing the right of any state to fight against subversive elements seeking to erode or overthrow its government. Many objections were advanced against the Soviet thesis, of which I shall recall the most important. It was noted that religious groups too were united by common beliefs and conceptions. It was stressed that the political and ideological conflicts at present dividing the world and even dividing groups within many states are liable to lead to massacres of entire groups, motivated by eminently political or ideological reasons. It was also pointed out that the exclusion of political groups could lead to acceptance of genocide committed for religious or racial reasons: a government committing acts of genocide against an ethnic or religious group could in fact have objected that in reality its actions were aimed only against the political ideals of the group or were dictated by political considerations (such as the need to suppress insurrection or maintain public order). They could thus have easily evaded the Convention's prohibitions.

The insistence with which the Soviet Union maintained its view and the support it derived from some Third World countries (apart from the other Socialist countries), as well as the slight enthusiasm with which the West (mainly the United States, France and Britain) opposed the Socialist theses led to the victory of the latter.

As I said earlier, 'cultural' genocide was not contemplated either. During the debates that led to the drawing-up of the Convention there had also been proposals to ban all acts aimed at 'destroying the language, religion or culture' of an ethnic, racial or religious group. Examples were given such as the prohibition of the use of a language in daily life or at school, destruction of libraries, museums, schools, historical monuments, and so on, or bans on access to these places. This proposal too was rejected, mainly because it was regarded as too vague: it was feared it might offer an opening for political interference by other states in the internal affairs of a government accused of committing acts of cultural genocide. In addition, it was argued that this field might be reserved for other international treaties.

The presence of these two lacunae in the definition of genocide does not, however, seem to me to be a very serious limitation on the Convention. There are two real limitations.

The first is that *dolus*, that is malice, or the 'intent to destroy a group', is *always* required as an essential element in genocide. This offers states an easy way out: they may deny the commission of acts of genocide by claiming that this element of intent was lacking. This was done by Turkey as late as 1985 in connection with the 1914–15 massacre of Armenians;[7] by Brazil in 1969 in connection with the destruction of indigenous populations in that country,[8] and by Paraguay in 1974 in replying to accusations of having massacred, or acquiesced in the massacre of, the ethnic group of the Guayaki (Aché).[9]

The other, and really unforgivable, limitation consists in the absolute inefficacy of the enforcement mechanisms, i.e. the mechanisms that ought to ensure respect for the prohibitions laid down by the Convention. Who is to punish the perpetrators of genocide? Who can accuse a state within which such acts have been committed if that state remains inactive? Summarizing, the Convention lays down four mechanisms: (1) trial before the courts of the state on whose territory acts of genocide have been committed: but clearly this is a purely imaginary guarantee since normally genocide is perpetrated by governmental authorities or at least with their acceptance, and those authorities easily succeed in 'neutralizing' courts; (2) recourse to an international criminal court to be set up: unfortunately, as was foreseeable, it never has been; (3) recourse to 'competent organs of the United Nations' to adopt the measures provided for by the UN Charter: in reality, this is a needless repetition of what could in any case be derived from the Charter, and furthermore, these organs can intervene only within the limits of their powers (so that, for instance, any military action against a guilty state could be decided by the Security Council only if the genocide amounted to a threat to peace, an act of aggression or a breach of peace, and only if the five permanent members were in agreement); (4) unilateral appeal to the International Court of Justice: this Court, however, can only ascertain possible wrongfulness and condemn the state responsible but does not have the force to impose that condemnation through coercive measures; what is even more important, all the Socialist countries, in ratifying the Convention, added a reservation rejecting the right of other states Party unilaterally to bring them before the Court. Subsequently, these reservations were found substantially lawful by the Court itself. In this way, a further blow was inflicted on the already extremely weak mechanism of international jurisdiction (it should however be pointed out that recently a fortunate development took place: in March–April 1989 Byelorussia, the Soviet Union and Ukraine withdrew their reservations. Unfortunately, three months before, the United States, in finally ratifying the Convention, had entered a similar reservation to the one withdrawn by the three aforementioned states.[10]

Why did the Convention's enforcement system turn out so inadequate? Because the majority of states that worked it out preferred to favour state sovereignty over the need to punish the perpetrators of atrocious crimes. They preferred to proceed at the normative level without taking the next, necessary step of accompanying that progress by equal progress on the level of implementation. The Convention, despite its merits (the detailed definition of genocide; the fact that it also bans crimes committed in peacetime; the fact that it also makes state officials punishable) remains in many respects 'a diplomatic exercise', vitiated by profound hypocrisy – or to put it mildly, with the words used in 1955 by Sir Hersch Lauterpacht,[11] 'the Convention amounts to a registration of protest against past misdeeds of individual or collective savagery rather than to an effective instrument of their prevention or repression'.

Legal developments after 1948

In the years following adoption of the Convention, the gap widened between the *purely normative dimension* and the *factual dimension*. At the level of what ought to be, considerable steps forward were taken; at the level of practical realization of what ought to be, there was no progress at all, and indeed the various cases of genocide that occurred all remained unpunished. Let us first of all consider the 'elephantiasis' of the normative aspect.

In this area, three important developments took place after 1948. Firstly, due not so much to the gradual acceptance of the Convention (which today has 96 contracting states) but more to many other events (declarations by states, decisions of domestic courts, and so on), there has gradually formed a *general* or customary rule on genocide, i.e. a rule binding on all states, even those that have not ratified the Convention. In practice, the prohibition sanctioned by that normative text has spread 'subjectively', in the sense that, step by step, it has extended to all subjects of international law – even to those that have not ratified the Convention. No state may today claim the right to commit acts of genocide on the grounds that it is not a contracting party to the Convention: the reply being that it is in any case bound by the general rule. Thus at the normative level, there is no longer any escape route for states: they must run the gauntlet of the prohibition. I would add that the general rule in question lays down obligations *erga omnes*, i.e. imposes on all states that they do not commit acts of genocide, and at the same time gives *every other state* the right to require that such acts are not committed. Any other subject of international law may, then, demand of a state that it not perpetrate acts of genocide, or at least put an end to them. All the states in the world may legitimately call for observance of the prohibition.

The second advance is that the general rule I am talking about has acquired higher rank than most other international norms; it has become part of *jus cogens* or peremptory law. This means that two or more states cannot legitimately conclude agreements providing for acts or measures of genocide. Accordingly, an impassable limit on the contractual and 'legislative' power of states has been set: if they nevertheless exercise such power, their acts are null and void. This means that the values consecrated by the rule in question, just like all the other prohibitions belonging to the body of *jus cogens*, have been found to be higher than, and to prevail over, those sanctioned in other international rules.

The third advance is still in the process of coming about, but is no less conspicuous. Genocide has been raised to the category of 'international crimes of states', with the consequence that reaction to its commission may be different from that to other 'ordinary' wrongful acts or delicts (such as non-observance of a commercial treaty, unlawful detention of a foreigner, breach of the law on diplomatic immunity, and so on). It is only the 'injured' state that may react to the latter wrongful acts, and it will normally confine itself to requiring reparation (for instance compensation for the damage, or at any rate immediate cessation of the wrongful act). By contrast, any state may intervene against acts of genocide, and moreover the countermeasures that may be taken include economic sanctions as well as other sanctions not implying the use of force, whether individual or collective (such as non-recognition of illegitimately created *de facto* situations, and so on).

Unfortunately, if we take a look at reality, we can see not only that these three steps forward at normative level have not led to any real changes, but that even the 1948 Convention itself has remained a dead letter.

The various cases of genocide and reactions by the international community

Since adoption of the Convention, a number of serious episodes of genocide have occurred, all, not by chance, *in the Third World*.

In 1960 in the *Congo*, the Congolese national army massacred hundreds of Balubas in the province of Southern Kasai, during a serious internal political crisis. In 1965 and 1972 in *Burundi*, the politically dominant, though minority group, the Tutsi, exterminated the Hutu group, a majority ethnic group in the population: in 1965 its leadership was liquidated and in 1972 between

100,000 and 300,000 Hutu were killed. In 1971 in *East Pakistan* the Pakistani army massacred the inhabitants of what is now Bangladesh. In 1970–4 in *Paraguay* thousands of Aché Indians were killed with the complicity of the government authorities. In 1971–8 Idi Amin's regime in *Uganda* massacred thousands of civilians, including many political opponents, but also members of ethnic groups (Acholi and Lango): the killings were so indiscriminate as to go beyond genocide in the strict sense (even though in my view their nature as genocide cannot be denied). Between 1975 and 1978 in *Cambodia* Pol Pot's Khmer Rouge exterminated some two million people, among them some ethnic or religious groups such as the Chams (an Islamic minority) and Buddhist monks. In more or less the same years in *Iran*, members of the Bahai faith were persecuted and killed. In 1974 the US scholar N. Lewis[12] claimed that in the 1960s and 1970s *Brazil* had in various ways pursued a policy of direct or indirect destruction of various Indian tribes inhabiting its territory. In 1978 acts of genocide were committed in *Equatorial Guinea*. In 1982 a massacre of Palestinians was perpetrated in Lebanon by Christian Falangist troops in the Palestinian camps of Sabra and Shatila, with complicitous inaction by the Israeli armed forces. In 1986–7 in *Sri Lanka* violence and acts of genocide were committed against the Tamils by the Singhalese majority (in turn victim of killings by Tamils), until the conclusion in 1987 of an agreement under the auspices of India (which, however, has only attenuated the race conflict).

As can be seen from the examples I have just cited, acts of genocide occur particularly in composite, conflictual societies in which economic and political problems caused by the creation of modern state structures and centralization of power are superimposed over traditional tensions and differences among groups and races. It has been noted that frequently genocide tends in these societies to follow a fairly customary 'growth pattern': polarization of the demands by minority groups, insistent calls for reform, recourse to armed resistance or terrorism by those groups, repression, and then massacres and exterminations by the government authority.[13]

Let us now consider what the international community has done in response to these various cases of genocide. All too little, alas. Broadly, *two forms of response* by other states or by the UN can be identified; to these should be added *internal response* by some states in which acts of genocide have been perpetrated.

The blandest of the international responses, is where some states or international organizations have invoked the Convention on

Genocide, or the general norm on the matter, during debates on grave breaches committed in a particular state. Reference to these norms has not however had any significant outcome, because other states have not taken it up, nor has the decision-making body within which the debate took place. I shall mention a few significant cases, dwelling first on one of them in particular, on which ample official documentation is available: the massacre of the Balubas in 1960.

On 9 September 1960 the Security Council debated the thorny issue of the Congo: following independence granted by Belgium, a civil war, largely fomented from abroad, had broken out. From the war, two rather contrasting leaders had emerged: Kasavubu, Head of State, and Lumumba, Head of Government. Both had on 12 July 1960 called for urgent intervention by the United Nations to bring an end to the internal conflict, restore order and stability in the country and ward off the dangers of secession (threatened by Southern Kasai and by Katanga). In August, Lumumba sent forces of the Congolese National Army (ANC) to the region of Southern Kasai, which had unilaterally proclaimed its independence. The armed forces occupied the capital, Bakwanga, and began requisitioning supplies and vehicles in preparation for entering Katanga, likewise secessionist. At this point, however, the soldiers began massacring the Balubas, the local tribe, savagely killing men, women and children. UN Secretary-General Dag Hammerskjöld, who had been immediately informed, felt that this amounted to 'a case of incipient genocide'.[14] Although harsh polemic had already arisen over the limits within which UN forces (ONUC) had the power to intervene, and though it had been established that they could not interfere in the Congo's internal affairs, Hammarskjöld felt that this prohibition could not 'be considered to apply to senseless slaughter of civilians or fighting arising from tribal hostilities'.[15] On 2 September he therefore instructed his representative in the Congo to call on that country's Foreign Minister, Bomboko, to take all necessary steps to control and punish the army in Kasai. He further authorized the UN armed forces to stop the massacre, using force if necessary. Subsequently, in presenting his fourth report on ONUC's actions and more generally on the situation in the Congo to the Security Council, Hammarskjöld recommended that: 'emphasis be put on the protection of the lives of the civilian population in the spirit of the [Universal] Declaration of Human Rights and the Convention on the Prevention and Punishment of the Crime of Genocide. This may necessitate a temporary disarming of military units which, in view of present circumstances are an obstacle to the restoration of law and order in the interest of the people and the stability of the nation'.[16] In the 'plan of action' he proposed to the Security Council, he mentioned among other things the advisability of clarifying the ONUC mandate in suitable terms, 'particularly with reference to protecting the life of the civilian population in the spirit of the [Universal] Declaration on Human Rights and the Convention on Genocide'. On 9 September Hammarskjöld came before the Security Council to give an oral report and illustrate his proposals. On that occasion he made clear reference to the massacre of the Balubas. Having stated that hundreds of members of that tribe had been massacred by the Congolese National Army and their villages burned, Hammarskjöld went on: 'These actions obviously cannot be viewed merely as examples of internal political conflict. They involve a most flagrant violation of elementary human rights and have the characteristics of the crime of genocide since they appear to be directed toward the extermination of a specific ethnic group, the Balubas.'[17]

A leading scholar, G. Abi-Saab,[18] has stressed that Hammarskjöld, in view of the bitter criticisms against him by Lumumba and the Soviet Union in the preceding days (he was accused of wanting to make the UN forces intervene against the central government of the Congo), nevertheless felt it advisable in some way to attenuate the terms of the accusation of genocide. He played down the responsibilities of the Congolese National Army, blaming the massacres on individual military personnel rather than on the army as such. In Hammarskjöld's own words: 'there is evidence that the soldiers have broken away from their command which has been unable to control their actions. Whatever the motives for bringing the troops to the region [Kasai], and whatever role they may have been intending to play in the domestic conflict, they have, of course, through such undisciplined actions, and once the authorities have lost control, ceased to be parts of a responsible army'.[19] He then added a question that put the ball back in the Council's court by giving it responsibility for deciding whether in the event of massacres the UN could act: 'Should it be supposed,' asked Hammarskjöld, 'that the duty of the United Nations to observe strict neutrality in domestic conflicts and to assist the Central Government means that the United Nations cannot take action in such cases [of massacre]?'[20]

The Council's answer was, alas, affirmative: UN troops had to abstain from intervening. This was so even although the solution put forward by the Secretary-General was diplomatically very skilful: given the suggestion that the Congolese military personnel guilty of the acts of genocide were, in a manner of speaking, no longer part of the army, thereby eliminating responsibility of the army and its leaders, the door was opened for punishing those responsible for the massacres as simple criminals, as individuals to be tried on the basis of the ordinary penal rules of any sovereign state. Despite this, as I have said, Hammarskjöld's proposal led to nothing. In fact the Security Council gave no weight to the Secretary General's indications, and in the course of time any allusion to the genocide of the Balubas disappeared. The contrasts among the Great Powers (the United States and other Western countries favoured Kasavubu while the Soviet Union had lined up behind Lumumba), the troubles between Lumumba (and the Socialist countries) and Hammarskjöld, the intrinsic difficulties of the situation, the need to reach a rapid solution to the conflict, and the intensity of the debate on the role of UN forces, all overshadowed the question of genocide, which fell into oblivion.

The consideration of the international response to the other cases of genocide that have occurred since 1948 requires less space. On the occasion when Bengalis were massacred in East Pakistan by the armed forces of West Pakistan, various states, especially India and the Soviet Union, referred at the Security Council to the massacres committed in what had become the state of Bangladesh. Apart from the fact that 'genocide' was not always mentioned explicitly, the main reason why these serious crimes were mentioned was essentially political: to justify India's armed intervention and the birth of the new state. Genocide was only one of the reasons adduced during the political debate. Another rather worrying circumstance was that Bangladesh had decided to put Pakistani prisoners on trial for acts of genocide and if necessary punish them; subsequently, for clearly political and diplomatic reasons, this decision was reversed and the Pakistanis were sent back to Pakistan, which, although it had formally undertaken to try them, did not follow up its promise.[21]

Let me finally mention the case of Cambodia. In 1979, when the world learned of the massacres committed in that country by Pol Pot's government, various states (Canada, Norway, Britain, the United States and Australia) presented detailed documentation to a UN body, the Sub-Commission on Prevention of Discrimination and Protection of Minorities, inviting it to discuss the extremely severe infringements of human rights committed by Pol Pot's regime. That body, however, confined itself to adopting a report in which, in rather 'neutral' terms, it reported the events that had occurred in Cambodia without speaking of genocide. The matter rested there.[22] Nor was there any follow-up to the accusation of genocide raised by the Soviet delegate to the Security Council in January 1979. Once again, the accusation – in my view objectively well-founded – was seen as an attempt to justify armed intervention by Vietnam (an ally of the Soviet Union) in Cambodia.[23] And the massacres remained unpunished.

Let me now move to the other form of international response to acts of genocide, that is, to the extremely few cases in which some international organ has adopted some measure. These in fact amount to only two. In 1977, faced with the UN's silence on the extermination of the Aché Indians in Paraguay, an organ of the Organization of American States, namely the Inter-American Commission on Human Rights, adopted a resolution drawing the attention of the Government of Paraguay to the reports of serious violations committed in that state against the Aché and inviting it to take steps to protect that population's rights.[24] As can be seen, genocide was not mentioned nor was the state concerned condemned. It nevertheless seems that the Government of Paraguay did take some steps to bring an end to the massacre of that ethnic group.

Still more singular is another 'international action' against genocide. In 1982, following the killing of hundreds of Palestinians in the camps of Sabra and Shatila, the UN General Assembly adopted a Resolution which, after mentioning the 1948 Convention, '*condemns* in the strongest terms' the massacre and '*resolves*' that it had been 'an act of genocide'.[25] In another book[26] I have already indicated my perplexity – to say the least – at this pronouncement by the General Assembly. It lends itself to two fundamental criticisms. Firstly, it is not based on an exhaustive enquiry into the rather controversial facts – and into the degree and extent of responsibility of, respectively, the Christian Falangists (who carried out the massacre) and the Israelis (who ought to have intervened to bring it to an end); that is, the Resolution is exclusively the fruit of a political debate and of political motivations (to criticize Israel). The superficiality of the General Assembly debate and the fact that states' reasons for favouring the resolution were exclusively political induced many Western countries to abstain from the vote. The second criticism is more radical. Confining oneself to saying that the massacre should be regarded as 'an act of genocide' without adding anything at all about the responsibility of the culprits or accomplices of the crime, or how they should answer for their crimes, means contenting oneself with purely verbal condemnations: in other words, with propaganda rather than with the pursuit of ideals of justice. Once again, an authoritative international organ has demonstrated its total impotence in the face of grave acts of inhumanity.

I feel that the inability of international organs to intervene to hinder acts of genocide[27] was effectively described by the President of Uganda in the speech he delivered to the UN General Assembly on 29 September 1979. His words were:

Our people naturally looked to the United Nations for solidarity and support in their struggle against the Fascist dictatorship. For eight years they cried out in the wilderness for help; unfortunately, their cries seemed to have fallen on deaf ears. The United Nations looked on with embarrassed silence as the Uganda tragedy unfolded. Meanwhile, the Amin regime continued with impunity to commit acts of genocide against its own people.[28]

A few words will be enough to mention the very rare cases in which repression of genocide occurred *at national level*. On 19 August 1979 a special court set up in Phnom Penh sentenced to death for genocide, in their absence, the leaders of Pol Pot's government. The same year, in Equatorial Guinea, the leader of the recently overthrown government, Macias, was tried for the genocide of two ethnic groups (the Bubis and the Fernandinos), and executed. In both cases, apart from the different outcome, a common feature strikes one: the trials were instituted by a government that had violently displaced the one to which the misdeeds were attributed. It would seem clear that this is the only condition that makes punishment by domestic courts possible.

The conclusions to be drawn

The balance-sheet of international action is sadly negative.

I have already said that all the grave massacres since 1948, by way of extermination of national, ethnic, religious or racial groups, took place in Third World countries. This is of course not a matter of chance. In those countries there exist antagonistic groups, tribes or ethnic groups, which have for centuries sought to gain the upper hand over their rivals. Economic and political conflicts and tensions, together with a weak central power or the fact that that power is in the hands of one of the rival groups constitute the occasion for bloody settling of accounts. Those countries lack the social structures that might mediate the conflict, channel hostilities or blunt their virulence; they also lack government machinery or state structures that might in some way act as a cushion between antagonistic groups, by imposing or facilitating compromise solutions. It is not that in other states conflicts between racial groups, between historically diverse 'nations' living together in the same state, have disappeared. It is merely that the long state tradition and the existence of structures able to act as safety valves normally prevent disputes and tensions reaching the stage of the *physical elimination* of members of the other group: at most, conflicts and dissent take the form of racist manifestations, of disorder that may be violent but is stopped by the central authorities (e.g. the events in Northern Ireland or those occurring now in the Soviet Union); or else various attempts are made to abate hatred between groups, and in particular to set up structures for mediation and dialogue. Work is also done in the field of preventing racial, religious, and ideological hatred, through educational and informative measures.

The capacity of Western and Socialist countries to hinder and prevent – to a large extent – acts of genocide within their territory ought to induce these countries to do something at the international level to come to the assistance of groups which, in developing countries, are by contrast the victims of massacres and destruction. Instead, those states, and the international community as a whole, stand idly by. The tendency not to assert at the political and diplomatic level the requirements of humanity as a whole, that is, the tendency to concern oneself above all with national interests, is manifest in this area too. This trend in the case of genocide is reinforced by awareness on the part of the possible 'interveners' of the obsessive emphasis placed by Third World countries on their right not to undergo outside interference. Unfortunately, in the case of genocide, this obsession of the countries directly concerned can in some respects serve to attenuate the 'bad conscience' of the states that ought to be calling for respect for the international standards protecting the rights of groups. Consequently, the various exterminations committed in so many countries either remain entirely unpunished or are punished by the new government (should the government responsible have been overthrown), or come to an end following intervention by a neighbouring state prompted by interests other than humanitarian ones.[29]

Faced with inaction by international organs and with the intervention of individual sovereign states (moved essentially by political, economic or military aims), there remains only one anchor of salvation: the hope that, if the horrors I have referred to are repeated, public opinion and non-governmental organizations may augment their pressure on governments to leave nationalistic considerations and *Realpolitik* aside in order, finally, to embrace the cause of human dignity.

5

The Savage States: Torture in the 1980s

Torture ancient and modern

The fact that torture is a widespread evil can be gleaned almost every day from the newspapers. Amnesty International, with its documented reports, has made us aware of the seriousness of the problem and of how widespread it is in the world. In one of its latest bulletins, 66 states (out of 171) are indicated as having more or less systematic recourse to the practice of torture in some form or other. Note that this means acts of torture inflicted not by individuals with a predilection for hurting people, but by government authorities (soldiers, policemen, and so on), acting in an official capacity, normally on precise instructions from their political and military leaders. This is what renders the phenomenon particularly repugnant.

Let us, then, ask why this happens, and why so frequently.

An initial answer is given by psychologists and psychoanalysts. Some of these trace torture back to the impulse for destruction, to the aggressiveness that is within us all; cruelty and the derivation of pleasure from inflicting pain on another, these are all fundamental components of every human being, they tell us. Recently, a noted German psychoanalyst, Alexander Mitscherlich, has stated that 'the image of the crucified [*das Bild des Gekreuzigten*] has for centuries been associated with our civilization. It was rarely seen for what it in fact was: the subjection of a man to torture with murderous intentions [. . .] One could have opened his veins or given him hemlock. But these less atrocious ways of killing were withheld. Painless death was denied him. Death alone would not have been severe enough punishment.'[1] The practical conclusion is that we should have no illusions: torture will not disappear, because we cannot suppress man's destructive instinct. At most, it may diminish, or take on other forms.

There is much truth in all this. Yet we are not satisfied. Above all, even at the strictly psychological level, it would seem that there is no agreement as to the role of aggressive impulses. For instance, Stanley Milgram, the American psychologist who carried out the famous experiments concerning obedience to authority, drew one important conclusion from his experiments: subjects who inflicted pain on their 'victims' were not compelled to do so by aggressive drives (in fact, whenever they were left free to choose whether to give the 'victims' electric shocks or not, they opted not to do so); according to Milgram, when they did give the shocks, they were acting chiefly in obedience to the orders they had been given.[2] Besides, one might object to the account by Mitscherlich and other psychoanalysts that in fact their interpretive 'key' explains very little, because it examines torture outside its historical and social context. *L'homme est méchant.* Agreed. But why does this 'inclination towards evil' take one direction rather than another? Why does the impulse to cause pain to others take different forms in different historical epochs? The answer can only be given by considering torture – like any other human phenomenon – in its historical framework.

Looking back through history, the first fact that strikes one is that in the past torture had a different role and a different meaning. For centuries it was used, justified, and legally accepted for *two purposes*: to extract the proof from the accused in criminal proceedings, that is, as a form of *judicial evidence* (the accused could legitimately be subjected to torture by judges, to make him confess to the crimes attributed to him), or as a *legal sanction* in order to give 'condign' punishment to the culprit. All in all, torture was used indiscriminately, i.e. in connection with every 'serious' crime. However, as we know, it took on particular importance in the context of Inquisition trials (at Rome and in Spain) against heretics, i.e. for purposes of religious persecution.

Severe blows were dealt the odious practice by Cesare Beccaria (*Essay on Crimes and Punishments* 1764) and Pietro Verri (*Observations on Torture* 1804). The main breakthrough came with Beccaria's work, rather than with Verri's rather muddled and wishy-washy one. In a few succinct pages, Beccaria criticized torture not only for its inhumanity, but also for its utter uselessness for extracting the truth from the accused. *Inter alia*, he noted that torture took no account of individuals' differing resistance to pain:

the requirement [. . .] that pain become the crucible of truth, as if truth's criteria lay in some wretch's muscles and sinews, only confuses all relations. It is a sure means to acquit the sturdy villain and condemn the weakly innocent [. . . .] The result of torture, then, is a matter of temperament and of calculation, and varies in every person in proportion to strength and to sensitivity; so that it would be more the mathematician than the judge that could solve the following problem:

given the muscular strength and nervous sensitivity of an innocent, find what degree of pain will make him confess to a given crime.

Beccaria forcefully brought out one other practical absurdity of torture:

One odd consequence that inevitably derives from the use of torture is that the innocent person is placed in worse case than the guilty; for if both are put to the question, the former cannot win, since either he confesses to the crime and is condemned, or is found innocent and has suffered an undeserved penalty; but the guilty person has a favourable chance, namely when having stoutly resisted torture he must be acquitted as innocent: he has exchanged a lesser penalty for a greater. Thus, the innocent can only lose, and the guilty may gain.[3]

Thanks in part to these writings and the enormous response they met with in all Europe, little by little torture disappeared from trials – or more precisely, was gradually banned in the most advanced states. In modern times it has reappeared, with somewhat different forms and aims. To be sure, it is no longer accepted in the criminal codes of states, and is indeed *strictly forbidden* everywhere. Nevertheless, torture is *de facto* widely used, both in the context of criminal proceedings *and above all outside judicial proceedings*; security services, police forces or military personnel in many states have recourse to it. As Amnesty International has clearly brought out, at present torture has taken on a largely new purpose: today, it is used chiefly as a means *to suppress political and ideological dissent*. It has gradually come to constitute the most inhuman form of struggle against political opponents, against those who do not share the ideology of the ruling group: to extort information or revelations of complicity, denunciations of friends or comrades, or to disseminate terror by acting as a powerful force to dissuade the spread of political opposition. In short, torture is *the perverse and cruel face of authoritarianism*, the quickest and most expedient way to 'deal with' those who are 'out of line'. With torture, authoritarianism comes out in the open and displays itself in all its obtuse negation of the 'other', of the 'dissident'. Torture is the pathological aspect of the denial of democracy. Democracy means: respect for the dignity of the person; torture means: humiliation or annihilation of the dignity of the person. Torture therefore thrives in all illiberal states, or in the authoritarian crannies of democratic states (Montesquieu in 1748 and Voltaire in 1766 had already noted that torture customarily accompanies despotism and tyranny).[4] It has constituted, or still does constitute, a 'mass phenomenon' in Argentina, Chile, Bolivia, Paraguay, Uruguay, Guinea, South Africa, Greece, Turkey, the Soviet Union and other largely auto- cratic countries; it has also constituted a pathological deviation in essentially democratic countries such as France (at the time of the Algerian war), the United Kingdom (at the time of Cyprus and in the early 1970s when repression in Northern Ireland got tougher), or Italy (I have in mind a recent trial of policemen accused of torturing terrorists, and the very recent accusations against other policemen in Sicily for torturing to death an alleged member of the Mafia).

'Classical' torture, in its role as a 'means to extort confessions', was described by Alessandro Manzoni in his 1842 *History of the Pillar of Shame*. (It recounts a historical episode: during the plague in Milan in 1630, a man was accused by a 'silly woman' of having smeared a wall with 'greasy, yellowish paste'; he was arrested and tortured to make him confess; under 'atrocious tortures' he accused other people, equally innocent, who were tortured in turn; some of the 'guilty' ended up condemned to capital punishment and were killed; at the execution site a column, the 'pillar of shame', was erected to remind posterity of the monstrous crimes committed by those poor wretches. The pillar was demolished only in 1778). The other 'face' of 'traditional' torture (torture as punishment) was rather more effectively described in Edgar Allan Poe's fantasy tale *The Pit and the Pendulum*, with its minute description of the 'refined' tortures inflicted by the Inquisition on a prisoner, to make him die in intolerable agony.

Contemporary torture has found its doleful reflection in such sober testimony as *La Question* by the French journalist Henry Alleg (which tells how in 1957 Alleg, accused by the French armed forces of being a communist and pro-Algerian was tortured in Algiers, though a European and a Frenchman, to make him reveal the names of other members of the resistance).[5] Another fundamental piece of evidence is *L'aveu* by the Czech political leader Artur London:[6] it describes the horrible methods used by the Czechoslovak security services to destroy the physical and spiritual resistance of certain politically active people – almost all of them Jews – tried in the 1950s (the time of the famous Slansky trial) to make them 'confess' lies, namely that they were in the pay of the Americans or were leading the 'Trotskyist conspiracy'.

Characteristics of torture today

I shall now seek to focus more closely on the salient features of 'modern' torture. First of all, it has become more 'sophisticated'. Although physical pain continues to be inflicted, with increasingly refined instruments, often endeavours are made to use methods that leave no traces – and therefore no evidence – in order to avoid any possible future accusations. There is therefore a move toward psychological torture. Suffice it to mention the five forms of torture inflicted by the British on detainees in prisons in Northern Ireland: they were deprived for long periods of food and water, or of sleep; or kept standing upright for hours; or kept hooded, except during interrogations; or tormented for hours, before interrogations, with high-level noise to disorientate them. According to Amnesty International, in the Soviet Union in the 1980s medical staff of some psychiatric hospitals with secret police connections administered powerful drugs to political dissidents to cause them pain and disorientation.

Besides the exploitation of increasingly sophisticated 'technology', other historical factors contribute to explaining the new role that torture is assuming today. First and foremost is the increasingly wide spread of *the highly ideologized autocratic model of state*. The division of the world into conflicting groups, and the opposition between ideologies fighting to the bitter end, make the coercive apparatus of authoritarian states theorize and take on a full struggle against ideological and political 'dissidents'. In Latin America and other countries (like Turkey) war is, or has been, waged on 'terrorists', generally accused of being communists or in the pay of communist countries; in the Soviet Union for many years the opposition have been 'dissidents', guilty of not sharing the official ideology, of being 'corrupted' or in the pay of the West, or of being dangerous 'anti-system elements'.

Another factor not to be underestimated is the transformation of the modern state into a *mass bureaucratic structure*. As the German political scientist F. Neumann noted,[7] the consolidation of anonymous bureaucratic apparatuses (in which every activity is compartmentalized and individual responsibility broken up, attenuated or entirely vanishes, along with the figure of the leader who takes every task and every responsibility on himself or herself) facilitates the spread of torture. In fact, the compartmentalization of tasks means that in police stations or units of the armed or secret services where such practices are employed, even the inflicting of mental or physical pain is subdivided among several people: some deal with kidnapping or 'disappearing' the 'culprit'; others see to his detention; still others give the orders for torturing him; others again carry out interrogations to extract confessions or information from the victim; and yet others manipulate the instruments that actually inflict the pain; others again deal with disposing of the victim's body, by throwing it from an aircraft into the sea, burying it in a nameless grave or destroying it in one of a thousand ways supplied by modern technology to the torturer.

All this serves to 'unload' the torturer's possible sense of guilt, to ease his conscience, in short to make it possible for him to commit acts that any human being endowed with a minimum of reason would have to regard as repugnant.

The three levels of international action

Let us now take a quick look at how the international community has reacted to the spread of torture. I shall distinguish three different levels: action by *governments*, by *domestic judges*, and by *private groups or individuals*.

Action at the *intergovernmental level* would be the most effective at suppressing torture, but it is also the hardest. The reason is easy to see: torture is today practised almost exclusively at the instigation or with the connivance of governments; but it is precisely these governments, in concert with states which abstain from the practice, that ought to prohibit it. There ought to be a kind of 'self-limitation' of states (it is well known that the international community has no parliament capable of legislating for those who resist new laws; in practice, an international rule is binding on a state only if it has decided to observe it). Obviously, it is not very likely that authoritarian governments will accept effective rules against torture. Of course, they neither admit to practising it nor refuse to adhere to conventions aimed at restricting its use. Their 'tactics' consist in seeking to weaken the conventions by taking away their specificity or incorporating loopholes.

To date, bans on torture have been proclaimed in various international instruments of a general nature. Leaving aside the law of war, it suffices to mention the 1948 Universal Declaration of Human Rights and the 1966 UN Covenant on Civil and Political Rights. The former is however a mere recommendation to states; the second, though binding, is equipped with inadequate supervisory mechanisms to ensure effective observance by contracting states.

More effective are the international instruments that states have chosen to draw up *specifically* on the subject of torture. In 1975, the UN General Assembly adopted by consensus (practically unanimously) a declaration aimed at banning torture,[8] which was mainly of moral and political value. It was followed in 1984 (after long negotiations, blocked for years by the Argentinian dictatorship) by a Convention,[9] i.e. a legally binding text (at least for states that ratify it).

What are the strengths and weaknesses of these documents? Firstly, the mere fact that they have been adopted constitutes enormous progress, given the premises I set forth above. Secondly, both documents contain a detailed definition of torture, which in itself represents a very important step forward, since otherwise torturing states might hide behind the ambiguity of the international standards and claim that what they are up to is not torture, but something different. Thirdly, these documents, in line with a tradition that goes back to the 1948 Universal Declaration, do not confine themselves to prohibiting torture, but also forbid inhuman actions on a less macroscopic scale: 'cruel, inhuman or degrading treatment or punishment'. This has meant a tightening of the normative mesh, so as to restrict states' room for discretion as far as possible. Fourthly, the 1984 Convention proclaims in black and white that any contracting state must punish torturers that fall into its hands, wherever, and against whomever, they commit acts of torture, or else extradite them to any state demanding this and entitled to try them; in short, the so-called criterion of 'universality of jurisdiction' has been adopted. This is a giant step forward by comparison with the old 'nationalistic' criteria of territoriality (proceedings can only be brought if the crime was committed on the territory of the state) or of the nationality of the culprit or victim (action may be taken only if the torturer or the tortured are citizens of the state).

Nevertheless, the severe limitations of these international instruments should not be overlooked. As I have already said, the 1975 Declaration had only moral and political value. The 1984 Convention can be binding only on states who decide to submit themselves to it. We thus fall back into consensualism, into the need for states to tie their hands voluntarily – not a likely thing for states that stubbornly pursue a systematic policy of contempt for human rights. Two other limitations of the 1984 Convention should not be ignored. Firstly, the provision prohibiting torture excludes pain or suffering legally inflicted by way of 'lawful sanctions' as the outcome of a trial; thus such pain or suffering is permissible even if it is in fact so serious as to constitute more or less manifest forms of torture. Secondly, the system of checks on the observance of the Convention was greatly weakened, at the explicit and unyielding demand of the Socialist countries (the Soviet Union, the German Democratic Republic and Ukraine): at present, the system is only 'optional', in the sense that a state ratifying the Convention may elect not to be subject to verifications by 'opting out' of the relevant provisions of the Convention.

Progress in a Western European context

The outlook is less gloomy if we move from the general picture to the regional one, in particular the Western European context. Here there is a very advanced treaty, the 1950 Convention on Human Rights,[10] Article 3 of which contains a sweeping prohibition on torture and inhuman or degrading treatment or punishment. Above all, there is an international guarantee mechanism (the European Commission and Court of Human Rights) which has carried out effective action in this field too. The European Commission and Court have produced voluminous case law, since they have been faced with a very large number of applications complaining of torture or of inhuman or degrading treatment or punishment. In several cases, both bodies concluded that the accused state had in fact committed the wrongful act imputed to it. This happened, for instance, in the case of Northern Ireland (in 1976 the Commission concluded that the 'five practices' which I mentioned above, to which the British authorities had had recourse in the early 1970s in Northern Ireland, constituted forms of torture;[11] subsequently, in 1978, the Court revised the assessment,[12] ruling instead that they represented 'merely' inhuman and degrading treatment, 'since they did not cause the suffering of particular intensity and cruelty that the term torture implies'. The fact remains that the United Kingdom was condemned – with the consequence, among other things, that it had solemnly to undertake not to repeat similar actions). Another famous case concerns Turkey: in 1976 the European Commission concluded that the fact of not supplying enough food and water nor providing necessary medical treatment to detainees in the zone of Cyprus occupied by Turkey amounted to inhuman treatment; likewise, it was deemed inhuman treatment that Turkish soldiers (in at least two cases officers) had committed rape in the same zone, without the Turkish authorities having taken adequate measures to prevent or repress such acts.[13] No less important are the decisions whereby the Strasbourg bodies held that acts of torture had been committed by Greece during the Colonels' regime[14] (a condemnation of mainly political and moral effect, since Greece withdrew from the Council of Europe) and by Turkey on Turkish territory.[15]

In addition there have been cases (not involving torture as such) where action by the Strasbourg bodies has proved important. The Amekrane case is one.[16] Mohamed Amekrane, a lieutenant-colonel in the Moroccan air force, took part in the attempted *coup d'état* against the King of Morocco on 16 August 1972. When the attempt failed, he fled by helicopter to Gibraltar, where he asked for political asylum. The British authorities, however, arrested him and sent him back the following day to Morocco, where he was sentenced to death and executed on 13 January 1973. Amekrane's wife (a German citizen), who on the day after the failed *putsch* had immediately fled with her children to her home country, asked the Strasbourg Commission to condemn the United Kingdom since, by immediately extraditing her husband, it had not only prevented him from disputing the legality of his (extremely brief) detention at Gibraltar before a British court, but had also subjected him to inhuman treatment (and moreover destroyed the appellant's family life). The Commission did not have occasion to go into the merits of the accusations, since in 1974 the British Government preferred to reach a 'friendly settlement': it paid the widow £37,500, though taking care to declare that it did not regard itself as guilty of any breach of the Convention. This solution was certainly far from being satisfactory. The fact however remains that without intervention by the European Commission the United Kingdom would not even have 'compensated' the widow.

In the *Tyrer* case the Commission took a firmer stance. The United Kingdom was accused of a breach, in the Isle of Man, of the provision of the European Convention on Human Rights forbidding inhuman or degrading treatment or punishment: on the island, the legal authorities had the right to have juveniles (between 14 and 21) sentenced to birching on the bottom. According to the British, this 'legal penalty' was aimed only at deterring further criminal acts. In 1976, the Commission concluded that birching 'as a punishment ordered by a court and administered as provided for in the Isle of Man is an assault on human dignity which humiliates and disgraces the offender without any redeeming social value. Furthermore the Commission observes that other persons involved may be humiliated or disgraced by the whole procedure.'[17] The Commission and later the Court[18] therefore found the United Kingdom guilty of a breach of Article 3 of the European Convention.

A very recent case concerned an application by a German national, Mr Soering, against the United Kingdom. Mr Soering was due to be extradited to the United States for murdering the parents of his girlfriend. He was 18 at the time of the homicides, and there was some evidence that his mental responsibility was substantially impaired. The application alleged that should he be extradited, this would mean that the United Kingdom would be breaching Article 3 which prohibits torture or inhuman or degrading treatment or punishment, as there was a real risk that he would be sentenced with the death penalty in Virginia, and hence subjected to the 'death row phenomenon'. The European Court of Human Rights found unanimously that:

[. . .]having regard to the very long period of time spent on death row in such extreme conditions, with the ever present and mounting anguish of awaiting execution of the death penalty, and to the personal circumstances of the applicant, especially his age and mental state at the time of the offence, the applicant's extradition to the United States would expose him to a real risk of treatment going beyond the threshold set by Article 3 [. . . .] Accordingly, the Secretary of State's decision to extradite the applicant to the United States would, if implemented, give rise to a breach of Article 3.[19]

This judgment is important in at least three respects. First, it represents a very strong stand on behalf of an individual who had admitted heinous acts of violence. Second, it establishes responsibility for acts occurring outside the jurisdiction of the contracting state. Third, and by the same token, it brings to the fore the enormous preventative potential of the Strasbourg machinery.

To be sure, even the important case law of the two Strasbourg bodies is not without its shady side. To mention a few cases, more than a little perplexity was aroused by the two Commission decisions of 1975[20] and 1978[21] regarding some members of the German terrorist gang known as the *Rote Armee Fraktion*. The Commission concluded that the treatment of these terrorists during their detention did not violate the rule on inhuman treatment (Baader, Meinhoff and others were kept for long periods in solitary confinement and for short periods deprived completely of any contact whatever with other prisoners or the outside world; it should be added that the defendants' conditions during the trials before the German Courts were particularly unsatisfactory: among other things, three of the four main advocates entrusted with their defence were removed by the Court on suspicion of connivance with the terrorists; moreover when the accused were in such physical and psychological conditions as to be unable to follow the hearings for more than three hours at a time, the German Court of Appeal nevertheless decided to continue the hearing, in part because the defendants' condition had been self-inflicted, namely by their hunger strike and refusal of medication). It is well known that the second decision was taken after three of the accused had already died in prison, apparently by suicide. An important objection can be applied to the Commission's decision: that body did not take cognizance that the 'cumulative effect' of the various detentive measures was such as to amount to inhuman treatment.

Doubts may also be expressed in connection with other cases, in particular one decided in 1981 (*B. v. The United Kingdom*)[22] and another decided in 1983 involving the Federal Republic of Germany (the *Kröcher and Müller* case).[23] In both cases the European Commission decided by a majority (eight to five) that Article 3 of the European Convention had not been breached, and in both the minority of Commissioners sharply dissented. A brief outline of the facts will be enough to show the scope of the two decisions. In the first case the appellant was a British citizen accused of fraud; being affected by paranoid schizophrenia, he had been interned 'at Her Majesty's pleasure' in Broadmoor state mental hospital, where he had actually remained for some three and a half years. He complained of the conditions of his detention, alleging that they were so severe as to amount to inhuman or degrading treatment (in particular, he drew attention to the serious overcrowding in the hospital; to the inadequacy of the sanitary installations; to the continuing fear of violence from other inmates and to the absolute inadequacy of the medical treatment, in particular psychiatric treatment). In their dissenting opinions, some Commissioners pointed out that the Commission had been wrong to rule out breach of Article 3: among other things, two Commissioners stressed that the serious effects of the treatment to which the appellant had been subject were entirely out of proportion to the reasons for which the treatment had been imposed on him, and another pointed out that whereas the purpose of the detention was mainly to treat the detainee's mental illness, he had in fact remained shut away in Broadmoor for a long time – in highly unsatisfactory conditions – without receiving adequate psychiatric treatment.

Still greater perplexity is raised by the decision in the *Kröcher and Müller* case. These were two German terrorists arrested in Switzerland and detained there. They complained about their conditions of detention, alleging that these were inhuman, especially during the first month (when they were kept in complete isolation, in a cleared wing of the prison, in order to stop them

communicating either with each other or with the outside, even
with their lawyers; they were further deprived of newspapers, radio
and TV and kept under constant visual surveillance; in particular
Ms Kröcher was kept under continuous surveillance by closed-
circuit TV to 'prevent suicide attempts'; electric light was kept on
in their cells night and day). The European Commission, though
regarding these measures as excessively severe, found that they had
been changed after the first month of detention, and that the
alleviation in the conditions was grounds for considering that
inhuman and degrading treatment had not been inflicted. The
minority Commissioners rightly stressed that, nevertheless, the
treatment inflicted on the two Germans in the first month was so
serious as certainly to constitute a breach of Article 3 of the
European Convention.

I would however hasten to point out that, especially recently, the
European Commission has been demonstrating greater severity
with states. Even where it does not rule that there have been
breaches of Article 3, it frequently censures governmental measures
and endeavours to have changes made. In this connection, three
recent cases seem to me to be illuminating: one concerns Italy (the
M. Chartier case)[24] another Denmark,[25] and the third the United
Kingdom.[26] In the first, the appellant, Michel Chartier, a French
citizen (arrested and sentenced in Italy for killing a public security
agent) was affected by hereditary obesity, complicated *inter alia* by
diabetes and respiratory and cardiovascular problems; he had for
this reason been interned in a 'remand home for the physically
handicapped'. He asked to be set free to be able to get treatment,
asserting that the Italian authorities' refusal to accept his request
constituted inhuman treatment. The Commission, having satisfied
itself that Chartier had received adequate medical treatment in the
remand home where he was kept, concluded (by thirteen votes with
two abstentions) that 'although rigorous in its effects, the appellant's detention' did not constitute inhuman or degrading treatment.[27] It nevertheless pointed out that 'because of his state of
health, the applicant's detention is undoubtedly a particularly
painful ordeal'; it then took note of the Italian Government's
undertaking to 'have the applicant hospitalized "in specialized
centres or clinics whenever that is desirable"' and added that it
'would appreciate any measure the Italian authorities could take
vis-à-vis the applicant in order to alleviate the effects of his detention
or to terminate it as soon as circumstances require.'[28]

The second case, as I have already said, involved Denmark. The
appellant, a Danish citizen, had been arrested and sentenced to life

imprisonment for complicity in the killing of a girl drug addict who had threatened to denounce him to the police for his involvement in drug dealing. He claimed that the fact of having been kept in solitary confinement during preventive detention (for almost two years) up to his trial and sentence had caused him mental disturbance and had constituted 'a kind of psychological torture'. The European Commission ascertained that the isolation had not been total (he could listen to the radio and watch television, borrow books, see prison medical staff as well as, of course, the warders, and receive some 'controlled visits by his family'). In the Commission's view, isolation was justified by the type of offence with which the prisoner was charged, given the danger of suppression of evidence or of recidivism. The Commission nevertheless concluded that the duration of isolation had been excessive (even though the isolation had not been so serious as to amount to inhuman or degrading treatment).

The third case worth mentioning is *Maxine and Karen Warwick* v. *United Kingdom*. In 1980, Karen Warwick, then aged 16, attended a school in Hereford. One day, after having taken an examination, she was seen by the headmaster smoking cigarettes together with two other girls in the street outside the school. Thereupon she and another girl were brought back to the school and told they were to be caned by the headmaster for smoking. The deputy headmaster was asked to witness these canings. She was then given one stroke of the cane on her left hand by the headmaster (in the presence of the deputy headmaster and the other girl). The caning caused two large bruises on her palm, which were still visible when she was examined by a medical doctor eight days after the incident. The girl and her mother complained about the punishment to various British authorities and then filed an application with the European Commission. The Commission decided by 12 votes to 5 that the corporal punishment amounted to degrading treatment. It stated among other things the following:

It [the Commission] attaches particular importance to the fact that the punishment consisted of a physical injury inflicted by a man, in presence of another man, on a 16-year-old girl, who under domestic legislation is a woman of marriageable age. In addition, the injury sustained by the applicant, the effects of which remained clearly visible for at least over a week, cannot be said to have been of a merely trivial nature. Nor can it be excluded that the punishment also has adverse psychological effects. Consequently, considering these circumstances as a whole, the Commission finds that the corporal punishment inflicted upon the [. . .] applicant caused her humiliation and attained a sufficient level of seriousness to be regarded as degrading within the meaning of Art. 3 of the Convention.[29]

Five members of the Commission filed a carefully reasoned – although to my mind unconvincing – dissenting opinion.[30] Subsequently, neither the United Kingdom nor, astoundingly, the Commission brought the case to the Court. As a result, the Committee of Ministers had to pronounce on whether or not there had been a breach of Article 3. Unfortunately it failed to reach on this point the requisite majority of two thirds and consequently on 2 March 1989 it simply adopted a resolution taking note that on the issue no decision had been taken.[31] This surprising result once again confirmed how unfortunate it is to leave to a political body the task of adjudicating legal issues.

In general, despite reservations regarding individual decisions, the work of the Strasbourg Commission and Court has to be regarded as praiseworthy, especially in recent times, when both bodies have taken a bolder approach.

Furthermore, considerable progress has recently been made, again in a European context, on the normative level: after years of discussions and negotiations, the Council of Europe has approved a convention that is in many respects revolutionary. It sets up a body of international 'inspectors', charged with visiting the territory of European states in order to satisfy itself whether torture is practised in prisons, barracks, high-security jails and other places of detention. The advance is very considerable, since this is the first time that governments have worked out and agreed upon an international treaty providing for *preventive supervision* in the human rights area. The weak point lies in the very nature of the legal instrument that brings in this scrutiny. As I said, it is an international convention; accordingly, like all legal instruments of this nature, it binds only states that have ratified it – that is, have expressed the desire to be bound by the agreement. The Convention came into force on 1 February 1989, and to date (April 1990) has been ratified by 18 states.[32]

Unfortunately, the progress achieved in Western Europe, largely attributable to the democratic tradition of the countries in the area and to the high degree of cultural and political homogeneity among them, cannot easily be extended to other areas of the world. The European experience may however be regarded as an important model from which other states might gradually take inspiration.

Action at non-governmental level

Courts in some countries have sought to contribute to the struggle against torture. Particularly important actions have been taken by some judges in the United States. One example is that of the *Filartiga* case (a young Paraguayan, Joelito Filartiga, was tortured to death at Asunción by a Paraguayan policeman who then fled to the United States where civil proceedings were initiated against the torturer, at the insistence of the victim's father and sister; finally he was ordered to compensate for the damage caused). Another is the *Siderman* case (the Argentinian family of Siderman, of Jewish origin and religion, was persecuted by the Argentine authorities: after the head of the family had been tortured, he fled to the United States, where he asked for and obtained, from US judges, a civil judgment against the Argentine authorities for the acts of torture).

In addition to these cases, mention should be made of the *Forti* v. *Suarez-Mason* case, recently decided by the US District Court in the Northern District of California. Two Argentinians resident in the United States brought a civil action against a former Argentine General who had been Commander of the Argentine First Army Corps between 1976 and 1979, during which time the complainants allegedly suffered gross breaches of human rights, including torture, committed by police and military officials under Suarez-Mason's command. In a decision of 6 October 1987, the Court held that torture practised by State officials constitutes a violation of the law of nations and consequently the Court had subject-matter jurisdiction under a US Statute (the 'Alien Tort Statute', 28 U.S.C. para. 1350). (By contrast, the Court rejected the plaintiffs' assertion that customary international law proscribed the administration of cruel, inhuman or degrading treatment, and consequently held that it could not grant relief upon this claim.)[33]

These cases, on which I shall not dwell (I have dealt with two of them elsewhere)[34] effectively show that domestic courts often act as a *substitute* for absent international machinery. They can turn themselves into the 'arm of the law', if not to issue penal sanctions, at least to award compensation for damage, and thereby indirectly denounce the misdeeds of governments and individuals in a public forum. Unfortunately, in many other cases judges have not wished, or did not know how, to become involved in such courageous action, so that the torturers' action has not been sanctioned at all.

Let us move to the third level of international action, to that of *private organizations and groups*, acting without any organic link with governments. This is the area where there are the most conspicuous results and the most encouraging prospects.

I shall mention only two of the many organizations that have denounced, testified and demonstrated against individual governments or groups of governments: Amnesty International (with headquarters in London) and the International Commission of Jurists (with headquarters in Geneva). The former has carried out most valuable, indeed indispensable, work of *gathering evidence* throughout the world. Through an all-pervading network of volunteers and 'officials', it has managed to verify the truth of accusations and evidence and to make public all the facts that seemed reliable. From this viewpoint Amnesty International has acted as a sort of international commission of inquiry, doing something that no government or intergovernmental organization (not even the UN) could have done. The results of these accurate inquiries have been used to bring pressure to bear on the government authorities concerned to set the torture victims free. These results have later been published in specific reports, or in the annual analysis published by the organization on the 'state of the world' in the human rights field. As well as asking governments to cease torture practices in individual cases and informing world public opinion, the organization has also rendered inestimable service to government delegates and experts on intergovernmental bodies (such as the UN Commission on Human Rights or the Human Rights Committee charged with verifying the application of the 1966 Covenant on Civil and Political Rights); Amnesty has supplied them with documents, reports and advice, and has generally raised consciousness and provided an enormous amount of information.

The International Commission of Jurists has had no less a role, though in another sector: it has in the main encouraged governments to draw up international treaties against torture, actively contributed to drawing them up, and carried out important studies and surveys. In particular, the Commission carried out a noteworthy action in actively promoting the drafting of both the 1984 UN Convention and – together with the *Comité Suisse contre la torture* – the 1987 Council of Europe Convention on the prevention of torture.

A few concluding remarks

The spread of torture in modern states, especially authoritarian ones or those with authoritarian 'pockets', has aroused a response among public opinion and the international community that is in many respects adequate. This response has taken practical form in 'institutional machinery' both at world level and regional level (especially in Western Europe). The 'law' has responded to new and more sophisticated forms of violence by endeavouring to proclaim bans and set up collective arrangements, in order to put some sort of brake on such violence. If the legal response is still in many respects inadequate, this is essentially due to a phenomenon I have already stressed: it is governments that authorize, tolerate or practise torture; by the same token, it is precisely those governments which ought to restrain themselves by proclaiming international prohibitions and setting up monitoring mechanisms. Unfortunately governments, especially the more autocratic ones, are not disposed to tie their hands with clear, sanctionable prohibitions, in areas where they need to terrorize, repress, punish and kill in order to continue to proclaim the anti-democratic ideologies they advocate.

Accordingly, trust must be placed above all in the more open, democratic states: they must exercise constant pressure over dictatorial regimes. Again, action by domestic courts and private organizations and groups remains indispensable, and will be so for many years. Above all it is they who are prepared to denounce and protest. The importance of protest is enormous. I wish in this connection to mention a parable drawn from that mine of human and political wisdom, Bertolt Brecht's *Tales from the Calendar*. In connection with the 'bad habit of swallowing wrongs in silence', Mr K. tells the following story:

A passer-by asked a crying boy what was wrong. 'I had got together two shillings to go to the pictures,' said the boy, 'when a boy came up and grabbed one out my hand.' He pointed to a boy a little way off. 'Didn't you shout for help?' asked the passer-by. 'Of course', said the boy, sobbing still louder. 'Didn't anybody hear you?' asked the man. 'Well, no', came the answer, 'I suppose not.' 'Then give me this one too,' said the passer-by, taking the other shilling from the boy's hand, and calmly walking on.[35]

Beware of not shouting loudly enough, and of lowering your vigilance.

However, there are some problems that have to be faced head on, though they scarcely lend themselves to easy answers, even in the light of existing international standards. I shall mention only one, which seems to me a particularly complex one, since it concerns emergency situations which according to quite a few people justify recourse to torture even by indisputably democratic governments.

Here is a first example. A few years ago, at the Geneva diplomatic talks (1974–7) to update the 1949 Geneva Conventions, one colonel from a Western Great Power told another negotiator off the record that he had sometimes found himself in the position of having an enemy prisoner tortured, knowing that that prisoner could supply essential information for saving a whole battalion. 'I was well aware of the inhumanity of what I had ordered,' said the Colonel, 'but against that one man's suffering, an enemy into the bargain, was the safety of hundreds of my men. For me they weighed heavier in the balance.' I expressed my grave doubts about the dangers of this kind of attitude (especially since the Colonel was sure that in similar circumstances in future he would not hesitate to do likewise; and since it was already known, from US Lieutenant Calley's 'memoirs', that in Vietnam American officers had frequently had recourse to the same logic). I asked him: 'What if that soldier had known nothing about the ambush that was being organized?' The main point is that once one puts one's hand to torture, what is there to dissuade that colonel or his subordinates from 'reprisals', from torturing enemies only because, before capture, they had inflicted grave losses on his men, or might *possibly* be able to supply information on troop movements? These and other doubts did not succeed in convincing him. Perhaps they will not convince my readers either.

Let me give a second example, again a concrete one. Should a person suspected of having placed (or of knowing where there has been placed) a time bomb due to go off soon in a public building be caught, can the urgency of the situation justify the infliction of torture or other mistreatment in order to obtain the information? In 1976, the European Commission on Human Rights decided authoritatively against torture of suspected terrorists, in the case of Northern Ireland. But quite a few people consider that the suffering of one person – terrorist or friend of terrorists – can be justified by the need to save dozens of innocent human lives.

These and other equally serious problems have to be discussed not only at legal level, but also, and especially, at moral, political and psychological levels. That is one of the ways to prevent a relapse into barbarism, by using the rational tool to which Camus referred in 1945 – the 'words' – by contrast to the other possible but irrational tool: 'the bullets'.[36]

6

Descent into Hell: Notes on Apartheid

Characteristics of race segregation in South Africa

That apartheid is an insane political and social system is now admitted even by many White South Africans. Everyone is *by law* stamped from birth on the basis of skin colour, and on that criterion will be a first-, second-, third- or fourth-class citizen (White, Coloured, Asian, Black). Blacks, though constituting 74 per cent of the population, cannot vote in general elections, cannot join a White trade union or political party, cannot go to cinemas or restaurants (non-deluxe) frequented by Whites, may use only those lavatories set aside for people of that colour, and cannot use the same buses as Whites. What is even more absurd is that Blacks have to live in different areas from Whites: they have to live in townships or homelands (the so-called 'Bantustans' or territorial settlements that have the nature of 'states'). Only the 120,000 Blacks that work as domestics are permitted to live in Johannesburg, but they have to sleep in separate buildings from Whites. If you go out after dinner in Pretoria or other large South African towns you will suddenly find yourself in a town made up entirely of Whites; you are no longer in Africa but in a piece of Europe ('we are not citizens of this country, just phantom inhabitants', as N. Motlana, a Black nationalist leader, has put it).

Some statistics will, I feel, quickly summarize the relationship between Whites and Blacks: there are 100,000 White graduates, but only 2,000 Black graduates; in the economy, Blacks occupy 5 per cent of skilled jobs and constitute 99 per cent of the unskilled labour.

All in all, South African society is the total negation of Rousseau's famous affirmation that 'all men are born equal . . . '. In South Africa there is inequality even before birth, since women are treated by doctors of different races and give birth in separate places, and the children, as soon as they come into the world, are 'pigeon-holed' in different human groups. Right from birth their destiny takes different paths, according to the colour of their skin.

How was it possible to reach this point? What induced Europeans, Christians by religion, to 'invent' and, with great determination, realize a social system that is so contrary to the fundamental principles of modern civilization and to Christian ideals? What made possible an experiment in social engineering so inhuman that it makes us deeply ashamed – even though we live on another continent – of being white and of being inspired by the fundamental values of Christianity? Let us first of all look at how that social system was born, and then go on to ask *why* it adopted structures so at variance with reason.

Segregation of the races was introduced shortly after the creation in 1910 of the South African Union, a state made up of the four present provinces (Cape Province, Natal, Transvaal and the Orange Free State) which was a dominion of the British Empire. As early as 1911, the Mines and Works Act introduced, or rather institutionalized, discrimination in the workplace by reserving certain jobs for Whites only. This was followed in 1913 by the Land Act, which barred Blacks from buying land outside the reserves, and hence laid the foundations for racial separation on a territorial basis. There followed in 1920 the Native Affairs Act, which created separate political institutions for Blacks, and in 1922 the Urban Area Act, which extended segregation to urban areas. The final realization of the discriminatory system, with the introduction of the term 'apartheid' and the detailed, almost maniacal regulation of race segregation, came about only after the Second World War. The major spur was the election in 1948 and in 1952 of the Afrikaner-dominated Nationalist Party. Its adherents tended to be much more racist than the English-speaking South Africans who had formerly largely governed the country. Between 1948 and 1952 there was a great flurry of legislation: with an *idolatry of law* that might surprise even the jurist, a barrage of normative texts were issued, meticulously disciplining the whole life of the various races, especially the 'inferior' ones, and rigidly regulating even the tiniest, most intimate details of daily and private life. In 1949 a law was enacted (the Prohibition of Mixed Marriages Act) which banned marriage between Blacks and Whites, and was followed by another (the Immorality Act) that extended the existing ban on 'unlawful carnal intercourse' between 'Europeans' and 'natives' to include intercourse and 'immoral and indecent acts' between 'Whites' and all 'non-Whites'; in other words, Whites could not have senti-mental or sexual relations with, still less get married to, members of any of the other three races (Black, Coloured or Asian). From then on Whites could make love only 'endogamously', totally isolated from other human groups. Insuperable barriers were thus set up against the possibility of merger and integration at least as between Whites and the other racial groups.

There followed in 1950 the Population Registration Act, which obliged every individual to register as a member of a racial group: mankind was legally and definitively subdivided into castes based on skin colour, and everyone from birth could join only one of these and would remain in that same caste for the rest of his or her life. The legislation was corroborated and strengthened by another statute, also enacted in 1950: the Group Areas Act, which formalized and perfected physical segregation with respect to residence and work by non-Whites. In this way, the various 'inferior' racial groups were, in addition to being marked for life, compelled to live in different territorial areas from Whites: as if the Whites' clean air would be dirtied or contaminated if they lived in the same town. Again in 1950, the necessary measures were adopted to prevent any rebellion. The Suppression of Communism Act (known since 1976 as the Internal Security Act 44 of 1950) made provisions for all attempts at sedition or disorder to be prevented and repressed. In fact, in defining the 'crime' of Communism, reference was made not only to Marxist doctrines, but also to any doctrine or scheme, which aimed at bringing about political, industrial, social, or economic changes by unlawful means. As we can see, the definition is so broad that it can cover any idea whatever that challenges or conflicts with the *status quo*. The 'high-point' was reached in 1952, with the Native (Abolition of Passes and Coordination of Documents) Act, which imposed on all Blacks over the age of eighteen the obligation to carry at all times an 'internal passport', whereby the authorities could keep tabs on all physical movement by members of the 'inferior race'.

With this series of laws apartheid was definitively established. Those that followed in subsequent years perfected and detailed the 'concentration camp universe' already in existence. The Black Education Act of 1953 had allowed the racist state to control the whole education system for Blacks; further legislation enacted in 1958 and 1959 extended segregation to sport and higher education.

The list I have just given of the main legislation providing the framework for apartheid speaks for itself, and clearly shows what this system of segregation means and how contrary it is to any ethical principle. I wish to make only three observations.

The first concerns the *content of the legislation*. Many South African leaders defend it by pointing out that in day-to-day reality Blacks in South Africa live better in material terms than those in other

African countries; their standard of living is higher. The truth of this proposition may be assumed. And yet, what those leaders do not perceive, or pretend not to understand, is that the condition of individuals is not to be judged solely by the yardstick of material standards of living. In other African countries Blacks are perhaps poorer, find it harder to get jobs, live in more squalid dwellings, have less chance of an education, but they are at least regarded under the law as human beings. In South Africa, Blacks are 'inferior' creatures by definition. The South African leaders I am talking about refuse to see that an essential part of the concept of the 'human person' accepted by all states and sanctioned in the 1948 Universal Declaration is that it is everyone's right to be regarded as *equal* to others, as a microcosm which only nature, *not* society, can differentiate from others.

My second observation concerns the choice of means to impose apartheid, namely the laws, viewed now not so much for their content but rather for their function as *instruments of social control*. What is striking in the action of South African leaders is the almost obsessive need they felt in the years from 1948 to 1952 to set up a complex, intricate legislative system to achieve their racist ideas. It has been rightly pointed out by Leo Kuper[1] that the South African Government went far beyond what the Nazis did as regards the legalistic, bureaucratic structure of their racism. The law, which Rousseau regarded as the supreme concentration of liberty and reason, has in their hands become a refined method of institutionalizing injustice and irrationality. It is indeed hard to find any other social system in which the normative dimension is so hypertrophied and in which the law has become such a powerful instrument of domination and social control. The imbalance in South Africa between the law is its aspect as an essential instrument for guiding the members of society, and the law in its highly oppressive aspect, was one of the essential points of the calm but bitter criticisms directed by Nelson Mandela (a leader of the African National Congress, the ANC) at the South African regime in his defence speech at his trial in Pretoria in 1962.[2] He was a lawyer by profession; accordingly, he was acquainted with the laws and aware of their significance.

Your Worship, I would say that the whole life of any thinking African in this country drives him continuously to a conflict between his conscience on the one hand and the law on the other. This is not a conflict peculiar to this country. The conflict arises for men of conscience, for men who think and who feel deeply in every country. Recently in Britain, a peer of the realm, Earl Russell, probably the most respected philosopher of the

Western world, was sentenced, convicted for precisely the type of activities for which I stand before you today, for following his conscience in defiance of the law, as a protest against a nuclear weapons policy being followed by his own government. For him, his duty to the public, his belief in the morality of the essential rightness of the cause for which he stood, rose superior to this high respect for the law. He could not do other than to oppose the law and to suffer the consequences for it. Nor can I. Nor can many Africans in this country. The law as it is applied, the law as it has been developed over a long period of history, and especially the law as it is written and designed by the Nationalist government, is a law which, in our view, is immoral, unjust, and intolerable. Our consciences dictate that we must protest against it, that we must oppose it, and that we must attempt to alter it.[3]

I now move on to my third observation. I noted earlier that, while racial segregation existed in South Africa as early as 1911, the systematic, all-pervasive construction of a society divided by extremely high barriers, of a world in which social communication, if it occurs, does so within rigidly fixed channels, took place only after 1948. That was the very year when the United Nations were proclaiming a new decalogue for the whole of humanity: the Universal Declaration of Human Rights. South Africa's abstention from the final vote was motivated, as I have shown in chapter 2, by a series of arguments marked by the most barefaced hypocrisy. The main reason for the abstention is that they did not wish to make even the minimal moral commitment that a vote in favour of the Declaration would have constituted. In fact, every one of the statutes I have briefly mentioned above is a major blow to the Declaration, a *specific, obstinate refusal to heed its appeals*. With the creation of apartheid, not only were immense, impenetrable walls erected between the various human groups in South Africa; an extremely high wall was also erected between South Africa and the rest of the world. What was valued, if not scrupulously observed in the rest of the world, was derided and trodden underfoot, or simply rejected in South Africa. Thus, the country gradually became transformed into a prison-state, into a tangible manifestation of how and up to what point reason (in the sense of abstract rationality) can pervert itself in arriving at the negation of the most important postulates of reason set out from the Enlightenment onwards.

Why apartheid?

The main reasons why South Africa has gradually transformed itself into a radically racist state are of an historical, religious and economic nature.

The *historical* motivations are the easiest to trace. Dutch settlement in South Africa, which goes back to 1652, was from the outset a typical manifestation of White colonialism, and hence of domination and enslavement of the native populations by the colonizers. This aspect is important, though account has of course to be taken of two atypical characteristics of European penetration in South Africa. Firstly, right from the end of the eighteenth century the 15,000 colonists of Dutch origin regarded themselves as separated from the motherland; they spoke a language (Afrikaans) that differed from Dutch, and gradually developed a culture of their own. In other words the Boers (which means 'farmers' and was what they liked to call themselves) soon began to distinguish themselves from other White colonizers (British, French, Belgian, etc.) in other areas of Africa, who were, and always felt themselves to be, mere extensions of a European country into the Third World. The second atypical feature of Boer colonialism was that the feeling I have just mentioned was strengthened by the British invasion (starting in 1795), which the Boers always regarded as a form of imperialist expansion by a European power at *their* expense (and not at the expense of the Zulus or Hottentots). It was in response to the British invasion (and the abolition of slavery in Cape Province by the British) that the Boers undertook the first great trek: in 1835 they went to Natal, led by Andreas Pretorius, overthrew the indigenous populations (Zulus) and wrested from them the land the latter had been living on for centuries. When the British definitively occupied the Cape in 1843, the Boers undertook the second trek inland, founding the Republics of the Transvaal and the Orange Free State, to which the British turned their attention after the discovery of diamond-bearing deposits in 1866 and gold-fields in 1886. The Boer War (1899–1902), between them and the British, led, as we know, to victory for the European power. This violent conflict between the 'old' White colonists (now firmly established in South Africa at the expense of the natives) and the 'new' British colonists is a fact that has always to be borne in mind in seeking to understand the present situation in South Africa.

The specific racist element, always present in any colonial domination, was accentuated by the *religion* of the Dutch colonists, the Calvinism of the Dutch Reformed Church. The fundamental pillar of this racism of religious origin was primarily a well-known passage in the Bible, in which Noah curses Ham and pronounces on him the dreadful sentence: 'Cursed be Canaan: a servant of servants shall he be unto his brethren' (Genesis, 9, 25). Reading that passage today, it might seem to us rather odd, or at least innocuous: Noah, drunk, goes to bed naked in his tent; Ham, his youngest son, sees him and goes to tell his brothers Shem and Japheth; they take a cloth and cover their father's nakedness without looking thereon; Noah wakes up, finds out what has happened and utters his pitiless curse on poor Ham (which today appears quite incongruous). But the Dutch Reformed Church interpreted the passage to mean that the Bible says that the Hamites (Africans) have to be the slaves of the Semites and Japhithites.

The other pillar of racism is the dogma of 'dual predestination', according to which each of us is born with the mark of goodness (the elect) or of infamy (the reprobate). This religious dogma is, as we know, the most unutterably terrifying: since God has not explicitly indicated the external signs that will distinguish the members of each category, how can we know whether we have been chosen by Him to be among the elect, or instead belong to the damned? It is hard to imagine a greater source of insecurity about oneself or about the world. It is also well known – since it was tellingly explained by Max Weber – that the dogma constituted a very strong impulse to the neurotic search for 'personal success', for showing oneself and the world that one belongs to the elect. This personal success, in the social and economic structure in which the religion operated, meant accumulation of wealth through work – tireless, obsessive, relentless work. But through an aberrant manipulation of religious dogmas, members of the Dutch Reformed Church came to raise the question: if it is not given to us to know for sure whether we belong to one category or the other, what sign could be clearer than the colour of the skin? And digging in the Bible one can find another passage that can be given a racist interpretation:

And I will establish my covenant between me and thee and thy seed after thee in their generations for an everlasting covenant, to be a God unto thee, and to thy seed after thee. And I will give unto thee, and to thy seed after thee, the land wherein thou art a stranger, all the land of Canaan, for an everlasting possession, and I will be their God   (Genesis, 17, 7–8).

The Afrikaners interpreted the passage in a very particular way: God has given them, and their race alone, the country they live in, which should therefore be preserved only for the elect, united with God through a solemn religious covenant. It is not by chance, as Gérard Chaliand[4] has rightly noted, that the Boers have experienced their history as a great *religious epic*: the great 'pioneering' treks were perceived by them as a journey into the land promised by God, as a kind of 'acting out' of the Bible. The whole construction of the South African state was conceived of and experienced by them as a sacred mission, as fulfilment of a divine commandment that it would be sacrilege to evade.

The irony of the influence of the Protestant religion in the building of apartheid, is captured by Winnie Mandela, the ANC leader's wife when describing her time in prison:

I forgot to say I had the Bible, because it was such a meaningless document in those circumstances. I read it four times. I never knew it was possible to read the Bible from beginning to end.

What was so ironical – we know how religious Afrikaners want to appear. Well, the way I got the Bible in prison – one of the Security men stood at the entrance, the door was flung open and he threw the Bible at my feet – 'There is the Bible, ask your God to release you from jail!'

Even for people who are not very religious, the Bible still inspires some form of respect. Now here are people who are supposed to be religious mocking this same God who they believe predestined them to be the rulers of this country. When they oppress us, they oppress us in God's name, they call themselves God's chosen people. In the name of *that* God he flung that Bible at me, and yet he stands in the pulpit every Sunday to preach what he has never believed in.[5]

And indeed, in 1947, when the word 'apartheid' (meaning 'separation') was used for the first time and the racial segregation already practised for decades came to be given a 'theoretical' basis, the programme of the Nationalist Party (still in power today) stated that 'apartheid is founded on the Christian principles of fairness and justice'.

To all these motivations of various types must be added certain *economic* ones. If a race is regarded as inferior, it will naturally be easier to impose humble, unpleasant and onerous tasks on it. Suffice it to recall that had cheap labour not been available, the extraction of gold (a costly operation in itself) would have been very difficult, and could not have made such an outstanding contribution to the industrial development of South Africa.

But, it will be said, all this does not explain one of the most aberrant manifestations of racism: the *segregation* of the races, by which the whole territory is divided on the basis of skin colour, and every race can live only in one particular area. There are historical reasons for this absurdity too. In the nineteenth century the Missionary Society of London, and later Lord Stanley (in his capacity as Secretary for the Colonies), conceived, and later implemented in South Africa, a system of 'native reserves'; it was claimed that these reserves would serve to protect the Hottentots, the Coloureds and the Black tribes from 'interference' by the British and Boer colonists. This 'model' was taken up by the new independent state (the South African Union) in 1913, and gradually transformed into the current inhuman system of racial segregation.

How did the international community react?

Between 1946 and 1951 the question of apartheid was considered and discussed at the United Nations only from the viewpoint of discrimination against citizens of Indian or Pakistani origin. However from 1952 onwards the United Nations began to deal with the policy of apartheid as such; that is, its character as a total negation of the human rights of the majority of the South African population. Accordingly, for some 38 years now the UN has been discussing the problem and adopting resolutions of condemnation, with meagre results, alas! The reason is well known to all. The only measures that might be able to produce devastating effects on the aberrant segregation system would be massive economic sanctions against South Africa, imposed uniformly by all states. But such sanctions could be implemented only following a binding decision by the Security Council and only if sustained – before, during and after – by the political will of the five permanent members of the Council (the United Kingdom, the United States, the Soviet Union, France and China), as well as other Western economic great powers (Japan, the Federal Republic of Germany, Canada and Italy). Unfortunately, this political will has so far been lacking, particularly in the United States and the United Kingdom. Why? The principal reasons appear to be those countries' close economic links with South Africa and their dependency on that state for certain minerals of great economic or military importance. I shall first consider the latter aspect.

It is well known that South Africa, as well as having huge quantities of gold, platinum and diamonds, possesses a number of minerals that are essential for the West: for example, the United States imports from South Africa 87 per cent of its manganese, 82 per cent of its platinum, 73 per cent of its vanadium and 48 per cent of its chromium, while France, for instance, imports from South Africa 41 per cent of its uranium and 40 per cent of its chromium. Moreover, at least for the United States, South Africa constitutes a fundamental Western bastion against Soviet penetration in Africa. Furthermore, economic bonds are very strong. American companies control 70 per cent of the computer industry in South Africa, more than 40 per cent of the oil and gas sector and one-third of the car industry. As far as Britain is concerned, one should remember the strong historic links with the Pretoria Government; but more important than these are the considerable investments of British industries in South Africa, as well as other circumstances (for instance, half of the annual imports of fruit and vegetables from South Africa to European Community countries go to the United Kingdom; some 800,000 South Africans have the right of residence in the United Kingdom should they ever decide to leave their country).

The balance-sheet of UN action is therefore a depressing one. In 35 years of action, the Organization has only been able to adopt one binding Security Council decision – on certain military sanctions – in 1977 (in essense, an embargo on arms supplies).[6] But these sanctions have had little effect, both because they are evaded by some countries and because South Africa is in any case fairly strong militarily, as well as being relatively self-sufficient. Economic sanctions have been on several occasions 'recommended' by the General Assembly (starting in 1976), but *de facto* adopted only by those states which in any case have few economic links with South Africa (while various Western powers have turned a blind eye).

It should not surprise us, then, that considering the failure of the sole tactic capable of inducing South Africa to bring an end to apartheid, the United Nations has ended up falling back on a *multiplicity* of measures, none of them decisive. These measures may yet, if taken together, produce some effect in the very long term, particularly by stimulating public opinion. The measures run from the adoption of countless resolutions and recommendations in a wide range of fields – sport, education, trade unions, the right of political organizations of the South African majority (such as the ANC) to wage armed struggle to realize the right to self-determination, to the creation of an assistance fund for apartheid victims and a fund for publicity against apartheid, the establishment of an education and training programme for people from South Africa or Namibia, and the adoption in 1973 of an International Convention on the Suppression and Punishment of Apartheid as a crime against humanity.[7] I shall dwell briefly on this last measure, since it seems to me typical of the kind of action on which the international community is tending to concentrate in the struggle against racial oppression in South Africa.

The main aim of the Convention is to define apartheid as a 'crime against humanity'. It renders responsible for that crime all 'institutions and organizations' and 'individuals' that commit it by encouraging or participating in the adoption of all the measures (legislative, political, administrative, and so on) that promote or maintain racial segregation. Punishment of those responsible is incumbent on the courts of states ratifying the Convention: they may initiate trials of those guilty of the crime whether they reside in South Africa or in some other country and whatever their nationality.

As can be seen, the scope of the Convention is enormous, and its impact could, at least in theory, be very considerable. However, the Convention, by its very nature, is binding only on states that have ratified it, that is, only those that have decided to subject themselves to its obligations. As was foreseeable, only Socialist countries and Third World countries, as well as a few Western countries with no links with South Africa, have ratified it.

All the major Western powers have stayed well away. These are precisely the states whose collaboration could have helped to punish those responsible for apartheid (since they are states visited by South African leaders, or on whose territory there are people and bodies that directly or indirectly encourage, or co-operate in, the maintenance of racial segregation). This outcome was readily foreseen by the authors of the Convention. That is, they knew that as an international treaty it would have only political or 'rhetorical' weight, and no real normative effect. We thus note that the same phenomenon, apartheid, has given rise to *two exaggerated versions of law*. In South Africa, the law has only a repressive dimension. If – as the French lawyer Georges Scelle said[8] – the legal norm constitutes the point where ethics and power come together and fuse, in South African legislation the ethical element is entirely lacking. At the international level, the exaggeration has been in the opposite direction: the international body of law – at least the one I am talking about – exists solely and exclusively in a non-operational dimension; using Scelle's idea, it is all ethics and no power. In South Africa the law acts as the quintessence of repressive force; at international level, the law symptomatically expresses the relative impotence of political myths. It is clear that only the enormity of the South African racist phenomenon has been able to split the law in two directions, and into a total separation of the two requisite dimensions, the ethical and the political.

Despite all the shortcomings I have noted, the balance-sheet of international action against apartheid still has some positive elements. Above all, one should not neglect *the long-term action* undertaken by the UN at the level of ideas, of convictions, of impact on public opinion, both in the world in general and within

South Africa. It does not seem to me mere chance that, in the long, articulate statement by Nelson Mandela in his 1963 trial at Rivonia[9] (which led the following year to his being sentenced to life imprisonment), he cited the Magna Charta (1215), the Petition of Right (1628) and the Bill of Rights (1689).[10] It is indubitable that the great international normative texts have contributed towards strengthening the moral commitment of those who oppose apartheid, and above all to their awareness of struggling for a just cause, a value that is shared by the rest of the world. But, as I have said, the long-term effect of UN appeals and condemnations has made itself felt outside South Africa too, in world public opinion, and in particular in public opinion in the great Western powers, which for years had accepted, or only mildly criticized, South Africa's actions. It is under the pressure of public opinion that those Governments have begun to revise their policies towards this segregationist country. In turn, it is because of these pressures that South Africa has adopted a series of measures including in particular the abolition of so-called 'petty apartheid'. Thus, segregation was abolished in banks and post offices and various public places including cinemas, theatres, libraries and some hotels, restaurants and beaches; the ban on inter-racial sexual relations and mixed marriages was eliminated, as were both official discrimination between Whites and Blacks at work in cases of equal qualifications, and the 'internal passport' (the document that previously allowed constant control over movements by non-Whites). More recently we have witnessed the release of Nelson Mandela, the unbanning of the ANC, the lifting of reporting restrictions provided for in the emergency legislation, and negotiations between the Government and the ANC.

Secondly, intergovernmental organizations have also begun to engage in more effective action, due to the greater willingness of the Western great powers to protest against the policies practised in South Africa. In fact, a few steps forward have been taken recently. For instance, on 26 July 1985, the Security Council, meeting at the request of France, adopted (the United States and the United Kingdom abstaining) a Resolution condemning the state of emergency which had just been proclaimed in South Africa.[11] In that Resolution the Security Council further 'invited' UN member states to adopt a number of specific sanctions (suspension of new investments; prohibition of the sale of Krugerrands and other coins minted in South Africa; restrictions in the field of sport and cultural activities; suspension of guaranteed loans on exports; prohibition of new contracts in the nuclear sphere; prohibition of sale of computer equipment that might be used by the South African armed or police forces). In June 1986 the European Council (that is, the Heads of State or Government of the 12 members of the European Community) adopted a Declaration expressing their concern at the internal situation in South Africa and outlining the main political conditions necessary in their view for dismantling apartheid.[12] The Declaration also stated that in the three subsequent months the Community should begin consultations with other industrialized countries on the 'further measures required', relating in particular to a 'ban on new investments and on the import of coal, iron, steel and gold coins from South Africa'. This is obviously a rather weak Declaration (and it is not surprising that on 10 July 1986 the European Parliament deplored the European Council's inability to adopt rigorous sanctions). However, the fact remains, that thanks to all these tiny steps, it may nevertheless be possible to make a breach in the massive structure of the segregationist system, in order gradually to wear it down and ultimately destroy it.

Is it possible to eliminate apartheid?

On 25 October 1982 Robert McNamara, in the columns of an important American newspaper, sounded an alarm, warning that if precautionary measures were not immediately taken South Africa might become the 'Middle East of the 1990s'.[13] His words were not heeded by the White minority, and now the problems are becoming steadily more complex. Are solutions still possible?

Broadly, there are two *political projects* being put forward, in various ways, in order to prevent McNamara's prophecy from coming true.

The first is that devised by Pieter Willem Botha (the former President) and the *White élite* led by him. A series of warning signals have convinced the White South African minority of the need for a 'strategy of movement'. The signals are well known: the growing agitation of the non-White population, repressed in blood baths at Sharpeville (1960) and Soweto (1974); the disappearance of the buffer-zone that sheltered South Africa from 'attack' by the states of Black Africa: first of all the collapse of the Portuguese Empire in Angola and Mozambique (1974), then the end of White supremacy in Rhodesia (1980), and now the independence of Namibia (1990); and hand in hand with these phenomena, growing international isolation. The South African governing party therefore embarked on a political project which revolves around the following ideas: firstly, gradual attenuation of apartheid; secondly, creation of geographical areas in which each of the major Coloured ethnic groups could pursue separate development (the homelands or Bantustans: there are at present ten of these, four of them have been declared 'independent'); thirdly, creation of national parliaments and 'councils of ministers' for Coloureds and Asians, which might be followed by similar institutions for Blacks; fourthly, creation of a federation between the Bantustans and the White state, within the framework of a broader community (like the EEC, based on economic and commercial integration). This project has the extremely serious defect that all real power would essentially remain in White hands. It is therefore a 'solution' that will inevitably be thrown out by internal and international pressure.

At the opposite extreme is the *radical political project* of the majority of the international community, as well as, in South Africa, the ANC (until recently an illegal organization, and led firstly by Nelson Mandela and then, during his imprisonment and to date, by Oliver Tambo). Their goal is simple: immediate destruction of apartheid and immediate introduction of the 'one person one vote' principle under which the Black population would take its place as the majority. How is this goal to be achieved? Internally, the aim was to achieve it through armed struggle by the ANC (the emphasis being on acts of sabotage against lines of communiction and public buildings) as well as on increasingly widespread and effective political action. Externally, it was to be achieved – according to this 'project' – through punitive economic sanctions capable of bringing the South African economy to its knees. Why have attempts to achieve this solution, in this way, failed?

First of all, as I said earlier, the Western Great Powers' dependence on South Africa for minerals of particular strategic importance renders doubtful their participation in the hardest-hitting sanctions (which consecutive US administrations have in fact opposed). Secondly, various African countries are highly dependent on South Africa in different respects: 90 per cent of the trade of Zimbabwe (formerly Rhodesia) goes through South African ports; 1,350,000 citizens of the nine neighbouring African countries work in South Africa and the money they send back helps the economies of their countries considerably; Botswana, Lesotho and Swaziland are dependent on South Africa for oil; finally, South Africa is the biggest trading partner for all nine Western Great Powers. It is therefore easy to imagine the disastrous economic consequences that international sanctions against South Africa might have for these countries. Thirdly, the introduction of Black rule in place of White rule in Zimbabwe in 1980 does not provide an encouraging precedent. The quasi-racist extremism of the South African Black party PAC (Pan-African Congress), and the lack of a Black ruling class (whose education has been prevented by the Whites), has made the White minority ready to resist the prospect at all costs.

The third solution would seem to be the *moderate* one, supported within South Africa by, among others, the Federal Progressive Party ('liberal' Whites, led by Helen Suzman). In essence, this would entail the immediate dismantling of apartheid, but with only a very gradual attainment of a political system in which the majority would be the non-White population (which amounts to 85 per cent, taking Blacks, Coloureds and Asians together), with some solid guarantees for the minority. At this point it might be objected that the guaranteed protection of existing property rights would merely entrench the present inequalities. There is still considerable work to be done, and any constitutional proposals should originate from those who have suffered most. Furthermore a Bill of Rights should do more than freeze a constitutional settlement, it must provide a programme for the future. These are the general lines of a project which at the moment few are helping to implement. In the light of the speeches by President de Klerk (to Parliament 2 February 1990) and by Nelson Mandela (Cape Town 11 February 1990) it now looks as though no one solution in isolation will take precedence over the others. Talks between the de Klerk government and the ANC may lead to the abolition of the worst aspects of apartheid. What form of government or constitution is appropriate for South Africa in the 1990s are questions which are unlikely to yield agreement from all sides. Taken together President de Klerk and the ANC do not represent all shades of opinion. Both sides have fierce critics and ideological, racial and tribal differences will not be easily resolved. Although these conflicts once seemed irresolvable, the prospect of negotiations now offers a glimmer of hope.

7

The 'Forced Disappearances' in Argentina: Barbarism and After

The events in Argentina between 1976 and 1983, during almost seven years of merciless dictatorship, well-known as they are, may illuminate one question of enormous importance: how can or should a democratic system react to inhumanity? How ought it to punish the guilty? What ought to be the object of the punishment: to do justice, or to prevent a return to barbarism?

A brief consideration of what happened in Argentina may throw some light on this complex of problems; it may perhaps also provide lessons for the future (lessons that will obviously apply only to the extent to which we succeed in being guided by rational choices and not by emotional impulses and pressures).

The years of dictatorship

The first military Junta took power in Argentina in 1976 (there were four in succession between 1976 and 1983). It decided to meet the problem of terrorism 'head-on'. In the years preceding the installation of the military dictatorship, gangs of left-wing subversives or 'terrorists' had devastated the country, striking above all at the armed forces and the police, but not even, in many cases, sparing civilians. The first Junta therefore decided to break up these groups once and for all. How did it propose to do this? Using essentially terrorist methods, which I shall briefly describe.

To combat the left-wing subversive groups, the military Junta set up a large network of operational centres and places of detention of a *clandestine* nature. This secret operational force was to act in parallel with the official agencies of coercion, the armed forces and police. The clandestine forces were made up of military personnel, and operated outside any legal system, but with coverage from the Junta and the tacit acceptance of the institutions. Why act outside the law, when the Junta could easily have changed the laws and created special agencies or anti-terrorism squads to act in the clear light of day? The answer is simple. The clandestine forces used methods that no code of criminal procedure, no military code or regulation, would have allowed. They swooped down suddenly on persons suspected of carrying out terrorist actions or being in some way, directly or even indirectly, linked to subversive groups, and seized them. The clandestine commandos preferred to operate by night, in mufti, without any distinguishing marks. Those arrested were taken to clandestine detention camps, interrogated and subjected to maltreatment and torture. To what end? To secure information on other subversives, but also in order to spread terror. Almost always, after having been tortured, those arrested were killed and buried at night in unmarked graves, or thrown into the sea from aeroplanes or helicopters. In some cases, after years of detention, they were released with warnings not to breathe a word of what had happened to them.

During the period in which the clandestine activity was most intense, namely between 1976 and 1979, according to figures from a Commission set up by Alfonsin in 1983 which I shall discuss below, 8,960 people 'disappeared' in this way; the secret detention and torture camps numbered 365. Personnel who according to the Commission were involved at various levels in the clandestine operations (in arresting, detaining, torturing or 'disappearing' the suspected subversives) numbered 1,300, almost all of them members of the armed forces or police.

And yet, as always, the figures say little about the quality of the horror. Let us, therefore, stop for a moment to reconstruct how the clandestine armed forces operated in practice. For this purpose, I shall use testimony from survivors and the judgment of the Buenos Aires Federal Court of Appeal of 9 December 1985 condemning the members of the first three military Juntas. (Interestingly a recent judgment delivered by the Inter-American Court of Human Rights, in the *Velásquez Rodriguez* case, found that in the period 1981 to 1984 the same methods were resorted to in Honduras. The Court's judgment (of 29 July 1988) gives a telling illustration of how clandestine military forces operated in Honduras, following the same pattern previously adopted in Argentina).[1]

As already indicated, arrests were made preferably at night. Groups of armed men, usually hooded or with their faces hidden in balaclavas, entered the home of a 'suspect', weapons in hand, and arrested him: the terrorized relatives were told that he would be taken away for interrogation, and that he would be 'handed back' as soon as the interrogation was finished. This was when the calvary began, for both the arrestee and the relatives (and the word 'calvary' has never been less of a metaphor than here). The arrestee and the relatives or friends entered a world of darkness. Those arrested were taken to an unknown place, with no distinguishing features, which they would not be able to later identify. They were interrogated by hooded figures who did not use each other's names. The interrogations were interspersed with threats, mistreatment and torture. The torture was not only the 'refined' type used by modern states: fake shootings and other inhuman treatment that leaves no physical traces. The Argentine military could also allow themselves the 'luxury' of old-style torture (electric shocks to lips, gums and genitals; sexual tortures, especially against women, and other similar methods); after all, in most cases, the tortured people were going to be 'disappeared', without leaving any trace. Torture was not the only way of destroying the detainees' humanity. No less devastating was the loss of identity, caused by the fact that they did not know where they were, nor who was interrogating and torturing them, nor who might be their companions in misery, still less whether their relatives and friends were informed of their fate. Isolation from the outside world was total. Only the physical pain inflicted by the soldiers made the detainees aware that they continued to exist (but for how long?), to be thinking human beings, even if only in the fog of pain.

The suffering of the relatives was different, but in some ways scarcely less acute. Obviously, they would immediately go to the police. The police would pretend to carry out enquiries, or even actually did so, only to reply that there was no record of the disappearance of the person arrested, nor had any writ been issued for his or her arrest. As far as the police were concerned, those arrested had simply evaporated into nothing. In many cases, relatives called in the magistracy, which began enquiries and legal investigations. These, too, invariably led nowhere. The Supreme Court received some 400 petitions for *habeas corpus* or applications to ascertain on what legal basis the 'disappeared' had been arrested and where they were detained: again, to no avail. The Court (the members of which had been appointed by the Junta) simply confined itself to asking the military leaders to carry out enquiries to discover the fate of the 'disappeared'. Despite all these legal proceedings, not one single member of the army or the police was ever tried by a military or civilian court. And the Government constantly denied the 'disappearances' and the crimes connected with them.

What I have just described may still seem rather remote. It will perhaps be helpful to describe some specific cases. I shall confine myself to one of the blackest episodes of the dictatorship: the arrest and disappearance of a group of seven secondary school pupils, guilty of protesting in September 1976 in order to secure renewal of their cards allowing reductions on public transport. This episode remained in the police archives under the code-name 'night of the pencils', and was exhumed in its full horror, after the return to democracy, by two Argentinian journalists, María Seoane and Héctor Ruiz Núñez,[2] mainly on the basis of the testimony of the sole survivor, Pablo Díaz, who was 18 when he was arrested.

The seven boys were kidnapped by the clandestine squads, following the usual lugubrious ritual: men with concealed faces waving weapons, indifferent to the terror of those being arrested and the distress of their relatives, who were told only the usual few words: 'We are taking them away for interrogation. We will bring them back soon, madam.'[3]

Let us read rogether a few extracts from Pablo's evidence to the Commission on the '*desaparecidos*' set up after the end of the military dictatorship.

First of all there was the total isolation: 'There you knew when it was night and when it was day from the tortures. Those were almost always at night, when there was no glimmer of light and you started to hear the screams of the women. That was when you knew night had fallen.'[4] Then the sense of total insecurity: another boy, having been arrested and interrogated, was carried off. 'You've saved yourself,' said the solider who had interrogated him, but added: 'but you'll live only if I say so.' And the impossibility of seeing the capturers: after ninety-seven days of detention and having been tortured several times, Pablo was taken to the infirmary. 'One of the guards ordered him not to look, because there was a lieutenant-colonel. "If you recognize him you're done for, kid," he told him.'[5] The doctor treated his wounds; then the guards photographed him and took his fingerprints. '"Well, kid,' the lieutenant-colonel said to him, 'now you're well we'll take you away from here. But I warn you: you don't know where you've been, you don't know who you've been with. You don't remember a thing, understand?" While they were taking him back to the cell, still with a rope round his neck, the guard told him: "We'll be transferring you tonight, but don't speak to anybody or you're done for. If you keep quiet, you'll be free'".[6] Pablo Díaz stayed in the hands of the clandestine forces for three years, nine months and ten days, with no trial and without his parents knowing whether he was still alive. Before being freed on 19 November 1980 (he never found out why and even today the reason is a mystery), an army major told him: 'You're going to be set free, but if you say anything about the kidnapping, you know what can happen to you and your family. Okay?'[7]

During the period of the military dictatorship the clock went back 300 years. One of the characteristics of the Western-type modern state is that every individual, as well as having a name, surname and proof of residence, is identifiable in his movements. If he has an accident, relatives and friends are 'activated', and the authorities carry out enquiries. In theory, the individual is not alone (at least externally) nor isolated from other members of civil society. Even if he is imprisoned in a place of detention, both relatives and the authorities keep track of his existence and his actions. Certificates, attestations and documents testify to his life and personal circumstances. Even the final event of his human existence, death, leaves its formal, external trace: certificates, stamps, markers of the death remain, a cross or some other symbol on a tomb, serve to indicate that a 'person' – having been materialized for a specific period of time in a specific place – has run his earthly course.

All this was negated in Argentina by the simple decision of a group of generals. The external 'certainty' of the existence of people was 'cancelled out'. A 'subversive' could disappear into nothingness: for civil society and the state, it was as if he had never been born or existed. If our world, our real and interior world, is an immense labyrinth which in theory offers thousands of possible pathways (that in practice are gradually reduced to a few and may sometimes even dwindle into blind alleys), then in Argentina in those years of horror, even the labyrinth disappeared. All those suspected of 'subversion' – or linked in any way, even remotely, with 'subversives' – did not have before them a labyrinth, where a minimum of choice still remains, especially in the early stages. They were offered only cancellation from the 'register', annihilation of body and soul, and, almost always, final disappearance. As the 1985 judgment of the Buenos Aires Federal Court of Appeal says, 'the victims were continually reminded that they were completely deprived of protection and subject to the whim of their captors.'[8] These in fact had a maximum of arbitrary power: they could maltreat, torture and kill *at their own discretion*.

There is another striking thing about the Argentinian system for eliminating 'subversives'. The modern state, as we know, is becoming increasingly bureaucratic. People's actions tend increasingly to be arranged and ordered by *laws* – abstract schemes aimed at regulating human conduct in the most minute details. At the same time, there is a trend towards keeping a record of every human action: of the orders from the authorities, of the reactions of those who have to obey, of conduct that departs from the directives. Many modern authoritarian states have pursued this trend obsessively. The Nazi state was obsessed with the need to preserve a written record of the actions of even the smallest, most minor cog of the state machine: and it is thanks to this obsessive deference to the need for written records that we have so much evidence today of the Nazi abominations. Another authoritarian regime, the South African one, is conspicuous for its obsessive attachment to the most formalistic legalism as I have already noted in chapter 6.

In Argentina the opposite took place. Everything was done *outside the law* and *without the written word*. I said earlier that, notwithstanding the possibility of promulgating new, stricter norms, the Argentinian military preferred to act clandestinely and unlawfully. They operated in a totally different *dimension* from that of the modern democratic state: the dimension of total arbitrariness. At the same time, they wanted to act in such a way as not to leave any written evidence of their actions: almost always the orders were *oral*, and almost always the persons upon whom these orders were executed 'were disappeared': in no case was any tangible sign of what had happened to remain. The military even used nicknames to refer to each other, in order not to be recognized in future by anyone who by some chance had escaped from their torture.

Let us reflect on these 'procedures' for a moment. To become aware of their implications, we must take ourselves back to some. trials in the past. The trials of the Inquisition left traces; we have available today even the interrogations and torture of Joan of Arc, preserved in the records accurately kept by her inquisitors and torturers. Why? Joan of Arc's persecutors were sure of acting for the Good, of being right. By contrast, the Argentinian persecutors realized that their actions, if known, would have aroused the reproof and condemnation of all. By the 1970s the progress of the civil conscience and especially the spread of the concept of human dignity dissuaded those persecutors from saying openly what they were doing. They arrested, tortured and killed illegally, but with the consciousness that they were breaking the most elementary rules of civil coexistence. It is not that they felt they had no justification – in their view the exceptionality of the phenomenon of terrorism called for an exceptional response. And yet they knew that public opinion, in Argentina and abroad, would not have accepted that justification.

The concept of respect for human dignity, then, was of little use: it merely induced the military to set up a system of clandestine repression in parallel with the overt 'legal' one of the state. How did the international community react? And after the fall of the military, what was the response of the free people of Argentina?

The reaction of the international community

News about the practice of 'forced disappearances' frequently leaked out of Argentina, and was immediately brought to the attention of world public opinion and of the United Nations organs dealing with human rights. Unfortunately the UN's reaction, and also that of many states, suffered from the various shortcomings typical of international bodies.

So far as the UN is concerned, the balance sheet is easy to draw up. The first detailed report of what was happening in Argentina had scarcely been published when the most independent, courageous body in the UN system, the Sub-Commission on Prevention of Discrimination and Protection of Minorities (composed of independent experts), adopted a resolution[9] on the subject (in circumstances I shall describe), albeit a rather weak one. Subsequently, in December 1978, the matter was raised in the General Assembly; the latter, however, confined itself to adopting a general resolution which,[10] without mentioning any names, invited states to put an end to 'forced disappearances' (a practice which was spreading to other countries of Latin America as well, with growing success). The first serious step was taken, on 29 February 1980, by the UN Human Rights Commission: it set up a Working Group on 'forced' or involuntary disappearances, charged with the task of gathering documentation and evidence. The Working Group immediately went about its job diligently, though without being able to visit the states 'concerned', and published reports (containing the information gathered), which were then brought before the Commission on Human Rights, discussed and made the subject of, again, general, rather vague resolutions. The Working Group's reports always contained detailed information on what had happened in Argentina.

Was this action useless, or even ridiculous, given the gravity of what was going on in Argentina? I shall reply with a few personal memories, which seem to me to be useful in that they indicate the limits, but also the potential, of the impact of international action.

The first documented reports on the forced disappearances and tortures in Argentina reached the UN Sub-Commission in August 1976, in the course of its annual session. Some representatives of Argentinian human rights groups consigned voluminous documentation to various members of the Sub-Commission, trusting that they would take some initiative. I was then a member of the Sub-Commission, and along with the French expert, Nicole Questiaux (later a Minister in the first year of Mitterrand's presidency), we decided to check the reports and, should they prove well-founded, draw up a draft resolution expressing the UN's concern at what was happening in Argentina.[11] A rather mild initiative; nevertheless, it aroused a great deal of alarm in the Argentine Embassy to the UN. The Ambassador immediately tried to speak to us, and even invited us to lunch. His invitation was flatly refused, but he continued to do everything he could to dissuade us from pursuing the initiative. His arguments, accusing the authors of the documentation distributed to us of being known terrorists, certainly did nothing to sway us. The following day, each of us was called before our respective Ambassadors in Geneva, who had received strongly-worded messages from their capitals: Buenos Aires had telephoned the capitals of our two countries, to have our Ambassadors to Geneva direct us to stop what we were doing. Fortunately, both the Ambassadors took note of our status as independent experts and simply conveyed to us the steps the Argentinian authorities had taken. The Argentinian Ambassador to Geneva, having heard of our decision not to retreat from our initial position, called another meeting, where he quickly moved from polite 'recommendations' to the most open threats (he was then chairman of the 'Group of 77', i.e. of the Third World states, a position that gave him considerable influence as regards our possible re-election and our 'diplomatic' future within the UN). These Argentinian protests and threats, far from discouraging us, only served to strengthen our resolve to persist. If anything, our action had seemed to us excessively small and trivial, given the seriousness of what was going on in Argentina. But if the Argentinian authorities had gone to such extremes to endeavour to avoid the passing of a resolution which would inevitably be general and weak, if they were so concerned about that resolution of a 'minor' UN body, that meant that body did count for something, and could have some effect, however minimal. Naturally, we exerted outselves to bring our campaign home – which is what happened – and, of course, we later paid the price, in different ways, for having dared to defy an authoritarian state.

I wished to recall this episode because it seems to me symptomatic of the potential for action by the United Nations. Despite the limited nature of the powers it enjoys, the world organization can to some extent influence public opinion (and in fact, in the case of the resolution we had promoted, the Latin American press quickly printed the essential parts of it, letting the whole continent know that a UN body in Geneva had taken a stance against what was happening in Argentina).

And I believe that, despite the shortcomings I have mentioned, the subsequent actions by the UN, along with action by individual states and, above all, the admirable courage of the *'Plaza de Mayo'* mothers, did have some effect. It was probably partly or mainly because of that action that – as the Federal Court states in its 1985 verdict[12] – from 1979 onwards the disappearances became rarer and in fact ceased in 1980, even before the fall of the dictatorship. Of course the guilty were not punished; but at least the most serious manifestations of their odious practices eventually stopped.

How the Alfonsín Government reacted

It is fairly rare for a change of government to entail that those responsible for serious crimes committed under the previous regime are punished. Normally, it is found preferable either to wipe the slate clean by means of an amnesty, or to confine oneself to purging only the guiltiest. To Alfonsín's great credit, he decided to break with this tradition – a well-consolidated one, especially in Latin America – and seek to expose the responsibility of the dictatorship, and punish the guilty – within the limits we shall see.

Alfonsín took action on several fronts. First of all, he repealed the 'national pacification law' adopted by the fourth military Junta on 22 September 1983, immediately before yielding power to a democratic regime: an amnesty law wiping out all the misdeeds committed in the 'dirty war' (as it had come to be called) against subversion.

The democratic President's second move was to set up a National Commission on the Disappearance of Persons (CONADEP), made up of eminent persons and chaired by the writer Ernesto Sabato. Its brief was to gather evidence on 'disappeared' persons and report within eight months. The reason why Alfonsín preferred to set up a special body rather than taking what might seem the more logical and natural step of having a judicial enquiry carried out by the magistracy is probably as follows. The Commission, being made up of people not compromised by connections with the previous regime, and indeed noted for their moral intransigence and their openness towards human rights, offered guarantees of impartiality and rigour that Argentinian judges could not always provide. In the event, the Commission drew up an important, voluminous report, entitled *Nunca Más* (Never Again).[13] This laid the foundations for the subsequent judicial enquiries. For instance, in the course of the trial of the members of the first three Juntas, the Federal Court of Appeal took account of the evidence gathered by CONADEP, stating, however, that, as it had not been given under oath, the applicable procedural rules required that it could be taken account of only if corroborated by other evidence. As the Court put it, it 'is not going to consider a fact as proven on the exclusive basis of the evidence furnished by CONADEP'.[14]

A third important measure taken by Alfonsín was to modify the Argentine Code of Military Justice in various ways. The biggest change was to limit the competence of the military courts, at the same time allowing appeals to be brought before criminal federal courts against decisions handed down by the 'Supreme Council of the Armed Forces'. In this way, the criminal courts would always have the last word. On the basis of this legislation, on 22 April 1985, a trial began against nine generals, the members of the first three Juntas. In relation to these nine generals the 'Supreme Council of the Armed Forces', previously entrusted with their trial, had decided to discontinue its proceedings because the directives on the basis of which the military leaders had acted during the dictatorship were 'incontestable'.

The Court handed down its judgment in the case of the nine generals on 9 December 1985.[15] Five were condemned to prison sentences ranging from four and a half years to life; the other four generals were discharged. This verdict was confirmed on 30 December 1986 by the Supreme Court, which confined itself to making slight changes to the sentences.[16]

The judgment of the Federal Court of Appeal is undoubtedly important both for its wide-ranging reconstruction of the facts and for its detailed refutation of the legal positions of the defence. While the refined jurist might find much to object to in the judgment, not only as regards its length,[17] but also as regards the lack of lucidity in the legal arguments adduced to support the condemnation of the generals, the judgment nevertheless remains important on at least two scores: accurate ascertainment of the various crimes committed by the armed forces led by the generals, and reconstruction of the essential characteristics of the anti-terrorist political line pursued by those generals. In other words, the verdict is very significant for its perspicacious and effective identification of a clandestine military structure in parallel with the official structures, though essentially under their leadership.

A number of other important trials followed those of the generals. Particularly noteworthy is the trial of General Ramón J. Camps, former Chief of Police for Buenos Aires Province, and five police officers; all were sentenced by the Federal Court of Appeal (on 2 December 1986) to varying periods of imprisonment.[18]

An idiosyncratic feature of these various Argentinian judgments is their immense length: for example, the judgment against Videla and the other generals, runs to about 110 printed pages (in very minute print), whereas the *Camps* case runs to over 1,000 typewritten pages. It is as if the Argentinian judges wished to react to the 'official silence' of the dictators, to the lack or absolute insufficiency of written documents in that period, by going to the opposite extreme. They have written torrential judgments in which they minutely explore any minor detail of the facts and indulge in prolix disquisitions on legal issues. From excessive silence one has moved to a sort of compulsive attempt to leave nothing undiscussed.

Let us now go back to the different stages which the Alfonsín regime has gone through with its legislative efforts.

The growing sense of dissatisfaction among the military, and the grave dangers that Argentinian democracy was facing induced Alfonsín to adopt a fourth measure: the 'full stop' law of 23 December 1986. This laid down a time-limit of 60 days for the initiation of proceedings for crimes committed before 10 December 1983 'related to the use of violent means of political action'. The sole exception was for crimes consisting of the kidnapping and 'hiding' of minors. At the expiry of the time-limit on 22 February 1987 some 150 suits had been initiated before eight federal appeal courts. The number of accused had thus been drastically reduced. Faced with the need to do justice, had democracy decided to capitulate?

To answer this question, one further, still more serious measure must be mentioned: the law of 'Due Obedience' of 4 June 1987. This is more serious than the previous measure because it constitutes a further 'step back' by the democratic government. In practice it 'absolved' from guilt all the higher, intermediate and low-ranking personnel of the armed forces who had committed crimes in the years of dictatorship. To clarify the terms and implications of this law, I must first explain what the situation was in Argentina before its adoption.

The 'acquittal' of those who had committed crimes on 'superior orders'

Let us start from the facts. It is clear that, while the clandestine repressive system set up in Argentina between 1976 and 1980 was the fruit of the military leaders' political design, its practical implementation was in the hands of subordinate personnel, from colonels down to privates. To achieve justice, after the dictatorship, these too ought to have been punished, in addition to the members of the first three Juntas themselves. What prevented this? Above all, there were obstacles of a legal nature. Let us look at them.

Argentine law in force in the period of dictatorship assigned all responsibility for any crimes committed in execution of an order to the person giving the order; this was laid down by Article 34(5) of the Argentinian Penal Code. Article 514 of the Code of Military Justice repeated the notion, adding only that the subordinate is responsible as accomplice 'only when he had exceeded compliance with such an order'.[19] As can be seen, these were laws that did not take the civil and moral progress of modern times into account; above all, they failed to take account of the great principles sanctioned in London in 1945 (with the international agreement to set up the International Military Tribunal to try the major Nazi criminals), and then reaffirmed at Nuremberg in 1946. In Argentina, faced with the dilemma between deference to authority or respect for the free judgment and dignity of the human person, the law chose the first alternative.

This was the legal situation that Alfonsín 'inherited'. What should he do? Apply those laws and thus set free all the intermediate and lower ranking military personnel who had committed so many crimes, or radically revise them in order to do justice?

Alfonsín's actions were taken in two stages. During the first stage, he secured certain amendments to the Code of Military Justice, which I have already mentioned, by means of law number 23049 of 14 February 1984.[20] One of these amendments, laid down in Article 11 of the law, introduced a *presumption*: military personnel who had no decision-making powers and who had remained within the limits of the orders they had received were to be *presumed* to have *been mistaken* as to the legitimacy of those orders. In this way, the attempt was made to 'update' Argentinian norms in the light of the Nuremberg principles (principles in virtue of which the subordinate is held responsible where the unlawfulness or criminality of an order given to him was manifest). In this case, yielding to the demands of the military, it was laid down that such subordinates were to be regarded as *excused*, since it had to be presumed that they had been in *error* as to the criminality of the orders received. Thus far, the 1984 amendment does no more than clarify any ambiguity in the previous laws, in favour of the military. The amendment did, however, add one important point: the 'presumption of error' by subordinate military personnel was rebutted if the acts committed in carrying out an order were 'atrocious' or 'aberrant'. Accordingly, intermediate ranks did become responsible for maltreatment, torture and murders, and should have faced trials.

This legislation aroused enormous resentment among the armed forces. The dangers that might have ensued for Argentina's fragile new democracy induced the Minister for Defence to take a backward step: on 24 April 1986 he issued a series of directives to the Prosecutor attached to the 'Supreme Council of the Armed Forces', among other things barring criminal proceedings against officers of intermediate or low rank who had committed atrocities, except where such atrocities had been perpetrated by *exceeding* orders given by superiors. One of the judges of the Federal Court of Appeal resigned in protest against these directives; but this, of course, did not change anything. All the same, the military were still not satisfied. Following the threats of a military coup in April 1987, Alfonsín had recourse to a final, extreme measure: on 4 June 1987, he secured adoption of the law of 'Due Obedience'.[21]

Let us examine this law, which, although it calmed the wrath of the military, aroused such criticism among public opinion. I should say right away that this law, addressing the crucial question of the value of higher orders, is valid only *for the past*; in other words, it constitutes a sort of *amnesty law*. This is an element that should not be underestimated; if its very regressive legal content – with which I shall deal in a moment – were valid for the future too, the law would amount to a very negative turn in the tormented history of the punishment of serious crimes against humanity.

What, then, does this law lay down? In practice, it absolves all the military, from privates up to brigadier-generals, for crimes committed in the dark years of the Argentinian dictatorship. The only people that remain punishable are the very highest military leaders – in practice, only the generals already condemned. In fact, some 250 Argentinian officers already in the process of being tried or awaiting trial were freed under this law. Among them were General Ramón J. Camps, Buenos Aires Police Chief under the dictatorship (who had been sentenced in the first instance to 25 years in prison as I have already stated); likewise, former army Commander Ernesto Barreiro and Captain Alfredo Astiz (notorious for having tortured many people, including two French nuns and a Swedish girl) and eleven of their co-accused, all of them active at the 'Navy Engineering School', which was one of the clandestine places of detention and torture in which the most horrific crimes were committed.

Let us now see how this law operates and how Alfonsín sought to justify it. Article 1 provides that 'it is presumed without proof to the contrary being admitted' that all military personnel 'are exempt from punishment' for crimes committed during the period of dictatorship, because 'in those cases it shall be deemed by operation of law that those persons acted under duress, in subordination [*en estado de coerción bajo subordinación*] to a superior authority and following orders, without having the possibility of resisting or refusing to follow those orders and of examining their lawfulness [*sin facultad o posibilidad de inspección, oposición o resistencia*]'. As if to render the impunity of the relevant military personnel absolutely clear, Article 6 then provides that Article 11 of law number 23049 of 1984 shall not apply to these personnel (this being the provision which, as mentioned earlier, laid down a presumption in favour of subordinates but made that presumption rebuttable in the case of 'atrocious' or 'aberrant' crimes). The road to absolution of the military personnel was thus followed right to the end, with no deviations. The absolute presumption in favour of the military, which applies even to pending proceedings ('regardless of the stage of the proceedings', Article 3) has only one exception: crimes of rape, kidnapping and hiding of minors, or change of their civil status, and appropriation of immovables through extortion (Article 2).

Let us now turn to look at Alfonsín's attempts to justify the law. These are conveniently summarized in his presidential message, in which he presented the Bill to both Houses of Parliament for approval.[22] The message contains three salient notions. The first is that

Whatever might have been the deficiencies that led to the present uncertainty as to the legal outcome of the review of the repression of subversion, it is obvious that society cannot remain indefinitely trapped [*atrapada*] in these conflicts. That would on the one hand hinder the possibility of setting about thorough reforms of the armed and security forces, which are essential, and on the other impede attainment of the objectives of peace and unity required for the consolidation of democracy.

This, clearly, is the essential political *ratio* of the law: it is only through a full pardon for the military that the process of consolidating democracy can be set in motion.

The presidential message continues with two considerations that relate more closely to the question of 'superior orders'. The first is the recollection that the repressive system set up in 1976 had as its essential presupposition the training of military personnel in accordance with an authoritarian method requiring blind obedience to superior orders. To this extent, there was a 'conditioning' of those military personnel who had no powers of command. This 'conditioning', notes Alfonsín, 'consisted in indoctrination aimed at denying the enemy's humanity [*la condición humana del enemigo*] and underlining the need to employ methods that brought about the formation of a moral climate in the context of which refusal to share this description of the enemy amounted to joining them'. The blame should therefore be put on the military leaders 'who used as their instruments the most authoritarian ideologies, imposing the rule that the end justifies any means whatever. In this way, subordinate personnel were induced to carry out orders, the legal and moral foundations of which they were not, in general, in a position to assess. The plan of action was based on the impossibility of reviewing higher orders, in the context of the blind obedience that an interpretation of Article 514 of the Code of Military Justice permits.' Alfonsín thus seeks the causes of passive obedience and finds them in the political, social and military conditions of dictatorship. He justifies subordinate military personnel by reference to the climate prevailing at the time: such personnel had been indoctrinated in such a way that they were unaware of the inhumanity of what they were doing.

Following this second argument Alfonsín goes on to develop a third concept which constitutes the very pivot of the legal – rather than political – justification for the legislation. In short, he says that the moral foundations of the 'doctrine of superior orders' must be reviewed and reformulated in a modern perspective based on respect for the human person. 'That makes it essential,' he says, 'for the future to remedy the indefiniteness of that provision [i.e. the abovementioned Article 514 of the Argentinian Code of Military Justice], so as clearly to incorporate in it the rule that obedience cannot justify the perpetration of crimes against humanity [*no hay obediencia para cometer crímines de lesa humanidad*]'. Thus far, one can only welcome this commendable, far-sighted proposal. Now comes the painful part. Alfonsín continues:

However, the rule of law [*las reglas del estado de derecho*] implies that what is to be taken into account is not the concept of obedience that ought to prevail in a democratic system that respects the dignity of the human individual, but *the concept which unfortunately prevailed in practice at the time when the acts were committed* [emphasis added]. It is on the strength of this last concept of obedience that one ought to draw a distinction between those who gave the orders for the construction of the perverse plan of operations described above and those whose responsibility it was to carry out those orders.

Given this premise, Alfonsín deduces a clear distinction between those who had 'decision-making autonomy [*autonomía decisoria*] and those who were 'subordinated to a system that required undiscriminating obedience to directives from above'. The former ought to be punished; the latter should go free.

Alfonsín's arguments in favour of the legislation, which I have just summarized, are astonishing to say the least. I can understand the considerations dictated by political necessities: between the 'pardoning' of 250 criminals and the danger of civil war entailing the possible toppling of democracy, the former is clearly the lesser evil. But what is absolutely unacceptable is the attempt to justify the distinction – as regards responsibility for crimes committed on superior orders – between military leaders on the one hand and all other 'subordinates' (from brigadiers-general downwards) on the other, on the basis that the 'rule of law' does not permit retroactive application of the principles of democracy. In practice, what Alfonsín was saying is that the principle *nullum crimen sine lege, nulla poena sine lege* (i.e. the principle whereby there may be punishment only within the limits laid down by the laws in force at the time the crime was committed) prevents the application of the new postulates of democracy, including those relating to superior orders, to Argentinian military personnel. Against this assertion two formidable objections may be raised.

Firstly, as long ago as 1946, at Nuremberg, the argument now invoked by Alfonsín was rightly rejected by the International Military Tribunal, with the observation that in any case the principle banning retroactive criminal legislation must always *yield* before the ethical requirement not to let atrocious misdeeds go unpunished.[23] Secondly, at the time these crimes in question were committed, between 1976 and 1980, *international law* did not exempt a subordinate from responsibility for crimes in cases where the criminality of the order given was manifest.[24] Alfonsín thus allows Argentinian law of the period of dictatorship to prevail both over the concepts of democracy introduced by his own government and over international law. This is a nationalistic, conservative position that runs counter to the most basic tenets of modern legal civilization; it also conflicts with the fundamental presuppositions of the democratic regime set up in Argentina in 1983.

There is at least one clear moral to be drawn from this sad story: when compelling political requirements impose the sacrifice of justice to *raison d'état*, one ought at least to refrain from contriving legal justifications. Instead of bolstering the political motivations, these may, as in this case, lead to very dangerous conceptions. It is the task of the jurist, as of any person concerned for the values of ethical progress, to demystify those conceptions and justifications and expose their full implications.

Let me complete the story of the law on the 'duty of obedience'. A challenge was mounted against it on 11 June 1987 by Juan Ramos Padilla, a federal judge in Morón (a suburb of Buenos Aires), on the grounds that the law was unconstitutional because it conflicted with the basic rule on the equality of citizens. Even though his courageous argument was rather limited, applying only to the trial of five military personnel accused of human rights violations in the Morón hospital, it was quickly cut short, as were the doubts as to the constitutionality of the law expressed by the judges of the Bahía-Blanca Federal Court. On 22 June 1987 the Supreme Court ruled that the law was in conformity with the Constitution.[25] This brought the whole matter to an end. It seems difficult, now, not to share the view expressed by Ernesto Sábato on 26 June 1987 to a *Le Monde* correspondent:[26] 'I am very saddened by the thought that the great ethical principles are being passed over. We have arrived at the paradox of imprisoning a man who steals a purse and letting torturers go free.'

8

A 'Contribution' by the West to the Struggle against Hunger: The Nestlé Affair

The facts

The fight to make the fundamental right to life a reality in the world is a truly titanic one, often enough to make the bravest despair. This is highlighted by an episode which, though very well-known, seems to me so important as to call for a brief reminder.

In 1974, a British charity, *War on Want* (founded in the early 1950s with the main aim of providing information on the problems of poverty in the world), published a brief study, *The Baby Killer*,[1] edited by Mike Muller, examining the pernicious effects produced in the Third World from the promotion and sale of powdered milk for infants. In brief, it asserted that the increasingly widespread distribution of powdered milk, encouraged and organized by large food industries in the West, was producing devastating effects. Why? For the very simple reason that all the hygienic and sanitary conditions, and more generally conditions of social progress, that may make replacement of mother's milk by powdered milk useful do not exist in most developing countries. For that milk to have beneficial effects, the baby's bottle must be sterilized, there must be drinkable water, and the accompanying instructions for using the bottle must be followed rigorously. But in many of those countries, none of this happens. Let us consider in more detail why.

'Wash your hands carefully, using soap, every time you prepare the child's feed'. That is how, according to *The Baby Killer*, the instructions for bottle feeding in the Nestlé pamphlet *Mother Book* start. But, the study continues, '66% of housewives in the capital of Malawi do not have running water. 60% do not have a kitchen inside their home.' 'Put the bottle and teat in a pan with enough water to cover them. Bring to the boil and boil for ten minutes', says another pamphlet, *Cow and Gate*, prepared by another large multinational and aimed at West Africa. In this pamphlet, the instructions I have just quoted are accompanied by a picture of a shining aluminium pan on top of an electric cooker. 'But,' observes *The Baby Killer*, 'the great majority of mothers in West Africa do not have electric cookers. They cook on three stones that support a pot heated over a wood fire. The pot for sterilizing the baby's bottle also has to be used to cook the family meal; sterilization and boiling water are likely to be forgotten.'

The *Cow and Gate* babycare pamphlet for Africa says: 'If you have a refrigerator, it is more convenient for you to prepare enough for baby for the whole day.' But how many African families, especially in rural areas, have access to a refrigerator?

In addition to the negative effects I have just pointed out, there is another one: the explanations for using powdered milk are of course in writing, and are contained in the pamphlets distributed along with the powdered milk. But the very great majority of Third World mothers are illiterate.

Another problem is the cost of artificial feeding, which is very high in developing countries. In 1973 the cost of feeding a three-month-old child was approximately equal in Burma to 10.6 per cent of the minimum working wage, in India 22.7 per cent, in Nigeria 30.3 per cent, in Pakistan 40.3 per cent and in Egypt 40.8 per cent. These percentages go up considerably when it comes to calculating the cost of artificial feeding for a six-month-old child, which needs more.

What are the consequences of all these concomitant factors? The answer is clear. The bottle is not sterilized and so becomes a breeding ground for dangerous germs; the instructions for use are not understood so that the milk is wrongly used; to make the milk go further it is diluted with water, often heavily polluted. The result is that the children are less resistant to infection and easily fall victim to gastric or intestinal complaints like gastro-enteritis; the malnutrition resulting from the use of diluted powdered milk often causes physical or mental damage, followed in many cases by serious illnesses and even death.

In short, the distribution of powdered milk in the Third World, instead of being a factor for progress, has brought deleterious effects; instead of raising the standard of life and nourishment of children, it has contributed to causing illnesses and malnutrition, the prelude to death. Who is primarily at fault?

The *War on Want* study laid the blame principally on the big foodstuffs multinationals. Indeed, an annual report from Nestlé itself helps us to understand why. Here is what it says: 'In general, sales [of infant feeding products] are developing satisfactorily, though the birth-rate in countries with a higher standard of living is continuing to fall, slowing down the increase in our sales. The result is increasing competition and an ever broader choice of products for the consumer. But in developing countries our products continue to sell well, thanks to population growth and the rise in standard of living.' Accordingly, the best market, on which the multinationals have to concentrate, is in the poor countries. The *War on Want* study specifically accused large-scale Western companies of using a host of questionable methods to sell their products: from recourse to mass-media repetition of slogans on the enormous advantages of artificial feeding ('your children will be more intelligent', and the like), to the use of 'saleswomen' (who, in the guise of nurses, 'counsel' mothers in dispensaries and hospitals, 'pushing' the various products under the pretext of giving advice on feeding), to the free distribution of 'samples' or of baby bottles to those who buy tins of powdered milk. The *War on Want* study concluded with an appeal directed at both the companies themselves and the governments of developing countries. It urged a return to breast-feeding, as not only healthier but above all more suited to Third World conditions; the multinationals were asked to stop publicizing their products in poor countries or carrying out sales campaigns, and instead to collaborate with intergovernmental organizations such as the World Health Organization (WHO) that are specially involved with problems of infant feeding in poor countries. The governments of those countries, it was suggested, should exercise effective control, and in particular ensure access to industrial products for those who really need them – infants who cannot be fed by their mothers, such as some twins or orphans.

The case brought in Switzerland by Nestlé

One of the multinationals mentioned in the English document was Nestlé, an enormous firm with its headquarters in Switzerland, with an annual budget higher than the Swiss Federal Government's (in 1974 its budget was 16.6 billion Swiss Francs as against 13.9 billion for the budget of the Swiss Confederation).[2] A group of individuals concerned with Third World issues, the 'Swiss Working Groups for Development Policy' (*Schweizerische Arbeitsgruppen für Entwicklungspolitik*, SAFEP), translated the pamphlet from English to German, entitling it *Nestlé tötet Babies* ('Nestlé Kills Babies'). This led to an enormous furore. But still greater furore was provoked in Switzerland and abroad by the charge against SAFEP brought on 2

July 1974 by Nestlé in the Bern Criminal Court (and the Court of Zug, another small Swiss town with an active SAFEP group). Nestlé invoked the Swiss Penal Code: in its opinion, the 'Working Groups' had defamed it by repeatedly disseminating through the press, in bad faith, allegations that 'injured' its 'reputation' (*Ehre*). In particular, according to the Swiss company, the 'Working Groups' had defamed it for four reasons: they had claimed in the title of the pamphlet that the company 'killed babies'; they had said that the activity of Nestlé and other multinationals operating in the sector was 'contrary to the principles of ethics, and immoral'; they had asserted that Nestlé was responsible for the death or permanent mental or physical impairment of thousands of children because of its advertising practices (i.e. the fact that it publicized powdered milk using unacceptable expedients); they had accused Nestlé of camouflaging its commercial representatives in the Third World as 'nurses', thereby deceiving mothers in those countries.

The trial dragged on for two years (from 1974 to 1976) before the President of the Bern Criminal Court, Sollberger, acting as sole judge. The two parties to the dispute of course made wide use of 'forensic' arguments, the one side to cut down the 'Groups', the other to refute the accusations decisively. Before sentence was pronounced, specifically at the third hearing (22 June 1976), Nestlé took a step that aroused much surprise and confirmed the impression that it felt rather weak in its legal action: it withdrew three of the four accusations referred to, leaving only the first one, that the 'Working Groups' had defamed it by having used as title for the German translation of the pamphlet an unproven, unfounded accusation: that Nestlé killed children. The 'Working Groups', in a periodical bulletin, hastened to underline the importance of this decision, noting that by virtue of it the three allegations against Nestlé covered by the part of the action withdrawn could now legitimately be levelled against Nestlé 'without being punishable or prohibited'.[3]

The verdict

Judgment was pronounced on 24 June 1976[4] and as was foreseeable, amounted to running with the hare and hunting with the hounds. In brief, the thirteen members of the 'Working Groups' were found guilty not of *defamation* (*Verleumdung*), but of the less serious offence of '*false accusation*' (*üble Nachrede*) (I shall explain why presently); with the consequence that each of them was condemned to a modest fine (300 Swiss Francs) with no jail sentence.

Before describing Judge Sollberger's reasoning, I wish to highlight one important point. When complex human affairs with manifold political and social implications are brought before the courts, a peculiar phenomenon not infrequently occurs: they become subsumed and, as it were, absorbed into the aseptic, impassive world of the law; they are stripped of their human dimension and translated into 'legal facts', that is, into facts with abstract, timeless connotations; facts described in rigid technical terminology: offences, lawful acts, powers, rights, obligations, and so on. It is for the magistrate concerned to obstruct this process of rarefaction of life. He may do so either by 'reading' the laws with modern eyes and a modern sensitivity, or by inserting into the formal parameters offered by those laws the real situation, warts and all.

What happened at the Bern trial? Judge Sollberger sought to take cognizance of the complex issues of the case and go beyond the rigid standards and formal choices imposed by law. He sought to be a rigorous jurist, and at the same time open to the moral arguments of the accused. But he did not have the courage to opt decisively for the thesis of one or other of the parties, and ended up saying that in some ways both were right, and in others both wrong – even if in the end the party in whose favour judgment was given was Nestlé. The result was a clumsy, vacillating verdict, a mixture of legal formalism and hypocritical moralism.

Let us see how this conclusion was arrived at. In doing so, I shall seek to review the reasoning adopted by the Swiss magistrate step-by-step.

As I mentioned earlier, Nestlé had withdrawn three of the four charges. Accordingly, the magistrate had to ascertain only whether, by asserting that 'Nestlé Kills Babies', the 'Working Groups' had defamed it. I should say straight away that the magistrate could easily have resolved the issue by noting that the German title of the pamphlet ('Nestlé tötet Babies') did not in any way reflect the pamphlet's content. The pamphlet did express criticisms of, and grave objections against, the advisability and 'ethics' of the conduct of various multinationals, but did not specifically accuse any one of them of 'killing'. The judge could have noted that the title in question, albeit unfortunate, inappropriate and out of place, was however to be read *in conjunction with* the pamphlet to which it referred; he could then have concluded that the 'Working Groups' had not intended to accuse Nestlé literally of 'killing' Third World children; the charge could have thus been dismissed.

Judge Sollberger preferred instead to proceed with the maximum formalism, and give the accusations against Nestlé the full weight attributed to them by the Swiss company.

The judge began by observing that the assertion that someone kills children, whether intentionally or negligently, has ethical implications and injures the person's reputation (*Ehre*) (by which is understood the 'respect to which the bearer of the reputation may lay claim, from an ethical and social point of view'). He then asked whether this injury to Nestlé's reputation constituted defamation (for which in Swiss law bad faith is required, namely full awareness that the charge levelled against somebody else is false and unfounded), or mere 'false accusation' (for which, by contrast, a lack of due diligence in ascertaining the truth is sufficient and neither awareness of the untruth of the utterance nor a special intention to insult or offend i.e. the so-called *animus injurandi*, are required). The judge found that the 'Working Groups' had not acted 'in bad faith' (*wider besseres Wissen*):

To be sure, they were above all concerned to make the public attentive to the problem at issue through as effective as possible a title. They wished to denounce the firm of Nestlé, as a Swiss firm, for its advertising practices for baby milk powder in developing countries, termed unethical and immoral. The defendants [i.e. the 'Working Groups'] saw these advertising practices as the basic cause of mothers being turned away from breast feeding and towards artificial nourishment of their babies, with the consequence, from hygienic and financial reasons, that babies fed in this way are more likely to fall ill and die than breast-fed babies. The causal chain constructed by the accused, with at the beginning the advertising methods of the firm of Nestlé for artificial infant nutrition and at the end danger to health, or death, of infants fed on dried milk, shows that subjectively the accusation of killing was meant specifically morally. The accused believed that they could draw this conclusion from the information and documents available to them, in particular the English original brochure, and believed they ought to concentrate on the firm of Nestlé because they, as members of a Swiss organization for development policy (see the object of the Association) felt themselves morally obliged to exert themselves on behalf of the infants concerned in underprivileged strata in developing countries, and to draw the attention of the public, and particularly the Swiss public, to the business practices of this Swiss firm.

The judge therefore noted that in any case the offence of defamation ought to be ruled out, since the accused could not 'be reproached with having made the accusation of killing in bad faith (*gegen besseres Wissen*) and at any rate they were not aware of the untruthfulness of their allegation'.

In this way, the Swiss judge resolved the first problem (i.e. assuming that the defendants were guilty, were they guilty of defamation or 'false accusation'?) in favour of the accused. At this point another problem arose. Nestlé had sought the application of the provisions of Article 173 of the Swiss Penal Code, so as to deny the accused the possibility of bringing evidence in exculpation. This Article of the Swiss Penal Code lays down, in paragraph 2, that persons accused of having injured someone else's reputation are not punished if they can prove either that their statements are in conformity with the truth, or that 'they had serious reason to regard them, in good faith, as true'. Paragraph 3 adds that the accused *is not allowed to furnish such proof* and is hence punishable, 'if the statements have been uttered or disseminated without taking account of the public interest or otherwise without justified cause, primarily with the aim of accusing someone of evil, especially when such affirmations relate to private life or family life'. Nestlé asked the judges to apply this last paragraph and therefore bar the 'Working Groups' from producing evidence in exoneration.

On this point too the judge found against Nestlé: the defendants had taken account of the public interest, there being a public 'right to information about the business methods of a firm of the size and importance' of the company that had brought the charge. The immediate consequence of this decision by the judge was important: the accused had the right at the trial to demonstrate the truth of their assertions, or at least their reasonable belief in their truth, that is, that they had 'done everything that could be expected of them to convince themselves of the truth of their allegations'.

We thus come to the crux of the matter, the pivotal issue around which the verdict turned: had the defendants told the truth in their pamphlet or had they not? With almost pedantic logic, acting on Article 173, paragraph 2 of the Swiss Penal Code quoted above the judge then dwelt first on whether the 'Working Groups' had during the trial demonstrated the truth of their assertions. Having concluded in the negative, he then went into the question whether the 'Working Groups' had nevertheless acted with due diligence and in good faith 'by taking all reasonable steps to convince themselves of the truth of their utterances'.

On the first point, the judge's reasoning was as follows:

The evidence taken has shown that incompetent use of milk powder can lead to the death or severe illness of infants. In the poor suburbs and also in the country, in developing countries the hygienic conditions for preparing bottled milk in accordance with the dried milk manufacturer's instructions are often lacking. The use of dirty, unboiled bottles and teats, and of dirty, unboiled water may lead to infections and to the death of infants. It is also known that milk powder is sometimes 'stretched' for economic reasons. The administration of over-diluted powdered milk may cause marasmus, a wasting disease resulting from lack of protein and calories, and this, along with other diseases to which the weakened infant is more susceptible, may have the consequence of death [. . . .] The quality of Nestlé milk powder is undisputed. An insufficient amount of the product, dirty water and lack of hygiene in the preparation of the bottle are the causes of the death or severe debilitation of infants. It is not therefore the product itself that leads to the death of infants in developing countries.

Up to this point the judge seemed to be reasoning in a way favourable to the 'Working Groups': they had clearly never meant to say that Nestlé powdered milk in itself and by itself kills; they had only asserted that artificial milk produced that result *in the particular social conditions of backward countries*.

Let us, now, look at how the Swiss magistrate's reasoning proceeded. He asked whether in its illustrative pamphlets on the use of powdered milk Nestlé adequately indicated the dangers of its use in poor countries. He stated:

No answer could be secured from the Private Prosecutor's representative [i.e. legal counsel for Nestlé] to the question whether the Nestlé company used the same advertising methods in developing countries as in Europe. The judge is of the opinion, following the taking of evidence, that they go considerably further there than in Europe. The advertising takes place, as far as has become known in this case, through posters in hospitals, and through coloured brochures which are distributed and lay the emphasis, as regards nutrition, on the bottle. The reference to breast feeding in these brochures may be sufficient for the state of knowledge in the West, but for mothers in developing countries it is by no means sufficient.
It is taken as proven that the Nestlé company employs nurses on advertising contracts, who advertise its products through their work. The witness Dr Ebrahim has impressively demonstrated this by referring to the so-called gift package, an advertising method that he terms most appalling, in which, along with a box of 'NAN' milk powder, a baby bottle with teat and an illustrated brochure are given free. The inducement towards artificial feeding instead of breast feeding could according to Dr Ebrahim have the consequence that, after only three

days, the breast may fail as a source of milk owing to lack of sucking and disruption of hormonal stimulation, leaving the mother dependent on bottled milk.

The judge then goes on to consider publicity for artificial milk by radio, press and posters, and notes that in poor countries, this is aimed at mothers with little education, who are 'not in a position to differentiate and are susceptible to propaganda slogans'. On this point, the judge concludes as follows:

To sum up, it may be taken as proven that powdered milk, the quality of which is not disputed, is necessary as a substitute or supplementary food for infants that cannot, or cannot sufficiently, be breastfed. Certainly, these products should be administered only where instruction, supervision and hygienic requirements are available. These preconditions for the use of powdered milk in developing countries are repeatedly mentioned in the documentation submitted [. . .]. It is accordingly incumbent on the Nestlé company completely to rethink their advertising practices for bottle feeding in developing countries, since their advertising practice adopted so far can transform a life-saving product into a dangerous, life-destroying one. If the Private Prosecutor wishes in the future to avoid the accusation of immoral, unethical conduct, it must alter its advertising practices.

After this thrust against Nestlé, one might think that the judge had completely embraced the thesis of the accused party. Not so. He hastened to add that nevertheless the accused had not succeeded in proving the fact that supply of powdered milk constituted homicide. For, so the judge reasoned,

This does not, however, constitute evidence of negligent or deliberate killing. The adequate causal connection [*Kausalzusammenhang*] between the purchase or other supply of milk powder and the death of infants fed on these products is interrupted by the action of third parties [*durch das Tun von Drittpersonen*] for which the plaintiff [Nestlé] cannot be held criminally responsible. In this sense, then, there is no negligent, far less deliberate, killing.

At this point the reader will be jumping up or rubbing his eyes, at the sudden apparition of figures (third persons) equipped with the magic power to break the 'causal chain' that would lead to finding against Nestlé. Who are these 'third persons'? The verdict itself does not say, but fortunately the judge clarified this in his oral explanation of his judgment given the same day it was handed down: they are 'the mothers using the bottle'. Nestlé could not be regarded as responsible for the actions of mothers; as the magistrate put it 'it is not the product but the circumstances that kill [*Nicht das Produkt sondern die Umstände töten*)'.[5]

At this point we cannot complain of mere legal formalism. What we have here is downright aberration. The judge began by accepting that Nestlé's publicity is misleading, since it induces mothers in poor countries to use a commodity which, though useful in industrialized countries, may become lethal in backward areas. He even rebuked the Swiss company, urging it to 'rethink' its methods of commercial penetration in the Third World. At this point it would seem logical to draw the consequence that Nestlé's conduct in poor countries, even if not undertaken with ill-intentions, in fact leads to the most pernicious effects. Conclusion: Nestlé is in breach of the obligations of diligence imposed both by legal standards and by the *de facto* circumstances; in short it – unintentionally – kills the infants to whom its powdered milk is administered. Nestlé's culpability (or more precisely, its managers' culpability) results from the cumulative effect of a whole set of actions, that is, it is the outcome of a complex of commercial operations and practices. And yet the judge, instead of arriving at this conclusion, introduced a *deus ex machina* to break the 'causal chain': the mothers themselves. But these mothers are in fact the *object* of Nestlé's conduct; they, along with their children, are the victims of that conduct. Assigning them the role of 'third persons' who in some way intervene between the 'agent' causing the damage and the direct victim of the damage (the children), means ignoring a fundamental fact (one even previously admitted by the judge himself): these mothers are not in a position freely to decide whether to use Nestlé's powdered milk and, if so, how, because they are misled both by their ignorance and the backward conditions in which they live, and by Nestlé's deceptive publicity (deceptive in that it is totally inappropriate to the conditions of those poor countries). The 'intervention' of the 'mothers' thus comes to appear as a mere expedient to wipe out the blame and guilt of the Swiss company. At this point, all the judge's previous considerations against Nestlé, the rebukes of lack of seriousness and so forth, appear as a sort of alibi to justify the final conclusion, which is, surprisingly, in favour of the multinational.

Having found that the allegations of the defendants against Nestlé were untrue, the judge moved on to the question whether nevertheless the defendants were to be acquitted on account of their having acted in good faith. He pointed out that a defendant would have to show that

he believed in the truth of his utterances after having conscientiously taken all reasonable steps to convince himself of its correctness and added that

the issue is whether the perpetrator made the utterance contrary to care (*sorgfaltswidrig*) or not [. . . .] The proof of good faith is based on the idea that anyone making utterances to the detriment of a third party is duty-bound to check those utterances.

After a detailed examination of the way in which this proof of good faith can be administered, the judge concluded that in the case at issue the defendants had not met the relevant requirements, on the following grounds:

The duty of care must be all the greater the more burdensome is the accusation and the more widely it has been disseminated. The accusation of killing is without doubt a serious one and the range of addressees was very wide, since the pamphlet met with a wide response, in particular in the press. And the defendants were just not any Tom, Dick or Harry thoughtlessly bringing the calumnious utterances into the world. On the contrary, they are people with a generally high level of education, with a high ethical estimate of their activity in development policy research and information, who accordingly wish to be taken seriously. By the fact that as wide a public as possible was addressed by using as spectacular and sensational as possible a wording, the duty of diligence [*Sorgfaltspflicht*] – on which in this case very high requirements must be placed on account of the serious accusation of killing – was neglected. If a sufficient extent of diligence or care had been applied, this wording would have been avoided [. . . .] The defendants applied too small an amount of diligence when they decided on the wording 'Nestlé kills babies'. On the basis of the documentation available to them when making up the title, they ought not simply to have plumped for this wording.

If, then, the accused were in the wrong, the proper penalty had to be meted out to them. The penalty turned out to be a moralistic homily in which the judge displayed understanding for the youthful ardour of the thirteen accused and at the same time pointed them in the direction of the proper path of moderation. Do criticize, yes – he says – since it is right that that should happen in a democratic society; but do not get hot-headed, do not let yourselves be led astray by immoderation or by polemical fits. Let us read his own words:

The people in the 'Bern Third World Working Group' find themselves in isolation in their endeavours, and have difficulty reaching the public; they stay within a small circle. Here lies the cause for their great leap forward. Through the exaggerated, unjustified heading [of the pamphlet] they secured publicity they would otherwise not have achieved. At any rate for the majority of them, their concern is honourably meant. They recognize the problem and seek in their own way to solve it. The way they chose is unfortunate, but that alters nothing as to the motives.

The accused are all of good reputation. Major previous offences are not recorded. Even though in the case of some of the accused a desire for social change and revolution may have played a part in the wording of the heading, it is not appropriate to dismiss the accused *en bloc* as left-wing revolutionaries. What comes from the left need not necessarily be evil in itself [*was von links aussen kommt, muss nicht an sich schlecht sein*]. Development work is necessary and information more necessary than ever. Factual criticism must exist and may indeed be aggressive, but it must remain within limits. That limit has been overstepped by the accused in their choice of title for their pamphlet.

In this way the judge demonstrated his 'openness'. He deigned to admit that being to the left of the political spectrum does not necessarily mean being a messenger of evil. And he showed 'indulgent' understanding for those who wish to change society: but these changes must come about in conditions of respect for established rules and forms. No dressing up as ragamuffins and going to the barricades. Things have to be changed wearing collar and tie and speaking politely.

Reading the final words of the judgment and thinking over the substance of the verdict one hardly knows whether to be angry or discouraged. This judgment constitutes an astonishing mixture of basic deference to the 'high and mighty', of pedantic formalism in applying legal standards, and of pharisaical respect for the rules of democracy. And yet, in the end, one cannot escape the fact that the machinery of the law has been used to make strength prevail over justice.

A defeat for the 'Working Groups'?

Despite all the criticisms, albeit circumspect, directed at Nestlé, Judge Sollberger's verdict clearly went against the accused. The latter came away from the trial beaten. To be sure, they immediately lodged an appeal (in accordance with the rules of penal procedure in force in Bern, appeals must be made within ten days). Later, however, they withdrew it, for three reasons: going on with the trial would have meant rather considerable financial expense; there was little hope that the Court of Appeal would alter the interpretation of the concept of 'homicide' upheld by the trial judge when dealing with the alleged negligent killing of infants by Nestlé; and in any case, a battle in the glare of public opinion would be more fruitful than prolonged legal proceedings, the outcome of which would be uncertain.

How did Nestlé react? Shortly after the verdict, on 2 July 1976, the Managing Director, A. Führer, sent all staff a letter applauding the result of the legal action undertaken against the 'Working Groups', and confirming the effectiveness of Nestlé's commercial penetration in the Third World, in conformity with advertising methods used by other companies too. He then undertook – though in rather generalized terms – to ensure that in the future these methods are better suited to the needs and conditions of poor countries.[6] In essence, Nestlé remained fixed in its positions.

Was the whole affair, then, an utter defeat for the 'Working Groups'? Not if we look a bit further than the trial. The furore aroused by the legal case and the campaign waged by the 'Groups' in the sphere of public opinion slowly began producing some of the results they sought, at three levels: in some of the poor countries directly concerned; within some industrialized countries; and within intergovernmental bodies concerned with such matters, particularly the World Health Organization (WHO).

As for Third World countries directly concerned, the Government of Guinea Bissau, on 15 April 1976, adopted restrictive measures on the feeding of children with artificial milk and similar measures were adopted in Malaysia in September 1976 and in Algeria in 1977.[7]

No less important was the impact of the 'Groups'' campaign in industrialized countries. As early as 1974 various firms, including Nestlé decided to adopt an 'ethical code' to regulate their business activities in the Third World: this comprised a set of non-binding and also rather bland rules (for instance, there were no restrictions on advertising); but it was at least one step in the right direction. The 'Code' was updated several times and gradually made more far-reaching in subsequent years.

Still more important was the action that was taken at government level. In the Netherlands the Ministry for Development Aid decided to review its whole policy regarding food aid. In the United States, in 1978, Senator Edward Kennedy initiated a series of hearings before a Senate Committee in the course of which strong criticisms were directed at multinationals operating in the food sector in poor countries. Again in the United States, a Catholic group, the 'Sisters of the Precious Blood', owners of 500 shares in an American company, the Bristol-Myers Company, presented a proposal to the shareholders' meeting which would have required the company's managers to submit a written report on advertising and commercial practices of the company in the infant feeding sector in the Third World. Unfortunately, this proposal was defeated by the majority of shareholders, winning only 3.5 per cent of votes. Subsequent legal proceedings brought by the Catholic group before the New York State District Court were dismissed, in a judgment of 11 May 1977. More effective was the boycott of Nestlé begun in the United States, again in 1977, by a pressure group, the 'Infant Formula Action Coalition', involving hundreds of consumer associations, trade unions, women's groups and religious movements, and gradually spreading to other countries as well.

Also significant, for better or worse, were the responses of intergovernmental organizations. In 1974, the World Health Organization Assembly approved a resolution inviting member states to review their policies regarding commercial promotion of infant feeding products. Subsequent resolutions culminated in the most significant document, adopted in 1981: the 'Code on international marketing of substitutes for mother's milk'. This 'Code' contains important rules on advertising of products and on the practice of giving mothers free samples (though it is ambiguous as regards information and education). It has, however, one serious, basic flaw: it is not binding, but purely exhortatory. States were not inclined to bind themselves in a field where enormous economic interests were involved. Moreover, despite its relative weakness, the 'Code' met with opposition from some states: the United States voted against it, and Argentina, Japan and the Republic of Korea abstained. The United States delegate, Elliot Abrams, noted that the 'Code' raised many problems for the Americans; in particular, it conflicted with certain freedoms established in the United States (freedom of speech and association), by forbidding certain commercial practices such as advertising, and also with American antitrust laws (by forbidding association among consumers and producers).[8] These criticisms clearly reflect the objections raised by the large multinationals, namely, that the WHO 'Code' is unrealistic and contrary to infants' health needs, and is, moreover, an attack on the market economy and on freedom of speech. Some representatives of those multinationals went so far as to assert that groups in favour of the 'Code' (often led or supported by religious associations) were 'Marxists marching under the banner of Christ'.

What are the lessons to be learnt?

In the long, impassioned campaign by private groups against Nestlé and other companies in the infant nutrition sector, darkness unfortunately ends up prevailing over light. Even though in 1983 Nestlé officially agreed to regulate advertising for its infant feeding products, we are still a long way from the demands of the 'Working Groups'. And there remains in any case one striking figure: in 1986 sales of substitutes for mother's milk in the Third World exceeded 2000 million dollars, as against 600 million dollars in 1978. The multinationals are omnipotent, we know, and they often have judges, governments, newspapers and television channels on their side. Furthermore, as recently demonstrated by a Tunisian research chemist,[9] they 'pollute' the Third World not only with milk powder, but also with pesticides and more generally with all sorts of chemicals. These produce lethal effects both on human beings (every year between 10,000 and 20,000 people die in the Third World as a result of exposure to pesticides) and on the ecosystem at large. All too often the fight against multinationals is therefore an unequal one: in front of them, we cannot but look like Chaplin's little man, so terribly unprotected and powerless. Ought we therefore to despair? I think not. Just like that little man, we can use the weapon of our intelligence. The persevering action against Nestlé of so many private groups and organizations has achieved something. And as for the broader problem of pollution caused by the North in the South, we ought to behave like the Tunisian chemist: we should do research and disseminate the results of our investigations as much as possible, we should publicly discuss those results and we should also propound constructive proposals.

Part III

Human Rights in a Gradually Unifying World

9

The Value of Human Rights in the Contemporary World

The 'Decalogue' of human rights: its significance in the world community

Fortunately, the most barbarous cases of disregard for human dignity, which I examined in the previous chapters and which we are usually forced to witness as impotent spectators, are relatively rare occurrences. I intentionally selected the worst, most repugnant and extreme instances because they serve as test cases by which to measure the effectiveness of the positive legal rules that embody the essential values of human dignity. In each case, I showed how the facts contradict these rules, or deny their effective application.

That these are extreme instances of barbarity must not lull our consciences. Indeed, on leafing through the newspapers every morning, the eye is caught by headlines reporting acts of terrorism, cases of torture or mass butchery, armed conflict in which human life loses all value, and civilians and enemy combatants alike are ferociously maltreated. Each time, our instinctive reaction is to ask: what is the use of all those universal proclamations of human rights, or of all the legal principles and international conventions that transform the proclamations into positive law?

As we reflect with trepidation on this question there are two reactions that we must avoid – one would lead merely to passive anguish, while the other induces excessive confidence and a naive hope that human rights will triumph sooner or later by virtue of their intrinsic value.

The first misguided reaction is to take the 'easy way out': it is hardly surprising – the argument runs – *since human nature is what it is*, that laws which were set down and approved after so much effort should be trodden underfoot every day by governments and private groups. Man is by nature evil; from earliest recorded time, religious texts have chronicled the irrepressible urge of men to kill one another, starting with the murder of Abel by Cain. Or, to put the argument in analogous terms: our passionate nature is like a wicked stallion that tramples its fellow (our courageous nature) and causes the charioteer (our rational nature) to lose control; or, man is weighed down by original sin; or even, mankind is prey to *amor sceleratus habendi*; or, in the words of Machiavelli: 'men are ungrateful, fickle, anxious to avoid danger, while avidly pursuing their own interests'; (or, to use again the Florentine secretary's words, 'the world was always inhabited by men with the same passions as their ancestors'); or again, all too often aggressive instincts prevail in man's psyche, and Thanatos replaces Eros; and so on and so forth. There is much truth in such a gloomy vision of mankind: who has not 'eaten cherries with the devil'? Yet it describes only one facet of man's nature and encourages passivity. Since man is what he is – so the argument goes – what point is there in raising dykes against his innate desire to dominate? He will always breach these barriers. One might just as well sit back and watch. Or, like Ituriel in Voltaire's *Le monde comme il va*, rather than destroy Persepolis for its wrong doing, since good and evil are inextricably mixed, we can decide to let the world go as it pleases because, though not all is well with it, all is not bad (*'si tout n'est pas bien, tout est passable'*).[1]

At the other extreme is the mistake of thinking that human rights are a kind of new, universal religion. With the decline of the great religions, many people hope – subconsciously, or at least very naively – to establish a new, non-metaphysical religion that is not other-worldly: a religion based in part on a secular creed, with no liturgy, made to measure for the inhabitants of this earthly metropolis. A religion that offers no promise of salvation, that does not mesmerise its followers with rites and magic, whose one aim is to exploit the qualities of human beings and give a central position to the individual and his needs as a rational and emotional creature: man as an extraordinary microcosm living in society, endowed with qualities that, at times, help him to live in harmony, at times, cause him to live in open conflict with his fellows.

However noble, this vision has the defect of stretching the meaning of human rights too far. They are, undoubtedly, a new form of *natural law for mankind*. By natural law I do not mean that body of principles jurists have always execrated and treated with scorn, namely that set of precepts selected at random by writers from the 'realm of reason' and consecrated as rules of behaviour overriding the dictates of positive law. What I mean is that there is a body of rules, by which we can discipline and evaluate our conduct, that have been distilled – with the consent of all states – from ideologies and philosophies, religious precepts and world views, and embodied, by those states, in an international code of behaviour. To call this code the new 'religion of mankind' simply because it sets out to reward certain human aspirations, whether of individuals, groups or peoples, strikes me as excessive and misleading. The risk is that the code will then be transformed into a myth (in the sense Sorel gives to the word, that is a construct of indefinite remoteness, '*[une] construction d'un avenir indéterminé dans les temps*').[2] There is a very real danger of sanctifying it as both utopian and doctrinaire, which it is not, nor should it be. Above all, if we believe in human rights as a 'religion' and then take a look at reality (where their existence is denied every day), we may feel obliged to become the missionaries of the new faith. Human rights would then be introduced into conflicts and disputes of a military and ideological nature between East and West, North and South: the 'religion' would become the handmaiden of strife. What started off as a rightful desire to have human rights respected, would become a 'crusade' and might, in the end, serve to cloak intolerance, manipulation and, even persecution – just as traditional religions were the premise for the burning of heretics, the persecution of 'unbelievers' and the conduct of bloody wars. Let us not forget the warning of that great French revolutionary, Robespierre, 'Nobody likes armed missionaries!'[3]

How, then, should we ragard human rights? As a *new ethos*, as an extremely important set of *secular, humanitarian precepts*, unencumbered by myth, though based on the main ideals of traditional religion (taken both from the West and the East) with a backbone of ideas borrowed from Western philosophy. This new ethos is intended to express the 'refusal of the natural biological order', as the great French scientist Jean Hamburger recently put it.[4] Indeed, nature is dominated by cruelty, disregard for the individual, injustice, aggressiveness and the predominance of the strong over the weak. The very concept of human rights is designed to react to these trends, to affirm and proclaim that there are tenets to be observed that do not follow from nature, but are instead aimed at coercing and dominating natural instinct. In a way, human rights constitute an attempt by the human being to make man as a 'social animal' prevail over man as 'natural animal'. This new lay ethos has been the foundation of a great new social structure of universal, not just local, application. What has been attempted is the crystallization of rules of behaviour for everyone, to be respected by all nations of the world: that is, by 5000 million people and 171 states. They establish how much freedom of action state administrations should leave individuals; when and how this freedom of action can be reduced; the indispensable characteristics of state administrations if they are to conform to standards acceptable to all nations; the steps to be followed by states in granting self-government to peoples, in allowing them to make certain fundamental choices, in removing social inequalities, in enabling the have-nots to obtain a minimum degree of welfare. Thus, human rights are based on an expansive desire to *unify the world* by drawing up a list of *guidelines* for all governments. They are an attempt to highlight the *values* (respect for human dignity) and *their opposites* (the negation of that dignity) that all states should take as parameters for assessing their actions. In a nutshell, human rights are an attempt by the contemporary world to introduce a measure of reason into its history.

Whether respect for human rights is a *sine qua non* for states wanting to take part in international affairs

What weight does this decalogue have in human relations? Can we say that human rights have become the *decisive criterion* by which all 171 members of the world community are judged? It is worthwhile being absolutely clear on this point. For this reason I shall take a few steps back in time and begin at the end of the First World War.

Once that massive upheaval was over, it was decided that the whole structure of international relations needed to be rebuilt, so as to avoid any recurrence of barbarity. Thus, the League of Nations was set up and its drafters hoped, thereby, to have curbed violence and set international relations on the road to peaceful coexistence. I have already mentioned how various states, particularly Britain and the United States, had turned down a Japanese proposal to proclaim the principle of equality (not among all human beings generally, but among all alien nationals of States members of the League in the territory of other States members). Though modest in scope, the Japanese proposal was rejected. Human rights had not yet 'taken root' in the international community. On the other hand, both the United States and France insisted that the 'democratic principle' (the principle whereby states should be based on 'representative institutions') ought to become a fundamental criterion for *admitting* new states to the League. In other words, it was felt that a democratic government was the watershed dividing states that were allowed to join the Geneva-based institution from those that were not. Wilson's idea of 'popular self-government' was accepted and merged with the concept of 'free states' propounded by France. Hence, Article 1, paragraph 2, of the

League Covenant set down that all states, including British dominions and even colonies, could join so long as they were 'fully self-governing'. The preparatory work[5] and jurists of the day all suggest that the expression meant respect for democratic values. Therefore, in 1919 it was not human rights as such, but respect for certain of these rights (in particular, the right to choose one's government), that became the litmus paper by which to distinguish 'civilized' states, which could join the new League of Nations, from others. I should add that the criterion fell into disuse a few years later when, first Abyssinia (in 1923), then the Soviet Union (in 1934), were admitted. The admission of the USSR provoked the protests of the Swiss representative, G. Motta, who objected that a modicum of 'political and moral concord' should not be sacrificed to the need for universal representation.[6]

After the Second World War, it was felt that the newly formed United Nations should be different from the old League, even from this point of view. Although, in the meantime, human rights had acquired the full value of an ideology, to the point of being embodied in the UN Charter in numerous explicit references, neither respect for human rights nor the 'democratic principle' was considered the *sine qua non* for membership in the new organization. The need for universal representation of the Organization was considered paramount and only one criterion of membership was envisaged: pacifism (thus, Article 4 of the Charter provides that the United Nations Organization is only open to 'peace-loving states'). A few years after the United Nations had been set up, an attempt was made to deny entry to a totalitarian regime: Spain. Poland took the initiative and recommended that Spain be refused admission because its government was not democratic and it did not respect human rights (at the same time, it was also pointed out that that state had joined the Axis powers and that the Franco regime was a potential menace to peace and security). In any case, even if the General Assembly did accept these arguments (at least in so far as respect for democratic principles and human rights were concerned), in later years it proved impossible for it to continue along these lines; in 1950, Spain joined the Organization (owing mainly to cold war pressures).

In the late 1970s, Cambodia received similar treatment (though in this case the issue was not a request for admission, but a decision on which of two governments should be recognized). In 1979, after Vietnam had invaded Cambodia, Pol Pot fled into exile with his government and the United Nations had to decide which government should be regarded as the legitimate representative of the

Cambodian people. Yet, although it had perpetrated heinous crimes and no longer had any effective dominion over the country, the UN accepted the credentials of the representatives of Pol Pot's government and his successors. Whatever the political motives for this decision (mainly dictated by a desire to condemn the Vietnamese invasion), the fact remains that the systematic violation of human rights was not considered sufficient grounds for refusing the credentials of Pol Pot's delegates. This merely confirms that respect for human rights is not a criterion for granting or refusing admission of a state or a government to the United Nations.

What, then, is the value of the human rights doctrine? As we have seen, the systematic violation of these rights is not considered an impediment to a state's *acquisition of the status of international subject* and does not prevent that state from becoming a *member of the United Nations* (further proof of this is that South Africa has been a member ever since the Organization was set up). Although, as I have just said, the concept of human rights has not been used as a determining criterion, it has had far reaching effects. It has been used to *delegitimize* certain states from a purely political point of view, because they have systematically violated human rights. South Africa, Chile, Israel and other states have been repeatedly condemned by the United Nations, even though they were fully recognized as *subjects* of international law and as *members* of that Organization. Thus, although they have been the object of repeated condemnation, these states may continue to enter into treaties, to send and receive ambassadors, to take part in debates in the various UN organs and to vote on UN resolutions. Nevertheless, most states no longer regard them as *full members* of the international community: most states prefer to eschew relations with them because they have violated certain values (human rights) which are considered of primary importance. Although these 'ostracized' states are equal to other states on the formal-juridical plane, they do not in practice enjoy the same *active diplomatic relations* as other members of the international community.

This is by no means the only aspect of international relations influenced directly by regard for human rights. As I hope to show in the next chapter, human rights have also worked a profound change on certain institutional aspects of the international community.

10

The Impact of Human Rights on the International Community

Human rights (in the broadest sense, which includes the rights of peoples) have had a *disruptive* effect in various areas of international affairs: I should like to take a quick look at each one of these and try to show, in each case, what the effects have been.

'Reciprocity' *versus* 'the demands of the community'

First, let us examine how the principle of reciprocity, which – as I pointed out in chapter 1 – has long been one of the main pillars of the international legal order, has been circumvented and eroded, if not removed altogether.

Once the right of peoples to self-determination and the rights of the individual had received international recognition, a new 'dimension' was introduced into world affairs. By this very token states decided the time had passed when they could behave towards one another as self-contained autarchic bodies, sensitive only to keeping their respective activities and rights on a par with those of other states, ignoring the general or collective interest (in other words an interest that superseded or transcended the interests of one or only some states). They have abandoned the logic of the mere *do ut des*, whereby a state is only bound to fulfil an obligation in so far as the other party does so too, or fulfils an equivalent obligation, and thus non-fulfilment by one state gives the other the right to disregard its duties.

The need to enable peoples subject to the domination of foreign powers or violently authoritarian regimes to choose freedom in the guise of self-determination, both on a national and international plane, has meant that states have had to look beyond the narrow confines of their own frontiers and national interests, and face the demands of subject peoples. Oppressor states have suddenly found themselves bound by legal rules they could not eschew: they were thus forced to free subject peoples and permit them to achieve self-determination. At the same time other states were given the right to ensure that the principle of self-determination was put into practice; and the peoples concerned were themselves authorized – subject to certain conditions – to take up arms and fight for their rights.

It is easy to see how such a new and, in a sense, universalizing legal network has destroyed the logic of reciprocity. Formerly, third states could not have taken a legitimate interest in oppressed peoples, except in special circumstances, such as when an international treaty permitted them to do so. Similarly, the whole structure of reciprocity is weakened if an oppressed people has a right to achieve self-determination. Peoples can now intrude on the cosy, bilateral relations of states. Peoples have nothing to give states, yet can make considerable demands on them: in particular, they can insist on being freed from an oppressive or foreign yoke. Thus, both the right of third states to help an oppressed people and 'intervene' on its behalf, and the right of that people to be free, are part of a new outlook: today, *community interests* transcend the narrow viewpoints of single potentates and reflect a broader humanitarian and collective desire for social progress.

The principle of reciprocity has been dismembered further by the doctrine of human rights, in the narrow sense. To proclaim that every state must respect certain fundamental standards on how to organize the structure of its government and on the amount of freedom individuals residing in its territory should enjoy, is of great consequence. What it means is this: from now on – at least as far as certain fundamental rights relating to the dignity of the human being are concerned – each and every state must now furnish proof to other nations and international institutions of how it treats not only foreigners, but its own citizens too. Each and every state is expected to make itself as transparent as a glasshouse. Any other international subject may peer inside; should he discover that all is not well, that there are instances of macroscopic 'deviation' from the accepted standards, he can call that nation to account and insist that the deviant behaviour be corrected in the light of international rules. What has been dismantled here is the traditional idea that each state could only look after its own nationals abroad, insisting that they be treated decently by other nations (on the understanding that if a foreign country maltreated these nationals, equivalent maltreatment would be meted out to the citizens of the 'deviant' state). Today, at least as regards certain fundamental areas, every state has an 'absolute' duty (towards other states) to behave in a given manner towards every individual under its authority, whatever his or her nationality. Conversely, any other state – even one that has no ties with the individual whose fundamental rights are being infringed – may insist that the offending state put an end to its arbitrary behaviour. The idea of *nationality*, which was an essential element in the principle of reciprocity, has, to a large extent, been replaced by the desire to protect the *human being* as such. There is a tendency to substitute for reciprocity a fraternal interest in safeguarding certain humanitarian values that transcend bilateral relations between states.

Peoples and individuals as the new subjects of the international community

The new doctrines we have been discussing have greatly influenced another area of international law: that of the subjects of the international community. As I said earlier, by tradition the only 'centres of power' endowed with legal rights and duties were the sovereign states themselves. They lorded it over their respective communities and did as they pleased. Today, peoples (or at least peoples subjected to colonial, alien or racist domination) and individuals have begun to emerge as their valid counterparts.

Many jurists and diplomats refuse to admit that these two categories have been given even a 'walk-on part' on the international stage; they feel that peoples and individuals are still subject to the authority of sovereign states. To contradict this view I shall quote two prominent statesmen. In 1947, the French delegate to the UN Commission on Human Rights, René Cassin (who played a considerable part in drafting the 1948 Universal Declaration), said that the defects of the Declaration should not be allowed to cast a shadow over its novelty, in that 'the individual becomes a subject of international law both in respect of his life and liberty'.[1] Then in 1986, President Raoul Alfonsín of Argentina stated in Strasbourg that 'far reaching change has been initiated in the very concept of international law [by the spread of human rights], by granting the individual the status of an international subject and by considerably restricting the idea of interference in domestic affairs when violations of human rights are concerned'.[2]

To my mind, individuals and peoples must now be considered – to a certain extent and for certain groups of states – international subjects. However, I must point out that these two categories do not play a primary role in international affairs, nor do they enjoy the same wide range of privileges as states. They are merely allowed to peep into the sacred enclosure where states act out their rites. In effect, their rights and powers are extremely limited. Moreover, they have no machinery by which to enforce those rights or assert those powers. A people can rebel when its rights have been violated or ignored, even by taking up arms; whereas individuals stand impotent, forced to put up with a state's arbitrary behaviour, or hoping another sovereign state will step forward in their defence. In essence this means that peoples and individuals are still spectators, even though they have acquired the right to protest vociferously: a meagre consolation. Yet many states regard this minor chink in the armour of their sovereignty as intolerable, an usurpation of their rights. They use all their concerted strength to prevent peoples and individuals from gaining a foothold on the international scene. This helps to explain why, for example, a number of Western states refuse to recognize that oppressed peoples enjoy any rights or have any power and, by the same token, why Eastern European states have so far refused to grant individuals any right to participate in world affairs.

Human rights and the rights of aliens

As I stated in chapter 1, for centuries individuals have received the protection of international law only as aliens, that is only when they were abroad and assuming their national state was ready and able to protect them. This led to the formation of numerous customary rules, mainly the result of a desire to protect Europeans and Americans when they travelled in southern climes, whether they were busy setting up commercial enterprises, or carrying on other lucrative business, or merely enjoying a holiday. International rules did not require states to admit aliens: all states, today as in the past, could refuse entry to whomsoever they wished (unless they had accepted treaty obligations to the contrary: as the members of the EEC have recently agreed to do). However, once an alien had been admitted, he enjoyed a series of rights: his legal personality was recognized; if arrested, he had to receive decent treatment; he had the right to access to justice; he had a right not to have his goods confiscated, and if they were seized, he had a right to receive proper compensation. If these rules were not complied with by the receiving state, the victim's state of origin could grant him 'diplomatic protection' and insist that the receiving state cease from violating his rights, give him proper compensation, or punish the guilty individuals concerned; if the receiving state persisted in its recalcitrance, then the other state could apply sanctions.

As the body of international rules on human rights was broadened, after 1948, one would have expected the traditional rules on the treatment of aliens to be absorbed into the new body of law. Since the new rules protect human beings as such, they should apply (though an exception must be made for political rights) to any individual, whether abroad or at home, regardless of whether he is the citizen of a given state: to be a 'human being' should logically include and surpass the idea of being an 'alien'. Alas, this is not so, for various reasons. First, very few rules on human rights have acquired universal validity (i.e. have become customary law). Most have remained mere treaty rules, with all the inherent limitations that this entails (that is, they are binding only on the states that have ratified these treaties: human rights treaties have been 'accepted' by several groups of states, groups that are on the whole rather small and certainly do not represent all the members of the international community). Accordingly, the old rules protecting aliens have served to protect individuals travelling abroad against possible maltreatment in the territory of states that have not accepted the 'new' rules on human rights. The second reason why human rights have not absorbed the rights of aliens is really 'subjective'. Various developing countries have pointed out that the rights of aliens arose from a desire to protect the nationals of the great powers abroad; this has made them wary of putting aliens on the same plane as their own citizens, fearing that the Great Powers would then encourage their nationals to exploit the resources of poor countries as they pleased.

Thus a strange dichotomy has been created between the rights of aliens and human rights (this dichotomy is, however, of little concern to those states, such as the United Kingdom that have ratified the principal treaties on human rights; except for some instances that directly concern aliens – for example, political rights, or the right to be admitted to a country – a foreigner has to be treated on an equal footing with any citizen in the receiving state). Yet, little by little, the rigid distinctions between these two sets of rights have diminished. Human rights have slowly changed the purport of rules on aliens. I shall now enumerate some effects of this influence.

First, certain international treaties on human rights contain provisions on issues that specifically concern aliens, especially as far as their possible expulsion is concerned. It is the aim of these rules to provide guarantees beyond those of traditional law, and thus increase the protection of an alien's rights. For example, collective expulsion is prohibited; moreover, any alien who is threatened with expulsion may appeal against the order and take his or her case to court.

Second, certain long-standing rules must now be interpreted or applied in the light of human rights. This is true of the fundamental principle against discrimination, which is a leitmotif of human rights. It is bound to affect traditional rules, which can no longer permit certain distinctions (based on race, religion, sex, national or social origin) that, to a certain extent, had been tolerated·before. The same goes for extradition: as embodied in traditional treaties, the extradition clause must now be 'reinterpreted' in the light of the new norms. To illustrate my point, let me refer to an important judgment of the Swiss Federal Court, in 1982.[3] On the basis of a 1906 bilateral treaty on extradition, Argentina had asked Switzerland to extradite five Argentinians who had been arrested for common crimes (the kidnapping for ransom of a Uruguayan banker and, later, of an Argentinian financier, in Buenos Aires). The two principal accused stated that, if they were extradited to Argentina, they would certainly face a politically biased trial; moreover, they would probably undergo torture, inhuman or degrading treatment (they had belonged, respectively, to the secret service and the Argentine police; they claimed that the first kidnapping had been carried out on orders from the secret service; furthermore, they had been members of a faction in the Argentine security forces disliked by the regime which had requested their extradition). The Swiss Federal Court remarked that these circumstances, together with the fact that Argentina was now under a repressive form of government, made it seem quite possible that, on extradition, these men would be subjected to inhuman treatment. The Court received further support for its judgment from the opinion of the International Federation of Human Rights, which informed it that, in the event of their return to Argentina, 'the accused would certainly be risking their lives'. The Court observed that even long-standing treaties on extradition must now be interpreted and applied in the light of two fundamental principles of human rights, which have now acquired the weight of *jus cogens*, that is peremptory law: one was the principle that no individual should be extradited to a country to undergo a trial in which considerations of race, religion or political opinion might play a role; the other was the principle prohibiting torture or any form of inhuman or degrading treatment. On the basis of these two principles, the Court declined to apply the bilateral Convention and refused extradition.

Third, the fact that the idea of human rights had become so widely accepted – as well as the fact that Third World countries, from which more and more people tend to emigrate, had begun to take an active interest in the protection of their nationals abroad – was instrumental in having a declaration on the rights of aliens (Resolution 40/144) unanimously adopted by the UN General Assembly in 1985. In the Preamble it is said that 'the protection of human rights and fundamental freedoms, as embodied in the international instruments, should also be guaranteed to those who are not citizens of the state in which they reside'; the Declaration also proclaims certain fundamental rights of aliens, obviously modelled – to a large extent – on the rights of all individuals, as embodied in the Universal Declaration and the UN Covenants. Here, the rights of aliens are reaffirmed as a separate category, distinct from rights of a more general nature: however, in the Declaration they have been reworded, reinterpreted and 'reorganized' in the light of human rights.

The techniques for creating international legal standards

Another area in which the two doctrines (human rights and the self-determination of peoples) have had a profound effect is that of the procedures followed to agree upon international rules. What has been affected is not the structure or method, but the content of procedures. Human rights and the principle of self-determination have not helped to introduce new techniques for creating international rules, nor was this ever intended by their 'supporters'. Rather, they have been instrumental in introducing a new set of principles and criteria that have helped to break with past attitudes and convictions.

In the first place, because of the gradual emergence of international customary rules (which are binding on all states), as well as the drafting of multilateral treaties on human rights, the International Court of Justice (the highest international judicial body) stated, in an *obiter dictum*, that in international law a distinction must be drawn between obligations based on reciprocity and obligations *erga omnes*, that is obligations every state is bound to observe *vis-à-vis* all other states.[4] The Court remarked that states are bound to observe certain obligations towards the whole international community: these obligations are vitally important for all states, so that they all have an interest in making sure they are observed. The Court went on to mention, as examples, the rules prohibiting genocide, as well as the rules and principles concerning 'the fundamental rights of the human person', including those banning slavery and racial discrimination. On a par with these, the Court mentioned one legal principle that was unconnected with human rights: the ban on aggression (yet another instance in which pacificist ideology is marching hand in hand with human rights, a fact that is hardly surprising). The effect of the Court's famous *dictum*, which merely reflected the existing state of affairs, or at least crystallized prevalent trends, made people realise that the essential principles of human rights have nothing to do with reciprocity. States are bound to respect these principles, whatever the behaviour of other states in this regard (for example, if a state is guilty of genocide, this does not give other states the right to do likewise). Moreover, any country in the world can call the delinquent state to account for its grave misdeeds and insist that it stop perpetrating these crimes.

The second area I would like to examine briefly concerns a set of principles – which to a great extent coincide with *erga omnes* obligations – to which the international community decided (in the international law. I refer to *jus cogens*, that group of principles endowed with special legal force because they cannot be derogated from, or contradicted, by treaty provision or customary rules. The right of peoples to self-determination and various other human rights – not to mention the ban on aggression – have all contributed to this new outlook in international affairs. Indeed, when states were discussing the creation of this new set of principles, the examples quoted most frequently by the delegates of various governments (and on which even the most fractious representatives agreed) concerned human rights and the self-determination of peoples.

This step forward in establishing a new category of principles was not merely an improvement on previous legal techniques, nor was it of interest only to diplomats and jurists. What, at first glance, may appear to be a new form of legal engineering, in fact reveals a radically new way of conceiving relations among states and relations between these and peoples and individuals. Actually it means that, for the first time, the international community has decided to recognize certain *values* (the dignity of the human person, self-determination of peoples, peace) that must *prevail* over any other form of national interest. These values show how the international community has made a fundamental choice between the various paths that lie ahead. These values also reflect collective needs, though within certain *limits*, as I shall hasten to explain. Just suppose that an international rule is drafted which is contrary to *jus cogens* (for example, a treaty for the extermination of an ethnic group, or for the subjugation of a people, or for suppressing the fundamental freedoms of a whole population). *In theory* that treaty offends not only the state or people against whom it operates, but the international community as a whole. Nevertheless, *in actual fact*, only those parties that are directly involved are entitled to react against the treaty and claim it to be null and void. In particular, in the case of bilateral treaties that are contrary to *jus cogens* (for example, a treaty in which two states agree to carry out acts of genocide together), no third state can protest and declare the treaty to be null and void. This power is still in the hands of the two contracting parties, which alone can declare the treaty null (for example, after a change of government in one of them).

Some readers may object that it is highly implausible for two or more states, intending to transgress some essential rule protecting the human person, to conclude a treaty in which their illegal behaviour is transcribed for all to see. It would be even less plausible for several states to agree to form a customary rule permitting torture, genocide or the oppression of a whole people. States that intend to behave in an immoral fashion do so in fact; they do not create a set of rules and standards for this purpose first. This being so, what is the revolutionary purport of *jus cogens*? The objection is justified, but only in part. It is true that over the last thirty years (that is, since *jus cogens* first came into being as a new legal category) no treaty has formally been declared contrary to the 'peremptory rules' of international law (even though various jurists have objected both to the Zurich agreement of 1960, which allowed armed intervention in Cyprus by the contracting parties, and to the 1978 Camp David agreements, which contained clauses allegedly infringing the right of the Palestinian people to self-determination). And yet we are considering the issue from too formal and technical a point of view and only in the short term. Many legal rules produce effects far beyond their immediate objective. They possess an ethico-political halo that is destined to glow in unthought-of areas. Above all, they are influential in the moral and psychological spheres, creating a new ethos in the international community, and new expectations not only among states but among individuals and peoples – the new twin poles of interest and action – not to mention public opinion. One only has to remember that in 1933, when the Peruvian delegate at the League of Nations stated that the treaty between his own state and Colombia was 'immoral', the French delegate sharply criticized the very idea that an international treaty could be considered null on grounds of 'immorality'.[5] Furthermore, sooner or later certain new international rules (including that on *jus cogens*) will affect other sectors of international law: this has just occurred in the field of state responsibility.

A third aspect of the creation, modification and extinction of legal rules that has been greatly influenced by the two doctrines concerns the 'demise' of treaties. According to classical law, the material breach of a fundamental provision of a bilateral or multilateral treaty by one state is sufficient cause for the other party, or parties, to denounce that treaty, that is, to terminate the treaty as between all parties. If one party breaks its promise to perform some act, the other party is free to do likewise. This is clearly one of the old precepts, derived from elementary rules governing human society, as well as from certain 'primitive' concepts that do not recognize any principle superior to that of 'do as you would be done by'. However, the international community has introduced a rule that completely transforms this state of affairs. In 1969, the Vienna Convention on the Law of Treaties (now slowly being transformed into a body of law valid for the entire international community) contained one, very important provision: Article 60. It reiterated the old rule that when one contracting party commits a substantial violation of a treaty, the other party (or parties) can suspend the treaty's operation, or even terminate the treaty. Yet paragraph 5 of that Article also provides that this rule does not apply to provisions for the protection of the human person contained in treaties of a humanitarian character. What exactly does this mean? It means that if a state violates provisions protecting human rights, this does not allow the other contracting party to terminate the treaty or suspend its operation. If France, for example, were to violate the human rights of British citizens residing in that country (either by arbitrary arrest, or by subjecting them to discriminatory or degrading treatment in prison) and by doing so were to violate a bilateral or multilateral treaty with the United Kingdom, the latter could not react by violating the human rights of French citizens residing in the United Kingdom. By the same token, if during a war between two states, one side attacks the civilian population of the other, the other belligerent cannot respond by doing likewise. It is expected to observe the treaties that protect the rights of civilians, even if they are enemy civilians. In such cases the rule on reciprocity no longer holds: the wrongful behaviour of one side does not entitle the other to regard its previous obligations as no longer valid. This is because the obligation concerns individuals: the interests of states take second place. What is now imperative is that the dignity and worth of the human person be protected.

Thus, an important new element has been introduced into the traditional interplay of state interests, to the advantage of individuals. The logic behind this new approach is that, even when the treaty rules protecting the individual are violated, they cannot be set aside by applying the traditional principle that 'there is no need to fulfil an obligation towards a party who has already violated it' (*inadimplenti non est adimplendum*). Such treaty rules can be set aside only when states take the ultimate step of declaring that the treaty in which they are embodied is to be considered terminated: a most unusual step for states to take. It is easier for states to violate a treaty (and subsequently deny that they have done so, or advance excuses, or declare that the transgression is transitory) than to make a formal declaration that the treaty is to be regarded as terminated. By counting on this attitude among states, Article 60, paragraph 5, of the Vienna Convention has set out to maintain the validity and effectiveness of all treaty rules that protect individuals.

International supervision

Let me now examine another important area in which the two doctrines, especially that on human rights, have had a profoundly innovating effect: that of the mechanisms set up to induce states to obey international rules of behaviour.

From the seventeenth to the twentieth century the international community had no *social* mechanisms by which to enforce compliance with certain standards of behaviour; it had to make do as best it could. This was a period when states exercised independent 'supervision': a somewhat primitive system by which each member decided for itself whether another member had violated its rights, how to react to the (alleged) violation, whether to resort to the use of force, or apply economic sanctions, or whether to do nothing at all. The system patently favoured the great and medium-sized powers, to the detriment of smaller ones, at least in relations with states larger than themselves. Then, improvements to the system were gradually introduced, particularly in the period between the two World Wars. These were in the form of arbitration courts; however, their powers were limited to ascertaining whether one of the parties had indeed violated an international rule; they could not force the parties to obey the law. Indeed, even though the court had declared a state guilty of an unlawful act, that state could ignore the court's decision and refuse to carry out its ruling – that is, if it felt strong enough to do so. Another limitation on the court's authority was that its jurisdiction depended on the consent of the two conflicting parties. In other words, judges in these courts did not have the same powers as those of domestic courts, in which disputes can be settled whatever the attitudes of the parties concerned, and even though one side may refuse to submit to the court's judgment.

The first timid attempts to remedy this imbalance of power were made in 1919, but the whole structure was turned upside-down by the emergent human rights ideology after the Second World War. How did this come about? Immediately after the First World War, the International Labour Organization (ILO) was set up and one of its aims was to regulate the condition of workers throughout the world. States were encouraged not only to draft and accept international conventions (on equal remuneration on the employment of women and minors; on night shifts; on freedom of association, and so on), but to fulfil these new obligations as well. This was no easy task, because respect for those conventions lay outside the strategy of reciprocity – at that time the only system by which implementation of international rules of behaviour could be *de facto* brought about in the international community. Indeed, the labour conventions required each state to apply the treaty rules within their own domestic sphere for the benefit of their own workers. Should one state refuse to fulfil its obligations, other states had little interest in 'intervening'. Only if that state had not fulfilled an obligation which involved respect for the rules of 'fair competition' (that is, if the state did not grant certain rights to its workers, or exploited them, thereby cutting its labour costs, with negative consequences for other states that respected ILO rules) would these states have an interest in direct intervention.

There was, therefore, an urgent need for new systems to enforce respect for international rules, which could be implemented not only by states but also by third parties. The international community was now sailing between Scylla and Charybdis. It was vital to ensure that the new ILO rules did not become a dead letter; it was equally important not to 'overburden' states with international sanctioning mechanisms – particularly unacceptable in an area, like that of labour relations, which by tradition belonged to the sphere of state sovereignty. The compromise solution was to set up *supervisory mechanisms* with two salient characteristics: first, they could be set in motion by bodies other than states (labour organizations, or employers' associations) or activated automatically, without any specific request; second, they merely established possible instances of violation and urged the state in question to cease its illegal behaviour, without issuing a formal condemnation or imposing any reparation.

The system adopted by the ILO was a rather isolated case in the years following the First World War (even though the same mechanism had been used by the League of Nations to protect the rights of minorities – a notable exception to then current practice). Yet, after the Second World War, great strides were made thanks to the idea of human rights, which posed the same problems as those of the ILO conventions. Alongside the international rules for the protection of the human person, a number of mechanisms have developed to ensure those rules are respected. Today, these form a tight network and are all centred on, or at least connected with, international organizations (the UN, the Council of Europe, the Organization of American States), and they can usually be set in motion by individuals or by non-governmental organizations.

Rather than taking a look at how the mechanisms work,[6] I would like to stress one point I consider vital. Because these mechanisms give *non-governmental organizations* a chance to lodge complaints with international agencies, they have thereby contributed enormously to the expansion and development of those organizations themselves. It has been a 'circular' process. Most of those non-governmental organizations promoted the international rules on human rights. They created the conditions in which they were drafted, they prodded recalcitrant states into fulfilling their obligations, or launched new ideas and proposals for their application. Remember the decisive role played by Jewish organizations in 1944–5: they championed, mainly in the United States, the need to insert a set of rules protecting human rights into the UN Charter. Thanks to their passionate lobbying, these rules were accepted by the states convened in San Francisco. Thus, the international rules, which non-governmental organizations worked so hard to achieve were, subsequently, to have the beneficial effect of legitimizing those organizations and of consecrating them as agents for the promotion of human rights. These rules have placed those organizations centre-stage on the international scene; they have encouraged them to strengthen their structure and acquire competent staff and have ensured that the organizations become a focus for public opinion. The organizations have, thus, become the mouthpiece of world conscience, the public censors and the goads of sovereign states. All this is closely linked to the supervisory mechanisms I mentioned earlier.

The upshot of all this is impressive: whereas once only sovereign states had a say in world affairs, non-governmental organizations – as well as individuals and peoples – now have a right to be heard. This does not, of course, mean that these organizations have now acquired full international subjectivity. They have no rights or powers. All they can do is to act as go-betweens for public opinion and states, reflecting the pressing need for a renewal of the structure of international affairs and for the defence of the rights of peoples and individuals, and projecting those needs onto the international scene. Yet they now play an extremely important role. In a world community that is still beset by anarchy and individualism, non-governmental organizations are a kind of 'safety-net' against any relapse into barbarism.

International responsibility

The consequences of any violation of international law by states is the fourth area to be influenced by the two doctrines. Formerly, state responsibility was regulated by a few rather primitive rules. Every time a state committed a breach of an international obligation thereby causing damage to another state (for example, by invading the territory of another state, or by refusing to grant certain immunities and privileges to its diplomats, by illegally detaining its citizens, or by sinking one of its ships), it was obliged to make reparation. Only the injured state could demand reparation; if the state that had committed the breach refused to pay compensation or to give full satisfaction, the former could apply the appropriate sanctions to the latter. Obviously, how the dispute was solved depended a great deal on the power of each state: if the victim was the more powerful of the two, the other state was unlikely to refuse reparation. Similarly, a strong state would probably baulk at making reparation, since the victim was less likely to resort to economic or military sanctions.

Take another characteristic of responsibility: it was a 'private' concern between the author of the breach and its victim. No other subject could intervene (unless such an intervention had been provided for in a treaty between the two states, or unless both states requested it). A breach of international law and its consequences did not involve the rest of the community. Individual states had to take the law into their own hands, while the rest of the community stood by, indifferent or completely impotent, however concerned some of those other states might have been about possible repercussions.

This area is yet another instance of how human rights – together with pacifism, which had made such decisive strides after the Second World War – have left a deep mark. In particular, two new trends may be traced back to the influence of human rights.

First, human rights played a part in diminishing the role of *damage* in the idea of a wrongful act under international law. Had it been kept as part and parcel of the wrongful act, it would have been possible for a state to put forward a claim against another state for the unlawful treatment of individuals only if the rights of *aliens* had been violated (that is, if one state ill-treated or improperly arrested the citizens of another state, or if it expropriated or arbitrarily destroyed their property) for such behaviour no doubt caused 'damage' to the injured state (even though only the individual citizen had been injured in reality). By contrast, no state can claim to have been damaged when the rights of a stateless person or of a refugee, have been violated, not to mention the frequent instances of citizens' rights being violated by their own state. In the latter case who suffers the injury? Obviously a legal obligation, which one state undertook to respect *vis-à-vis* all other states (or other contracting parties), has been violated. Yet the violation of this obligation has not caused any other state injury (other than a *legal* one). In a nutshell, if one were to hold that a state is responsible only when its non-compliance with an obligation goes hand in hand with damage, then it would not be possible to speak of responsibility for the violation of human rights. This aberrant conclusion has helped people to realize that damage is not an indispensable element of state responsibility under international law.[7]

Second, human rights have had a hand in the creation of a category of *special violations* of international law. States have slowly come to realize that, besides 'ordinary' wrongful acts under international law (for example, when frontier guards cross over into the territory of another state; the improper arrest of a citizen by the police of one state in another state's territory; the illegal expropriation of foreign property; the violation of another country's air space, and so on), there are other, more serious acts. These include genocide, the grave and systematic abuse of human rights, the use of force to prevent a people from achieving self-determination, wars of aggression (once again human rights and pacifism are never far apart). Slowly but surely, people have come to accept the idea that such acts are so serious that a purely private and 'individualistic' reaction has to be replaced by a collective, 'public' one. This has led to the crystallization of a new category: the 'international crimes of states', which may be said to possess two characteristics. First, they are particularly grave violations of fundamental rules; second, the reaction of states involves the adoption of collective measures, best carried out under the aegis of such international organizations as the United Nations. This collective response may range from a refusal to recognize the situation created by the culprit state to the application of concrete economic or even military sanctions (if the unlawful act involved the use of force).

As you can see, thanks to the ideology of human rights and the principle of self-determination of peoples, when states commit a breach of particularly important rules, their wrongful behaviour is of concern to the whole international community, which can react by taking the appropriate measures. To date this is true only on paper. States are wary of invoking the idea of international crimes of state, because nationalism and isolationism are still paramount. This must not discourage us. The very fact that the rules exist on paper is a great step forward; the next one will be to ensure that they are applied.

The law of warfare

Lastly, let us take a look at yet another area that has been influenced by human rights. This is the set of rules and principles that seek to regulate the conduct of war between two or more states, as well as civil war and wars of national liberation.

The traditional legal principles on war tried to regulate the conduct of hostilities between two or more monarchs; they were based not only on military requirements, but on a spirit of chivalry (ensuring a minimum of fair play between the belligerents by prohibiting perfidious or treacherous behaviour and demanding that the armed forces distinguish between civilians and combatants) and on an idea of reasonable and reciprocal behaviour (it is not reasonable for one side to murder all the prisoners it takes, unless it wishes the other side to do likewise).

To be sure, humanitarian precepts were not ignored by these rules and principles. On the contrary. One of the fundamental principles of the law of warfare prohibited the use of weapons that caused unnecessary suffering, in other words, suffering that was not justified by the purpose of putting the opponent out of action. Moreover, many of the rules concerning prisoners of war insisted on their receiving proper and humane treatment. However, these humanitarian principles gave way to military considerations and to the logic of war as soon as this suited one or more of the parties involved. Thus, the ban on the use of weapons that cause unnecessary suffering has merely succeeded in prohibiting the use of savage weapons that do not have a decisive effect on the outcome of hostilities (such as barbed bayonets, shotguns, or dumdum bullets): it has not prevented the use of other, no less cruel, weapons that are highly effective from a military point of view. Furthermore, international law itself allowed states, in given circumstances, to set aside the humanitarian guarantees that had been embodied in the laws of war concerning civilians, the wounded, the sick and prisoners of war. Indeed, one of the main principles of these laws was the right to resort to *reprisals* should the enemy violate these laws. In times of war it is, obviously, far more difficult to ascertain the facts of a case, which are never easy to discover, even in peacetime; this makes it easy for one belligerent to insist that the other has violated these laws, thereby justifying the use of reprisals. The very essence of reprisals is that they deny all the guarantees that ought to protect individuals: they open the door to a whole set of heinous acts such as the bombing of cities and the killing of prisoners of war, wounded soldiers and civilians.

This barbarous state of affairs was in part modified after the Second World War, when it was realized that the human person had to be protected. The shift in purpose was reflected in a change in terminology: today people talk less of the 'laws of war' and more of the 'humanitarian law of armed conflict', evidence of a new approach to the question.

The impact of human rights has been felt at various levels. First, reprisals against prisoners of war, wounded, sick or shipwrecked personnel, as well as against civilians held by the enemy from the moment hostilities began, have been banned; the ban was introduced in 1949. In 1977 the prohibition was extended to cover another important area: that of civilian populations living in enemy territory during the war, the obvious victims for reprisals. Unfortunately, this latter-day ban has not been accepted by all states. Indeed, during the recent war between Iran and Iraq, both sides made frequent use of precisely this kind of reprisal and the international community was powerless to put a stop to such behaviour.

Another area affected by human rights is that of inhuman weapons. Here states have preferred to be specific, rather than condemn whole categories of weapons in vague formulas. Thus the use of napalm in certain circumstances has been prohibited, as well as the use of booby traps and even arms that so far exist only on the drawing board – bullets that cannot be traced by X-ray once they have penetrated the body.

Yet another terrain affected by human rights is that of war victims, including prisoners, wounded, mutilated or shipwrecked members of the armed forces and civilians who have fallen into the hands of the enemy. Their daily treatment is minutely regulated from an exclusively humanitarian point of view, with no reference to the traditional rights of belligerents as foreseen in the laws of war.

The creation of a new category of international crimes connected with war represents a further step forward. These are crimes against humanity: racial or political persecution, deportation and other inhuman acts perpetrated during a war or in connection with hostilities. Thus, the area of unlawful, inhuman acts that must be punished has been enlarged.

At the same time an important new principle has been introduced: that of universal jurisdiction for war crimes and crimes against humanity. Previously, only the state to which the criminal or the victim belonged, or the state on whose territory the crime had been perpetrated, could punish the criminal. Today, any state can try and punish anyone who has committed such crimes – unless it extradites him or her to another state: this is the principle *aut judicare aut dedere*. On paper this is a tremendous step forward; however, in reality not much has been done to apply the principle.

Let me just mention one last area that has been decisively affected by human rights: that of civil wars. In the past, armed insurrection against the state was of concern only to the country directly involved: on the whole, other nations steered clear of such distressing outbursts of violence; at most, a state might decide to give the beleaguered government a hand in putting down the rebellion. Only in exceptional circumstances, when a civil war was particularly long-lasting and ferocious and the international community could not pretend to ignore it, did the rebels receive fleeting international recognition, especially when the government they were trying to overthrow decided to recognize them as belligerents. However, even these rare occurrences were covered only by the traditional laws of war, with all their limitations and, therefore, with scant regard for the rights of the human person. After the Second World War, there came a turning point. There were two reasons for this. On the one hand, it was the result of pressure from the socialist bloc, because these states wanted to grant international protection to rebels fighting against colonial powers, in the hope that greater recognition would drive a wedge into the heart of colonialism and help to dismember the colonial empires. On the other, the movement for human rights had made people far more aware of the need to introduce humanitarian values into the laws governing civil war. That turning point was the famous Article 3 contained in the four 1949 Geneva Conventions on war victims. Article 3, which was gradually to become a rule applicable to all states (including the few who have never ratified the Conventions), does not give the rebels political legitimacy, nor does it grant them specific rights regarding the conduct of hostilities. In the eyes of the state against which they are fighting, the rebels are classed – as indeed they had been in the past – as common criminals; in other words, Article 3 has not transformed them into international subjects. Nevertheless, they now enjoy the protection of a set of humanitarian guarantees should they be captured (and, similarly, they are also expected to apply those guarantees to any prisoners they themselves have taken). Moreover, civilians, the wounded and sick, who have not taken part or can no longer take part in hostilities, are also covered by these guarantees. All these very important humanitarian rules were later to be broadened in scope and made more precise, always from a purely humanitarian point of view, in the Second Additional Geneva Protocol of 1977.

So far I have dealt only with the repercussions of human rights on the laws of war. Now, let me mention the impact of the principle of the self-determination of peoples on these laws. This principle has acted as a strong leaven upon the creation of a new category of armed conflict, half-way between inter-state war and civil war: wars of national liberation. Between 1960 and the mid 1970s, states from the Third World and from the socialist bloc fought hard in the United Nations to establish the existence of this new category; their efforts produced the First Additional Geneva Protocol of 1977. Here, a war in which an oppressed people is fighting for self-determination against a colonial or occupying power or a racist regime is elevated to the rank of international conflict. Consequently, such hostilities are covered, not by the laws of civil war, but by the laws of inter-state war (which are far broader in scope, more detailed and more favourable to the oppressed peoples involved).

The incursion of human rights ideology and the principle of the self-determination of peoples into two of the most common and savage phenomena today – civil wars and wars of national liberation – can be hailed as the greatest advance in the field of armed conflict. Unhappily, here as elsewhere, there is a vast gap between law and its daily application. Jurists, diplomats and humanitarian organizations have played their parts in getting these rules onto paper. It is up to government officials, the military and those bodies that represent public opinion to see that these legal imperatives are applied in reality.

Concluding remarks

In the course of this chapter, I have drawn attention to the transformations brought about by the human rights ideology and by the principle of self-determination and shown how they are hedged in by limitations. Nevertheless, these transformations have been far reaching. The idea of reciprocity has been cut down to size, if not eliminated. The traditional individualism of states has been partially weakened by a new awareness of the collective needs of the community. Formerly, the international community was guided by the maxim Spinoza suggested in 1677: 'Whereas freedom or inner strength are the virtues of the individual, a State knows no other value than its own security (*animi* [. . .] *libertas, seu fortitudo privata virtus est; at imperii virtus securitas*).'[8] Yet today states are also guided by other values for fear of being censured, denounced, criticized and, in extreme cases, delegitimized by a majority of the other members of the community. As I said earlier, we now possess a scale of values that states are obliged to respect. At the top of that scale is peace, respect for the dignity of the human being and the right of peoples to self-determination.

To a large extent these innovations are still in the chrysalis stage. From a purely legal point of view, the international community has passed from mere *Dasein* (existence) or mere *Mitsein* (coexistence of subjects) to *Gemeinsein* (interactive coexistence of a social group). In reality, alas, the community is made up of subjects who may, indeed, co-operate, but who are also frequently at odds with one another. Otherwise, why should sovereign states stand silently by while fellow members of the international community commit serious misdeeds? Why do they have nothing to say when they learn that people have been tortured, atrocities and massacres have been perpetrated, or that the most elementary rights of mankind have been violated? Why are they so laconic before the spectacle of bloody civil wars, or international armed conflicts that drag on, year after year, while the blood-soaked land is laid waste, or before the enslavement of whole peoples to whom the very right to life is denied? The reason for such callous behaviour can only be that national interests and geopolitical strategy still determine the behaviour of states. Like a gigantic wave, the doctrines of self-determination and human rights have swept over the world community, smashing old prejudices and antiquated structures, and shaking the ground on which long-accepted views and ideologies once stood firm. But the main structure of the old community has withstood this buffeting and the surrounding landscape has not radically changed. The wave has left numerous eddies of ideas and has resulted in a new vision of relations between international subjects. The contemporary landscape is now littered with notices (prohibiting certain acts and encouraging others) with a social purport that would have been unthinkable 50 years ago. Yet the 'Westphalian model' – the political and organizational system that linked members of the international community from the peace of Westphalia (1648) to the Second World War – has not been replaced by the new model for the organization of international relations inaugurated by the United Nations Charter in 1945. This failure must not plunge us into despair. The new 'organizational model', though incomplete, does at least indicate the routes to be avoided, as well as the main thoroughfares that it would be best for states to follow.

11

What Should We Do?

The path of human rights does not run smooth and straight: every day we stumble against the irrational; reason is pushed to one side and rights are trodden underfoot. Many are the forces that oppose human rights: authoritarian regimes, heavy-handed and all-inclusive government structures, as well as private groups (think of terrorist organizations) that treat defenceless and innocent people with ruthless violence. All those who belong to such authoritarian structures or violent private groups refuse to allow anyone to question or threaten their aggressive impulses and lust for power. The faint voice of human rights can hardly be heard over their clamour.

What then can be done? Any answer, which is not too glib, must start with the statement that it will take more than a day or a year to ensure respect for human rights: the time required is long. The international protection of human rights resembles such natural phenomena as earthquakes, magmatic transformations, glaciations, climatic changes, all of which happen imperceptibly, beyond the observation of a single lifespan, and can be measured only in terms of generations. The effects of human rights are slow moving, though – unlike natural phenomena – they are not self-propelling, but advance only through the efforts of thousands of people and hundreds of non-governmental organizations and states. Their progress is not straightforward, but is continually interrupted by backsliding, by returns to barbarism, and by periods of stagnation and prolonged silence.

It is hardly surprising that human rights should take so long to become established. Though not a religion, human rights do possess many of the characteristics of the main religious faiths. Centuries elapsed before the great religions began to expand; they were beset by obstacles, by persecution and a categorical refusal to accept their tenets. Yet, in time, they came to dominate the minds of men and to condition the behaviour of people and states, generation after generation. The essential precepts of these religions were trampled underfoot by opponents and followers alike. Day by day their most sacred principles were violated; nevertheless they continued to expand. All this is true of human rights, which many states habitually disregard; yet, they stand out as one of the great forces of natural law.

Let me add that in at least one area of the world – in Western Europe, or, to be more precise, among the states that belong to the Council of Europe – after a long period of gestation, important results have been achieved. Here, an international system of guarantees has been set up that has already lowered the rate of abuses and violations and will stand as a solid dyke against authoritarianism and the abuse of power. Specific historical, cultural and political factors have made this achievement possible in an area that has thus become relatively free of turmoil. The creation of international organs to ensure that member states of the Council do not indulge in lawless or arbitrary behaviour has already helped to strengthen the protection of human rights in Europe. It is, however, a unique example of what can be done, though some timid imitations have begun to emerge in other parts of the world.

Now, let us take a look at the forces that – whether consciously or unconsciously – oppose human rights in the international community: they constitute the Bastille we will have to take by storm. Underlying this opposition are three separate sets of factors, which are all connected with the structure of the modern state.

The first of these is that rather singular fact which I have already mentioned several times: the guarantors who are to ensure respect for human rights are the states themselves; in other words, those who violate human rights on a daily basis are also expected to police their own behaviour. This is one of the strangest aspects of the international community: the protagonists, in whom all power is vested, are sovereign states; they dominate, direct and regulate the affairs of larger or smaller groups of individuals, the people over whom they rule. For centuries states have had almost unlimited power of life and death over individuals; they have behaved like despots outside the law, who have a right to do as they wish with the possessions and lives of their subjects. Today, states have gradually accepted certain *self-imposed limitations* to their powers by promising to guarantee the freedom and rights of their citizens. This means that, if we wish to ensure respect for the rights and freedom of individuals, we *must try to win over* those who are the worst offenders in this area, those who easily give in to a desire to wield unlimited and arbitrary power over their own subjects. It is rather like begging a seventeenth-century slave merchant to accept

184 Human Rights in a Gradually Unifying World

reducing his earnings or renouncing his trade. This disconcerting state of affairs could hardly exist if the international community had an independent sanctioning system to punish abuses and unlawful behaviour. Instead, as we all know, the international community is rather like Voltaire's description of the wonderful land of Eldorado depicted in his novel *Candide*, where Candide and his faithful servant Cacambó arrived after many misadventures: a land with no courts of justice, no parliament, no prisons. The country survived without these institutions only because its citizens were free; precious stones and gold lay scattered among the pebbles in the streets, while towering rocks and perilous cliffs protected the inhabitants from rapacious European nations. Alas, the international community has neither parliament, nor courts, nor prisons, but only because no single state or group of states has ever managed to possess enough ships and cannons (today we would say missiles and nuclear arms) to enable it to rule supreme over all other nations. In such an anarchic community, any sovereign state may choose first to bind its hands and, later, to loosen those bonds as it pleases. It is hardly surprising, then, to discover how often states ignore – to a greater or lesser extent – the rights and fundamental freedoms of the individuals they govern.

This, I must insist, is the insidious rock against which all those who follow international affairs, sooner or later founder. So long as states refuse to renounce their sovereignty, so long as no supra-national (yet democratic) authority is set up, it will never be possible to ensure *universal* respect for the dignity of the human person. The international community is still profoundly different from a national community. This point is well illustrated by the Italian philosopher, Norberto Bobbio, when he writes that 'all states are forced to arm themselves, whereas all or almost all the citizens of a well-governed state go about unarmed'.[1] The international community is still made up of sovereign states and so it will be for many decades to come. We might as well accept this, together with the inevitable consequences – although, as Hedley Bull, that acute student of political science, pointed out many years ago, 'not all these consequences are negative'.[2]

The second set of factors is part and parcel of the *structure of the modern state*. My remarks on the previous point may have created a slightly misleading impression: a state is not a kind of monster, ever ready to pounce upon its subjects and maul them, or even devour them. A state is not 'evil' by nature. The simple fact is that there exist states that have adopted an oppressive policy (discriminatory or racist, for example) or have an authoritarian regime, and consequently trample the rights of individuals and groups under-foot. What is more, even states with an open structure or a pluralistic party system, or at any rate based on parliamentary democracy, are now such a complex structure as to be unable to solve the multitude of problems that beset them with the necessary speed and accuracy. As we all know to our cost, the modern state is a colossus, with a highly formal bureaucratic organization, where the relations between government and citizen are labyrinthine and often far from transparent. Consequently, it is often extremely difficult for sovereign states to obey international precepts on human rights in the daily exercise of government. Furthermore, taken as a whole, the state is an extremely complicated organism: the central administration is flanked by a whole set of organizations and groups (such as political parties, trade unions, regional and local bodies, financial groups and private associations) over which the government often has little control.

Furthermore, a state may be troubled, from within, by subver-sive groups or even by terrorists, who threaten the lives and possessions of its citizens. Indeed, the proliferation of these groups is one of the most vexatious phenomena of modern life, because the impotence of governments in dealing with them is all too frequently apparent. The increase of 'private violence' is due, not so much to a decline in the power of the modern state, as to the increasing needs, aspirations and pressure of groups that were once voiceless or at the silent service of the state, but now demand new power and authority – although the means by which they intend to attain that power and authority are exceedingly perverse. A fact that one ought not to gloss over in silence is that this increasing violence of private groups is *also* the result of the spread of the human rights ideology itself.

Such an intricate and ramified conglomeration of bodies, which may work in harmony, but are usually at loggerheads with the central administration, form a cumbersome and unwieldy machine. It is easy to see how even the most democratic of states may be incapable of ensuring that its citizens enjoy their fundamental rights and freedoms.

My third set of factors refers to the *specific history* of each of the three main groups of states in our present-day international community.

Although Western countries tend, on the whole, to recognize human rights (especially political and civil rights), this recognition is often seriously flawed. (Here, again, one must not forget that Western Europe is in many respects a veritable 'oasis' in the desert). One has only to remember the often purely formal participation of people in the political institutions of their country. However genuine and free the elections, however respectful of the tenets contained in the 1966 UN Covenant on Civil and Political Rights, how much do the people who choose their representatives really count? How far are their opinions and will shaped by the intermediate organizations and groups that control most of the economic and social levers? To what extent does heavy-handed authority survive in the community, in the family, the school, the factory, the trade union, the church, the army, and so on? Are there forces at work to destroy, or limit, the profound inequalities between ethnic groups, social classes, religious communities, or regional administrations?

On the other hand, socialist states have been labouring for years under the burden of the Leninist concept of the state, due, in part, to the very size of the economic tasks these states had set themselves. Political pluralism is only just emerging and the state machinery is gradually becoming less oppressive and omnipresent. However, it is still too early to say whether the concepts of democracy, the rule of law and respect for human rights will become quickly rooted in the new ground, or whether the departure from authoritarian rule will instead be rather slower.

As for Third World nations, they are now passing through a phase in their development in which the concentration of power and a considerable degree of authoritarianism often seem essential ingredients for a strong economic structure, capable of self-sufficiency, or at least of a development that is less and less dependent on industrialized countries. To these economic justifications for authoritarian government one must add the effects of conflict between ethnic and other groups, the absolutism of leaders whose ends are the satisfaction of personal ambition, tension between military hierarchies or between them and political groups, and savage competition between economic groups dependent on foreign countries. All this adds up to a fairly depressing picture. Most Third World countries are ruled by military regimes and despotic administrations, if the regime has not actually de-generated into a dictatorship. The rights of individuals and groups, sometimes of whole peoples, are systematically disregarded.

All these three factors must be taken into account if we are to make realistic plans for the progressive enhancement of human rights throughout the world. These factors are still, and will be, objective barriers to respect for those rights.

What should be done and how should we go about the task?

Once again, let me return to a crucial question, one which cannot be avoided. The very nature of the struggle for human rights, to which I alluded earlier on – namely the fact that it will take considerable time to achieve solid results – together with the numerous trip-wires along our path, make one point crystal clear: the struggle cannot be undertaken except by myriads of individuals and groups. What we need is a vast army in which, however, there are neither generals, nor strategists, nor leaders. It will have to be an army of commoners, of people who contribute in a thousand different ways and at different levels to the patient, humble tasks that must be accomplished day by day: like the mothers of the *Plaza de Mayo*, united in their obstinate protest against the unacceptable. The battle of ideas is no less a part of the struggle. The most enduring human movements are first given voice and then defended with the sword (*ad acquirendum dominium hominis lingua, ad defendendum arma* [. . .] *videntur proficere magis*), in the words of Tommaso Campanella, who was tortured and imprisoned precisely because the authorities feared his ideas.[3] To open people's minds, to illuminate the straight and narrow paths that lead in the right direction, to criticize omissions and mistakes in what has been achieved so far; all this is of great help. It is equally important to ensure that the wells of public opinion are not poisoned by people becoming inured to authoritarianism and bullying.

But, you will object, these obstacles make the journey too long, too arduous, and place the prize beyond our reach. Why should we give our utmost only to come up against governments and terrorist groups that disregard the most elementary rights? I could answer by appealing to the impersonal, peremptory force of the 'categorical imperative'. Yet I would rather give a simpler and more humane answer: to be able to reduce, if only infinitesimally, the burden of suffering in the world can make it a little easier for each of us to weigh the achievements of a day's work. Remember the last scene in *The Trial* – a novel that holds the key to our existence – when K, 'awaiting trial', is dragged at night by two representatives of the Law to a lonely stone quarry. Before he is stabbed in the back for unknown crimes, a window in the house opposite is thrown open – like 'a flicker as of a light going up' – and a figure appears and spreads its arms wide. 'Who was it?', the man who is about to be killed wonders. 'A friend? A good man? Someone who sympathised? Someone who wanted to help? Was it one person only? Or were they all there? Was help at hand?'[4] Perhaps it is enough for one about to die – in a prison, a concentration camp, a mine, a torture chamber, a city destroyed by bombs, a village oppressed by drought – to know he does not die alone; the figure in the window is not indifferent: he will at least protest. Not much by way of consolation, but better than dying completely alone and forgotten.

Appendix 1

The Universal Declaration of Human Rights (1948)

1. Universal Declaration of Human Rights[1]

Adopted and proclaimed by General Assembly resolution 217 A (III) of 10 December 1948

PREAMBLE

Whereas recognition of the inherent dignity and of the equal and inalienable rights of all members of the human family is the foundation of freedom, justice and peace in the world,

Whereas disregard and contempt for human rights have resulted in barbarous acts which have outraged the conscience of mankind, and the advent of a world in which human beings shall enjoy freedom of speech and belief and freedom from fear and want has been proclaimed as the highest aspiration of the common people,

Whereas it is essential, if man is not to be compelled to have recourse, as a last resort, to rebellion against tyranny and oppression, that human rights should be protected by the rule of law,

Whereas it is essential to promote the development of friendly relations between nations,

Whereas the people of the United Nations have in the Charter reaffirmed their faith in fundamental human rights, in the dignity and worth of the human person and in the equal rights of men and women and have determined to promote social progress and better standards of life in larger freedom,

Whereas Member States have pledged themselves to achieve, in co-operation with the United Nations, the promotion of universal respect for and observance of human rights and fundamental freedoms,

Whereas a common understanding of these rights and freedoms is of the greatest importance for the full realization of this pledge,

Now, therefore,

The General Assembly

Proclaims this Universal Declaration of Human Rights as a common standard of achievement for all peoples and all nations, to the end that every individual and every organ of society, keeping this Declaration constantly in mind, shall strive by teaching and education to promote respect for these rights and freedoms and by progressive measures, national and international, to secure their universal and effective recognition and observance, both among the peoples of Member States themselves and among the peoples of territories under their jurisdiction.

Article 1

All human beings are born free and equal in dignity and rights. They are endowed with reason and conscience and should act towards one another in a spirit of brotherhood.

Article 2

Everyone is entitled to all the rights and freedoms set forth in this Declaration, without distinction of any kind, such as race, colour, sex, language, religion, political or other opinion, national or social origin, property, birth or other status.

Furthermore, no distinction shall be made on the basis of the political, jurisdictional or international status of the country or territory to which a person belongs, whether it be independent, trust, non-self-governing or under any other limitation of sovereignty.

Article 3

Everyone has the right to life, liberty and security of person.

Article 4

No one shall be held in slavery or servitude; slavery and the slave trade shall be prohibited in all their forms.

Article 5

No one shall be subjected to torture or to cruel, inhuman or degrading treatment or punishment.

Article 6

Everyone has the right to recognition everywhere as a person before the law.

Article 7

All are equal before the law and are entitled without any discrimination to equal protection of the law. All are entitled to equal protection against any discrimination in violation of this Declaration and against any incitement to such discrimination.

Article 8

Everyone has the right to an effective remedy by the competent national tribunals for acts violating the fundamental rights granted him by the constitution or by law.

Article 9

No one shall be subjected to arbitrary arrest, detention or exile.

Article 10

Everyone is entitled in full equality to a fair and public hearing by an independent and impartial tribunal, in the determination of his rights and obligations and of any criminal charge against him.

Article 11

1. Everyone charged with a penal offence has the right to be presumed innocent until proved guilty according to law in a public trial at which he has had all the guarantees necessary for his defence.

2. No one shall be held guilty of any penal offence on account of any act or omission which did not constitute a penal offence, under national or international law, at the time when it was committed. Nor shall a heavier penalty be imposed than the one that was applicable at the time the penal offence was committed.

Article 12

No one shall be subjected to arbitrary interference with his privacy, family, home or correspondence, nor to attacks upon his honour and reputation. Everyone has the right to the protection of the law against such interference or attacks.

Article 13

1. Everyone has the right to freedom of movement and residence within the borders of each State.

2. Everyone has the right to leave any country, including his own, and to return to his country.

Article 14

1. Everyone has the right to seek and to enjoy in other countries asylum from persecution.

2. This right may not be invoked in the case of prosecutions genuinely arising from non-political crimes or from acts contrary to the purposes and principles of the United Nations.

Article 15

1. Everyone has the right to a nationality.

2. No one shall be arbitrarily deprived of his nationality nor denied the right to change his nationality.

Article 16

1. Men and women of full age, without any limitation due to race, nationality or religion, have the right to marry and to found a family. They are entitled to equal rights as to marriage, during marriage and at its dissolution.

2. Marriage shall be entered into only with the free and full consent of the intending spouses.

3. The family is the natural and fundamental group unit of society and is entitled to protection by society and the State.

Article 17

1. Everyone has the right to own property alone as well as in association with others.

2. No one shall be arbitrarily deprived of his property.

Article 18

Everyone has the right to freedom of thought, conscience and religion; this right includes freedom to change his religion or belief, and freedom, either alone or in community with others and in public or private, to manifest his religion or belief in teaching, practice, worship and observance.

Article 19

Everyone has the right to freedom of opinion and expression; this right includes freedom to hold opinions without interference and to seek, receive and impart information and ideas through any media and regardless of frontiers.

Article 20

1. Everyone has the right to freedom of peaceful assembly and association.

2. No one may be compelled to belong to an association.

Article 21

1. Everyone has the right to take part in the government of his country, directly or through freely chosen representatives.

2. Everyone has the right to equal access to public service in his country.

3. The will of the people shall be the basis of the authority of government; this will shall be expressed in periodic and genuine elections which shall be by universal and equal suffrage and shall be held by secret vote or by equivalent free voting procedures.

Article 22

Everyone, as a member of society, has the right to social security and is entitled to realization, through national effort and international co-operation and in accordance with the organization and resources of each State, of the economic, social and cultural rights indispensable for his dignity and free development of his personality.

Article 23

1. Everyone has the right to work, to free choice of employment, to just and favourable conditions of work and to protection against unemployment.

2. Everyone, without any discrimination, has the right to equal pay for equal work.

3. Everyone who works has the right to just and favourable remuneration ensuring for himself and his family an existence worthy of human

dignity, and supplemented, if necessary, by other means of social protection.

4. Everyone has the right to form and to join trade unions for the protection of his interests.

Article 24

Everyone has the right to rest and leisure, including reasonable limitation of working hours and periodic holidays with pay.

Article 25

1. Everyone has the right to a standard of living adequate for the health and well-being of himself and of his family, including food, clothing, housing and medical care and necessary social services, and the right to security in the event of unemployment, sickness, disability, widowhood, old age or other lack of livelihood in circumstances beyond his control.

2. Motherhood and childhood are entitled to special care and assistance. All children, whether born in or out of wedlock, shall enjoy the same social protection.

Article 26

1. Everyone has the right to education. Education shall be free, at least in the elementary and fundamental stages. Elementary education shall be compulsory. Technical and professional education shall be made generally available and higher education shall be equally accessible to all on the basis of merit.

2. Education shall be directed to the full development of the human personality and to the strengthening of respect for human rights and fundamental freedoms. It shall promote understanding, tolerance and friendship among all nations, racial or religious groups, and shall further the activities of the United Nations for the maintenance of peace.

3. Parents have a prior right to choose the kind of education that shall be given to their children.

Article 27

1. Everyone has the right freely to participate in the cultural life of the community, to enjoy the arts and to share in scientific advancement and its benefits.

2. Everyone has the right to the protection of the moral and material interests resulting from any scientific, literary or artistic production of which he is the author.

Article 28

Everyone is entitled to a social and international order in which the rights and freedoms set forth in this Declaration can be fully realized.

Article 29

1. Everyone has duties to the community in which alone the free and full development of his personality is possible.

2. In the exercise of his rights and freedoms, everyone shall be subject

only to such limitations as are determined by law solely for the purpose of securing due recognition and respect for the rights and freedoms of others and of meeting the just requirements of morality, public order and the general welfare in a democratic society.

3. These rights and freedoms may in no case be exercised contrary to the purposes and principles of the United Nations.

Article 30

Nothing in this Declaration may be interpreted as implying for any State, group or person any right to engage in any activity or to perform any act aimed at the destruction of any of the rights and freedoms set forth herein.

Appendix 2

The Main International Organizations Active in the Field of Human Rights: A Practical Guide

Intergovernmental Organizations

1   United Nations

I have already explained in chapter 1 how, towards the end of the Second World War, human rights 'broke through' onto the world stage and were then proclaimed in the United Nations Charter in 1945.

The Charter, apart from demanding respect for those rights and realization of the self-determination of peoples as being among the goals that both the organization and member states ought to pursue, entrusted a number of UN organs with the task of acting in this sphere. The most important body from the political viewpoint is the General Assembly (made up of delegates of all 159 member states); one of the Committees through which it operates, namely the Third, spends some three months every year discussing the issue of human rights, approving resolutions, adopting international conventions and denouncing governments. The other organs are all subordinate to the Assembly: the Economic and Social Council (made up of 54 governmental delegates) and – dependent on it – the Commission on Human Rights, consisting of 43 states. The Commission is the key body in this connection. It meets once a year in Geneva for some six weeks, to discuss draft recommendations or international conventions, specific questions (for instance forced disappearances or torture) and denunciations against individual states. It is clearly a political body (made up of governmental delegates), a fact that considerably limits its actions. More stimulating and innovative is the activity of a subordinate body of the Commission, made up of experts acting on an individual basis (even though elected by the states sitting on the Commission): the Subcommission for the Prevention of Discrimination and Protection of Minorities (26 members).

Beside the Commission on Human Rights is another political body with more specific competences: the Commission on the Status of Women, made up of 32 government delegates.[1]

Apart from the bodies just mentioned, there is a secretariat within the UN called the Centre for Human Rights[2] with, among other things, the task of preparing the necessary material for meetings of the various competent bodies, publishing and distributing texts adopted, maintaining contact with non-governmental bodies and so on. One may approach the Centre for documents or other information on UN activity in this field.

The action of the various UN bodies has been outstanding in the area of drafting international normative texts. Suffice it to mention the 1948 Universal Declaration, the Convention on Genocide, also of 1948, the two 1966 Covenants (on Economic, Social and Cultural rights and on Civil and Political rights, with the attached Optional Protocol); the 1965 International Convention on the Elimination of all Forms of Racial Discrimination (the one ratified by the largest number of states of all: 124), the 1984 Convention on Torture, and many others, as well as various extremely important resolutions on the principle of self-determination of peoples (embodied also in Article 1 of the two 1966 Covenants).

It should be noted that the UN has followed a twofold approach in its norm-setting activity. On the one hand it has drawn up *general* texts (such as the Universal Declaration, the Covenants and the Resolutions on self-determination of peoples just cited). On the other, it has concerned itself with *specific sectors: slavery* (1956 Convention); *traffic in persons* and the exploitation of the *prostitution* of others (1949 Convention); *genocide* (1948 Convention, cited); *racial discrimination* (1965 Convention, cited); *other forms of discrimination* (against women: 1981 Convention); *religious freedom* (1981 Declaration on the Elimination of All Forms of Intolerance and of Discrimination Based on Religion or Belief); *protection of detainees* (Standard Minimum Rules for the Treatment of Prisoners, 1955; Code of Conduct for Law Enforcement Officials, 1979; Guidelines for Medical Doctors Concerning Torture and other Cruel, Inhuman or Degrading Treatment or Punishment in Relation to Detention and Imprisonment, 1982); *freedom of information* (Convention on the International Right of Correction, 1952); the *right to development* (1986 Declaration); the *political rights of women* (1952 Convention); *marriage* (1962 Convention); the rights of *the child* (1959 Declaration); the rights of the *mentally retarded persons* (1971 Declaration); the rights of *disabled persons* (1975 Declaration), and so on.

The text of these and other no less important normative documents can be found, in English or French, in the periodically republished UN collection, *Human Rights: a Compilation of International Instruments*, obtainable from the Geneva Centre for Human Rights mentioned above.

No less effective than the standard-setting activity on fundamental rights of individuals has been UN action on *practical implementation of the principle of self-determination of peoples* (in the 1950s and 1960s the UN contributed enormously towards promoting the political independence of almost all peoples under colonial domination). While some peoples are still without the status they aspire to – the South Africans, the Palestinian people, the Sahrawis, the Eritreans, the Afghans – this is not the fault of the UN, but of the inherent difficulty of the problems, and above all of the lack of political will, among the states that count, to reach a just solution in conformity with the aspirations of those peoples.

UN action has been less conspicuous in the field of *implementation* of human rights *stricto sensu*. The various treaties provide for specific supervisory systems (this is true for most of the conventions I have mentioned above). Altogether, however, they are somewhat ineffective, since in this case more than others the myth of state sovereignty is opposed to forms of international monitoring of the domestic behaviour of individual states. In addition to the supervisory machinery provided for in specific conventions, there exist within the UN two general monitoring procedures; they can be set in motion by 'communications' from individuals or groups of individuals, concerning 'a consistent pattern of gross violations of human rights': one procedure, public in nature, was provided for in 1967, and the other, 'confidential', in 1970. Both hinge on the Commission on Human Rights, and may go as far as an investigation (if the state challenged accepts that it be carried out on its territory), or to the drafting of a report on any violations found. So far these two procedures have functioned in several cases, arousing a wide response among international public opinion (for instance, *Le Monde*, the *International Herald Tribune*, the *Guardian*, or the *New York Times* often report them in detail).

To conclude, UN activity in the field of human rights from 1945 to date should be regarded as important, despite lacunae, deficiencies and silences. We should not ignore two important facts when objectively appraising UN actions. Firstly, the UN is an *intergovernmental* institution, set up by states and operating only with their consent and support. Bearing in mind what I have said above on the fundamental antinomy we meet in the area of human rights protection (that states, the greatest violators of those rights, are the entities one must approach to secure respect for them), it seems clear that the UN can act only up to a certain point, since its hands are tied. Secondly, the UN is *world-wide*, that is, it brings together states that are very heterogeneous in economic, political, military and ideological conditions. Obviously, it is very difficult to draw up a single 'message' for states so 'remote' from each other: one is compelled to dilute the message, often making it feeble and generic, if it is to reach such diverse destinations as China and Sweden, Pakistan and the Federal Republic of Germany, Fiji and the United States, Iran and France, Paraguay and Poland, Singapore and the Soviet Union.

2 Council of Europe

This is a Western intergovernmental organization set up in 1949, which at present groups together 23 states: the twelve members of the European Communities plus San Marino, some Nordic countries such as Iceland, Norway, Sweden and Finland, central European countries like Switzerland,

Austria and Liechtenstein, Mediterranean countries like Malta, and two Asian countries, Cyprus and Turkey.

The Council of Europe emerged from an idea launched initially by Winston Churchill in 1943. From the beginning, the Council was conceived as an international institution aimed at uniting and strengthening the democracies of Western Europe in the political, ideological and cultural field, and at promoting respect for human rights. The foundations for the institution were laid at the Hague Congress of 1948, held by a number of private bodies advocating the unity of Europe (among other things, that Congress launched the idea of creating a 'Human Rights Charter' and a 'Supreme Court' to guarantee respect for them). But when it came to translating the various ideas into fact, a clear conflict emerged – it was to mark the birth and for many years the functioning of the Council of Europe – between the pattern hoped for by the British (a Europe founded on co-operation and hence hinging round meetings of 'responsible ministers' of the various states) and the model advocated by the French and Belgians of a Europe founded on integration (and therefore hinging around a European parliamentary assembly). The Treaty setting up the Council of Europe represented a compromise: beside an intergovernmental organ (the Committee of Ministers) there is a collegiate body (the Consultative Assembly, made up of members of national parliaments). However, only the first body has decision-making power.

Partly at the insistence of the Italians, the Preamble to the Treaty setting up the Council of Europe stressed one important factor: the founding states were devoted to 'the spiritual and moral values which are the common heritage of their peoples and the true source of individual freedom, political liberty and the rule of law, principles which form the basis of all genuine democracy'. This gave explicit formulation to one of the reasons for setting up the Council: to promote or strengthen democratic freedoms and human rights, in the hope of thus being able not only to prevent a return to the barbarism of Nazism and Fascism, but also oppose the growing influence of the socialist regimes of Eastern Europe.

However, even before the first session of the Consultative Assembly (August 1949), doubts arose among Council of Europe Member states on the advisability of setting up a European Court of Human Rights: there were fears of encroaching upon state sovereignty in such a delicate area. Fortunately, Winston Churchill secured approval from the Assembly for a motion to compel the Committee of Ministers to enter the question of human rights on the Assembly's agenda. The Governments met and embarked on prolonged negotiations; in 1950 they approved an extremely important international treaty, the European Convention on Human Rights, subsequently updated and supplemented by several Protocols.

The Convention protects some important civil rights (the right to life; the right not to be subjected to torture or inhuman or degrading treatment; the right to personal safety, to fair trial, to respect for private and family life; freedom of conscience, religion and expression; freedom of association; the principle of equality). The Protocols (additional conventions) protect a number of rights including the right to free elections, the right to education and peaceful enjoyment of possessions.

So far as international monitoring of respect for these rights and liberties is concerned, the Convention ended with a compromise between requirements of state sovereignty and the humanitarian demands of individuals. The international supervisory mechanism it institutes might thus at first sight seem cumbersome and somewhat strange. Individuals cannot approach the international court directly, but must pass through a series of 'filters' (which are designed to allay the fears of sovereign states). The mechanism operates in the following fashion.

Any individual or group of individuals claiming to have been a victim of a violation by a Contracting State that has accepted Article 25 of the Convention[3] may lodge a complaint with the European Commission of Human Rights (note that it is not necessary for the plaintiff to hold the citizenship of one of those states: they may be stateless, Chinese, American, Tunisian, Kenyan, Soviet, or any other nationality, as long as they show that they have suffered wrong from the authorities of one of those states). The Commission, made up of eminent experts from each of the Contracting Parties acting in entirely independent fashion, carries out an initial examination of the complaint. If the complaint is procedurally correct and does not seem *prima facie* manifestly ill-founded, the Commission considers the merits. If it concludes that the applicant's grievances are well-founded, the Commission may propose that the two parties (the applicant and the Government under accusation) reach a 'friendly settlement' (for instance, the Government makes compensation for the damage, or gives a flat-rate indemnity, or undertakes to abolish the government measures complained of). If this attempt fails, the Commission draws up a report which is forwarded to the Committee of Ministers (a political body). If the accused state has not previously accepted the Court's jurisdiction or should the case not seem to the Commission to be important or particularly significant or controversial, the Commission's report remains before the Committee of Ministers of the Council of Europe. However if the Commission or the relevant state decide to bring the case before the Court the case will come before 23 independent judges. Thus, the outcome of the procedure may be a judgment from the Court ('acquitting' or 'condemning' the state) or a decision of the Committee of Ministers. It should be noted that in the event of 'condemnation' the state may also be required to furnish 'just satisfaction' to the victim of the violation (for instance, a sum of money), and that the Committee of Ministers has the further power to supervise the 'condemned' state's execution of the Court's judgment or its compliance with the measures prescribed by a decision of the Committee of Ministers.

In addition to individuals, non-governmental organizations and groups may lodge a complaint with the Commission (provided they themselves are the 'victim' of an alleged violation; in other words, they cannot act on behalf of individuals in a sort of *actio popularis*). Contracting States too are entitled to an application with the Commission: thus, one of the 23 states may bring an accusation against any other Contracting Party, for alleged violations of human rights of a national of the applicant state, of a national of the respondent state, or of any individual (whatever his or her nationality) under the jurisdiction of the respondent state.

By December 1989 15,911 applications were registered, decisions were taken in 14,241 cases and 670 cases were found admissible. The court have delivered 151 judgments on the merits. The Committee of Ministers has decided 129 cases.[4] There have been very many cases in which states challenged have been found guilty of having violated the Convention or one of the Protocols.

The seat of the Commission and Court is Strasbourg (France), and the address is c/o the Council of Europe, Boîte postale 431 R 6, F-67006 Strasbourg-Cedex. If one intends to apply to the Strasbourg bodies, it is useful to write to the Commission, the Secretary of which will send a form to be filled in for the application. It is also important to bear in mind the procedural requirements to be observed before entering the application (for instance, it is necessary to have exhausted all appropriate domestic remedies; moreover, the application must be submitted within six months of the last national decision). The Council of Europe will, on certain terms, provide a contribution towards the legal costs.

In the Council of Europe framework, economic and social rights are also protected, though less effectively. In 1961 the 'European Social Charter' was adopted, which came into force in 1965 and today binds a number of European states. The Charter protects various rights relating to the economic and social sphere: for instance the right to work, to fair working conditions and to fair pay; the work of women and children; trade union rights and the right to social security. The legal provisions that deal with these rights do not in fact confer upon individuals any 'subjective rights' in the proper sense (i.e. legal entitlements that can be asserted directly *vis-à-vis* governmental authorities); instead, they are formulated as general principles that should guide the legislative and administrative activity of Contracting States; in short, they constitute 'programmatic standards', more than directly applicable precepts. To facilitate participation by states in the Charter, it is laid down that they may accept only some of its provisions (the United Kingdom has accepted 62 out of 72.[5] Italy has accepted all of them, as has Spain).

In order for the Charter not to remain a dead letter, an international supervisory mechanism has been set up which is rather complex and intricate: several bodies take part in it. The outcome of verification may consist in a recommendation to a Contracting State, adopted (by two-thirds majority) by a political body: the Committee of Ministers of the Council of Europe.

Despite the 'programmatic' nature of the Charter's provisions and the complexity of monitoring their implementation, results obtained to date are to be regarded as fairly positive (in several cases, Contracting States have amended national legislation following observations or criticisms by the international supervisory agencies).

3 Organization of American States (OAS)

In terms of human rights, the Latin American countries tend to adopt an attitude that may seem somewhat contradictory. On the one hand they have on more than one occasion been promoters of broad international protection for such rights: for instance, in 1945 they made an impressive contribution to the proclamation of those rights in the UN Charter, and urged the Western countries, among them the United States (which after having taken important initiatives in this field was to some extent back-pedalling) to expand protection for human rights as far as possible. Probably, this tendency is to be attributed – at least in part – to the Catholic tradition of those countries, to their strong links with Western Europe and the United States, i.e. with those countries where the rights were born, and also to a political reason: the most enlightened leaders of Latin America realized that the 'international anchoring' of human rights, i.e. spreading and guaranteeing them at 'supranational' level, might obstruct or at least hinder autocratic regimes on the American continent. In other words, they hoped that the international community might at least limit – from the outside – the abuses produced by the governmental changes and *coups d'état* so frequent on that continent. The other aspect, in apparent contradiction with the first, is the very spread of authoritarian regimes, frequent recourse to states of emergency, or at any rate the large-scale violation of important human rights. In short, in Latin America there is a strong tension between two poles – that of what 'ought to be' and that of everyday reality. On the one hand there is a desire to proclaim precepts on human rights forcibly, and on the other these precepts are often being trampled on left, right and centre.

To seek to strengthen the first pole – the 'normative' aspect – the American Convention on Human Rights was concluded in 1969, under the auspices of the OAS (an intergovernmental organization with headquarters in Washington, bringing together the United States, Canada, Mexico, the Central American countries and those of South America). At present the Convention, which only came into force in 1978, binds twenty states (among them Mexico, Nicaragua, Honduras, El Salvador, Venezuela and Argentina, but not the giants of North and South: the United States and Brazil).

The Convention proclaims a number of civil and political rights in detail, and sets up an international supervisory mechanism centring around two bodies: the Inter-American Commission and Court of Human Rights. Each of these bodies is made up of seven people, who act as independent experts. The Commission fulfils three chief functions: (1) it considers applications submitted by individuals against alleged violations by a Contracting state; (2) it draws up and publishes general reports on the human rights situation in specific countries of the Americas; (3) it carries out 'promotional' activities (among other things, seeking to broaden the range of Contracting States to the Convention).

Both when considering individual applications and drawing up general reports on specific countries, the Commission does not hand down verdicts, but may only formulate 'conclusions' or 'recommendations'. The Court is instead a jurisdictional body proper, with two chief functions. The first is to give rulings on actions brought by a state (or by the Inter-American Commission) against another state; this power is, however, subordinate to an important condition: the accused state must have accepted this power (to date, only Argentina, Costa Rica, Ecuador, Honduras, Peru, Venezuela, Colombia, Uruguay and Surinam have deposited a declaration of general acceptance of the Court's jurisdiction). The second function of the Court consists in issuing 'advisory opinions' on matters concerning human rights: these (non-binding) 'opinions' may be asked for by any Member state or any organ of the OAS.

To date, the Commission has considered large numbers of complaints from individuals, drawn up reports on states (for instance on Cuba, Chile, Nicaragua, Argentina, Haiti, Paraguay and Uruguay) and made on-the-spot visits to several countries. The Court has delivered a number of 'advisory opinions', and one judgment – the case of *Velásques Rodríguez* v. *Honduras* (1988) where Honduras was found to have violated a number of articles of the Convention. The case concerned one of the many 'disappearances' which take place in South America (see chapter 7).

Taken all round, the results of the action of these two bodies are modest, especially if compared with the frequency and enormity of the violations that occur or have occurred in so many countries of the Americas. However, the Commission and the Court do, to some extent at least, contribute to denouncing the most serious abuses and to putting pressure on governments to stop them. It is hoped that gradually this action will become incisive and effective, especially if combined with action carried out at other levels (economic, social and political) to solve certain fundamental problems of the development of democracy in Latin America.

The seat of the Organization of American States is 17th and Constitution Ave NW, Washington DC 20006, USA; telephone: (1)(202) 458 3000.

4 Organization of African Unity

This intergovernmental organization was set up in May 1963 in Addis Ababa by the heads of state of 32 independent African countries. At present all African states except the Republic of South Africa and Morocco (which left on 12 November 1984) are members, as well as the Sahrawi Democratic Republic.

In 1981 in Nairobi, the organization's main body, namely the Assembly of heads of state and of government, unanimously adopted the African Charter of Human and Peoples' Rights.[6] The Charter entered into force on 21 October 1986, the date when it secured the necessary number of ratifications (a simple majority of OAU states). To date it has been ratified by 34 countries.[7]

In 1987 the African Commission on Human and Peoples' Rights, provided for by Article 30 of the Charter, was set up. In August that year, the Conference of heads of state and of government of the OAU elected the 11 members of the Commission, by secret ballot. The first meeting of this body was held in Addis Ababa on 2 November 1987. In subsequent meetings the Commission has adopted its Rules of Procedure and a number of resolutions on organizational matters.[8]

The seat of the OAU is in Addis Ababa. The postal address is PO Box 3243 and the telephone number is (251)(1) 15770. There is also a permanent office in Brussels at Avenue de Cortenbergh 66, B-1040 Bruxelles, Belgium. Telephone (32)(2) 7349603/7369830.

Non-Governmental Organizations

5 Amnesty International

This is a non-governmental organization set up in Great Britain following a 1961 initiative by a British lawyer, Peter Benenson, who made an appeal for amnesty for all political detainees in the world. The success of the initiative (initially conceived as a publicity campaign intended to last only one year) led to the setting up of a permanent institution, which soon acquired sufficient credit and respect to be awarded the Nobel Peace Prize in 1977, the UN Human Rights Prize in 1978 and the Council of Europe's Human Rights Prize in 1983.

The organization's headquarters is in London at 1 Easton Street, WC1 8DJ, tel. 071-251-8371, and there are national sections in many countries, particularly the Federal Republic of Germany, Sweden, The Netherlands, France, Britain and the United States.

Amnesty International concerns itself above all with respect for civil and political rights. In particular, it seeks to secure the release of 'prisoners of conscience' (all those detained for their political or religious opinions, for reasons of conscience or because they are victims of discrimination). An essential condition for assistance from Amnesty International is that the 'prisoners of conscience' do not practise or support violence. Amnesty International is also opposed to the detention without trial of political prisoners, to the death penalty and to inhuman or degrading treatment (in particular torture) of any detainee (see chapter 5).

Amnesty International acts through large numbers of 'local groups' made up of five or more members of the organization; each group 'adopts' several 'prisoners of conscience'. To guarantee impartiality and independence, it is a requirement that cases dealt with involve several countries, excluding that to which group members belong.

Other operational activities of the organization include missions to countries where human rights violations occur, either to attend trials, or

to make an on-the-spot investigation into whether such violations have
been committed and induce the authorities to make them stop.

Amnesty International further publishes reports on individual states or
specific topics (for instance torture), as well as a very important *annual
report* on the human rights violations it has concerned itself with in various
states in the world. Finally, Amnesty International actively participates in
debates in intergovernmental organizations (such as the UN, the Council
of Europe and the OAS), urging states to extend, clarify or strengthen
international protection of human rights. An indispensable role is
assigned to Amnesty International in the UN (for instance, in relation to
the Committee on Human Rights charged with guaranteeing application
of the 1966 UN Covenant on Civil and Political Rights; Amnesty
International supplies Committee members with detailed, reliable documents on violations that have taken place in countries on which the
Committee has to express its opinion on the basis of states' reports).

6   Anti-Slavery Society for the Protection of Human Rights

Founded in 1823 in Great Britain, this non-governmental organization
has had an enormous influence on legislation and practice concerning the
abolition of slavery. Their aim is to eradicate slavery and forced labour in
all their forms, to promote the well-being of indigenous peoples and to
protect human rights in accordance with the Universal Declaration of
Human Rights (1948). They produce a newsletter and an annual
publication called the *Anti-Slavery Reporter*

The headquarters is at 180 Brixton Road, London SW9 6AT; tel.
071-582-4040.

7   The International Commission of Jurists

This is another non-governmental organization. It was set up in 1952 and
deals with all human rights (and not only with some categories). Its action
takes place at several levels. Firstly, it promotes the drawing-up of
international treaties (it played a very important part in encouraging and
promoting the drawing-up of the African Charter of Human and Peoples'
Rights of 1981; together with the *Comité suisse contre la torture*, it had a
decisive role in promoting the elaboration and adoption of the European
Convention for the Prevention of Torture, of 1987) and the working out of
international documents or declarations (for instance the 'Study on the
independence and impartiality of the judiciary, jurors and assessors and
the independence of lawyers'). Secondly, it carries out visits and missions
to various countries (its delegates have, for instance, been to South Africa,
Pakistan, South Korea and Japan) to examine the general human rights
situation on-the-spot, attend trials or discuss individual issues (it should
be noted that as a result of its reports on the condition of the mentally ill in
Japan following various missions to that country, the Japanese authorities
amended part of the legislation governing this specific area). Thirdly, it
participates actively in meetings of international organizations of an

intergovernmental nature (for instance, the UN and Council of Europe), in order to denounce human rights violations in certain countries or propose lines of action.

By contrast with other similar organizations the International Commission of Jurists does not deal specifically with the forwarding of individual complaints to the relevant intergovernmental organs.

The address of its headquarters is: P.O.B. 120, CH-1244, Geneva, Switzerland; tel. 22/493545.

8   International Federation for Human Rights (Fédération Internationale des Droits de l'Homme)

This non-governmental organization is composed of national affiliates in 36 countries. It was founded in 1922 in France to uphold the principles of justice, liberty and equality. Members conduct missions of enquiry, act as 'judicial observers', make protests and representations to governments concerning violations of human rights. The Federation also publishes reports on individual countries (e.g. Afghanistan, Iraq, South Africa). In the Swiss case, discussed in chapter 10, the evidence and opinion of the Federation played a crucial role.

The address of its headquarters is: 27 rue Jean-Dolent, 75014 Paris, France, tel. 033/43319495; 6 Rue J.-C. Amat, 1202 Geneva, Switzerland; tel. 022/313332.

9   International League for the Rights and Liberation of Peoples

This is a non-governmental organization set up in Rome in 1976 by the Italian leftist politician and member of the Italian Parliament, Lelio Basso. He had been a member of the Russell Tribunal, set up by the British philosopher Bertrand Russell to judge United States activities in Vietnam (sessions in 1966 and 1967). In 1973, Basso in turn set up the Russell Tribunal II, to investigate human rights violations in Latin America (sessions in 1974, 1975 and 1976). In 1976 Basso conceived three closely linked institutions: the International League for the Rights and Freedom of Peoples, the Lelio Basso International Foundation for the Rights and Liberation of Peoples, and the Permanent Peoples' Tribunal (which started operating only in 1979).

All three bodies differ from other non-governmental organizations operating in this area, in three main respects. Firstly, they deal more with the rights of peoples (and minorities) than with rights of individuals. Secondly, they do not, like the other organizations, intend to be 'neutral'; they have 'chosen their camp', in that they adhere to the Socialist ideals advocated by Lelio Basso and pursue objectives of 'anti-imperialist' struggle. Thirdly, they intend, in the main, to carry out activities of study, research, denunciation and political debate; in particular they aim to stimulate ideological debate and theoretical elaboration of the great themes of peoples' rights.

The League has as its main aim the spreading of ideas and the organization of public events and debates. It is organized in national sections (Italy, France, Switzerland, etc.) and within each country in regional or provincial sections. The Foundation operates above all in the area of research, and draws up declarations and general texts (on 4 July 1976 an international conference in Algiers, organized by the Foundation, proclaimed the Universal Declaration of Rights of Peoples, which has since had some follow-up in various international venues). The Peoples' Tribunal organizes 'trials' against states accused (by private groups, non-governmental organizations or national liberation movements) of violating the fundamental rights of peoples. This is, of course, a 'court of public opinion' (on the model of the Russell Tribunal). Accused governments normally refuse to appear before it, disputing its legal competence and moral authority. To date the Tribunal, chaired by an eminent Belgian jurist (Francois Rigaux, Professor at the Catholic University of Louvain) and made up of political scientists, jurists, natural scientists and sociologists, has 'delivered' various 'consultative opinions' (for instance on the Western Sahara and on Eritrea) and 'verdicts' (for instance on Argentina, the Philippines, El Salvador, Afghanistan and on the genocide of the Armenians).

The headquarters of the three institutions is in Rome at Via della Dogana Vecchia 5 – 001186; tel. 06/6541468, 6879953, 6543529 or 6547516.

10   Interights

The International Centre for the Legal Protection of Human Rights is a London-based law centre concerned with the practical application of human rights law in national, regional, and international courts and tribunals. It provides assistance to lawyers as well as providing legal representation itself in selected cases. Additionally Interights has submitted *amicus curiae* briefs before domestic and international courts in cases concerning the interpretation of human rights instruments. Interights has played a significant role in cases before the European Commission and Court of Human Rights as well as the Inter-American Court of Human Rights (the *Velásques Rodríguez* v. *Honduras* (1988 case). In recent years the emphasis has been shifting from Europe to the developing countries of the Commonwealth, Caribbean and Asia (it is worth pointing out that the 12 independent Commonwealth Caribbean countries together with Bermuda have the European Convention on Human Rights enshrined in their Constitutions). In addition to this specialized legal advisory work Interights maintains a library and conducts workshops on human rights law.

Its headquarters is at 46 Kingsway, London WC2B 6EN; tel. 071-242-5581.

11 The Minority Rights Group

This non-governmental organization was founded in Great Britain by liberals, academics and media people including David Astor, former editor of *The Observer* and the Rt. Hon. Lord Grimond. It has been active since the early 1970s and now has groups all over the world.

The Minority Rights Group aims to secure justice for minority and majority groups suffering discrimination, and to help prevent the escalation of group conflict which often arises out of such discrimination. These aims are achieved through a series of reports designed to promote greater understanding and alert public opinion throughout the world. Over 70 reports have already been published, covering subjects as diverse as: Northern Ireland, Eritrea, Namibia, Burundi, the Palestinians, Arab women, Jehovah's Witnesses and female circumcision. In addition the Minority Rights Group organizes meetings and lectures as well as presenting evidence to bodies such as the United Nations Sub-Commission on Prevention of Discrimination and Protection of Minorities.

In 1982 the Minority Rights Group was awarded the United Nations Association Media Peace Prize.

The address of its headquarters is 29 Craven Street, London WC2N 5NT; tel. 071-930-6659.

Notes

INTRODUCTION

1 F. Kafka, *Briefe 1902–1904* (1958), Fischer Taschenbuch Verlag, Frankfurt, 1983, p. 28 ('ein Buch muss die Axt sein für das gefrorene Meer in uns').

CHAPTER 1 THE EMERGENCE OF HUMAN RIGHTS ON TO THE WORLD STAGE

1 G. Vico, 'Sul diritto naturale della genti' (1731), in *Opere* (ed. by F. Nicolini), R. Ricciardi ed., Milan-Naples 1953, p. 934.

2 J. Locke, *The Second Treatise of Government* (1690), chapter III, 'Of the State of War'.

3 J. Lorimer, *The Institutes of the Law of Nations*, vol. 1 (William Blackwood, Edinburgh and London, 1883), pp. 101–3.

4 R. Ago, *Lezioni di diritto internazionale 1936–37* (mimeograph Genoa, 1937), pp. 35–8.

5 P. S. Mancini, *Diritto internazionale – Prelezioni con un saggio su Machiavelli* (Giuseppe Marghieri, Naples, 1873), especially pp. 1–92, 169–220.

6 P. S. Mancini, *Sulla politica coloniale* (Tipografia della Camera dei Deputati, Rome, 1885), offprint of the speech at the Chamber of Deputies.

7 J. C. Bluntschli, *Allgemeine Staatslehre*, 6th edn (Berlin, 1866), p. 107 ('Jede Nation ist berufen und berechtigt, einen Staat zu bilden').

8 See D. H. Miller, *The Drafting of the Covenant*, vol. II (G. P. Putnam's Sons, New York-London, 1928), p. 324.

9 Ibid., pp. 323–5. The passage quoted is at p. 324. Baron Makino added the following considerations:

'There are other considerations of a more direct nature which merit earnest thought. The future States members of the League, comprising all kinds of races, constitute a great family of nations. It is in a sense a world organisation of insurance against aggression and war. If one member's independence and political integrity is menaced by a third Power, a nation or nations suitably placed must be prepared to take up arms against the aggressor, and there are also cases of enforcing common obligation which would entail contribution of armed force. These are indeed serious obligations to which each State member, in accordance with its capability and power, mutually pledges itself, and must be prepared to fulfil them for the benefit of their brother nations. This means that a citizen of one nation must be ready to share the military expenditure for the common cause and, if need be, defend other peoples by his own person. Seeing these new duties arising before him as the result of his country's entering the League, each national would like to feel and in fact demand that he should be placed on an equal footing with people he undertakes to defend even with his life.

In this war, to attain the common cause, different races have fought together on the battlefield, in the trenches, on the high seas, and they have helped each other and brought succour to the disabled, and have saved the lives of their fellow men irrespective of racial differences, and a common bond of sympathy and gratitude has been established to an extent never before experienced. I think it only just that after this common suffering and deliverance the principle at least of equality among men should be admitted and be made the basis of future intercourse.' (ibid., pp. 324–5).

10   As for the opposition of Great Britain and Australia, see A. Zimmern, *The League of Nations and the Rule of Law 1918–1935* (Macmillan and Co., London,1936), p. 258 (Zimmern's account is based on the 'Intimate Papers' of Colonel House, a close associate of President Wilson). For the debate at the 'Commission on the League of Nations' see Miller, *The Drafting of the Covenant*, vol. II, p. 325.

11   Miller, *The Drafting of the Covenant*, p. 389. See at pp. 387–9 the forceful speech of Baron Makino. See also the subsequent statements of Baron Makino, at pp. 574 and 701–4.

12   Ibid., p. 392. According to the minutes, 'eleven votes out of seventeen were recorded in favour of the [Japanese] amendment'. The French delegate pointed out that a majority vote was sufficient for the passing of the proposal, but President Wilson rebutted this view with a lengthy procedural statement.

13   Ibid., p. 389.

14   British opposition was particularly strong (see Miller, *The Drafting of the Covenant*, vol. I, pp. 461–5) but the US opposition was no less strong. In this respect A. Zimmern, *The League of Nations and the Rule of Law 1918—1935* pp. 261–2 mentions the following: 'By this time [namely by the time the Japanese had submitted their emasculated proposal] both he [President Wilson] and Colonel House [the US representative on the War Council and a friend and close advisor to President Wilson as well as a US delegate to the Commission on the League of Nations] had shifted their ground [i.e. moved from favouring the Japanese proposal to its rejection], no doubt as a result of the discussions of the matter in the United States. Delay had wreaked havoc. During the debate [in the Commission on the League of Nations] House, who always sat next to the President, had passed

him a note in these words: "the trouble is that if this Commission should pass it [the Japanese proposal], it would surely raise the race issue throughout the world". This gave the President his cue. He said that already discussion of the matter had "set burning flames of prejudice" and pleaded with the Commission to do its best to damp them down. "How can you treat on its merits in this quiet room a question which will not be treated on its merits when it gets out of this room?"' (the words of President Wilson reported by Zimmern are taken from an account made by a stenographer).

15   Ibid., p. 389.
16   See League of Nations *Official Journal*, Year XIV, July 1933, pp. 833–935 and October 1933, Special Supplement no. 114, pp. 1–3 and 22.
17   Mr Von Keller, ibid., p. 839.
18   Ibid.
19   Count Raczynski, ibid., p. 841.
20   Ibid.
21   Ibid.
22   League of Nations, *Official Journal*, 14, 1933, p. 842.
23   League of Nations, *Official Journal*, 14, 1933, p. 846.
24   League of Nations, *Official Journal*, 1933, *Special Supplement* no. 120 (Minutes of the Sixth Committee – Political Questions), p. 28.
25   Ibid., p. 42.
26   General Assembly Resolution 1514 (XV) *Declaration on the Granting of Independence to Colonial Countries and Peoples*, adopted 14 December 1960.
27   General Assembly Resolution 2625–XXV, *Declaration on Principles of International Law Concerning Friendly Relations and Co-operation among States in accordance with the Charter of the UN*, adopted 24 October 1970.

CHAPTER 2 THE UNIVERSAL DECLARATION OF HUMAN RIGHTS FORTY YEARS ON

1   See entry *Droit naturel*, in *Encyclopédie ou Dictionnaire raisonné des Sciences, des Arts et des Métiers*, vol. 5 (Paris, 1755), p. 116.
2   B. Constant, 'De la Liberté des Anciens Comparée à celle des Modernes' in *De la Liberté chez les Modernes* (Hachette, Paris, 1980), pp. 491–515.
3   See *Droit naturel*, in *Encyclopédie ou Dictionnaire raisonné des Sciences, des Arts et des Métiers*, p. 116.
4   See G. Pico della Mirandola, *Oration on the Dignity of Man* (1487), transl. A. R. Caponigri (Regnery Gateway, Chicago, 1956), especially pp. 6–9.
5   'The Sinews of Peace', Westminster College, Fulton, Missouri, 5 March 1946 in *Winston S. Churchill His Complete Speeches 1897–1963*, vol.

vii, 1943–1949, Robert Rhodes James (ed.) (Chelsea House Publishers, New York, 1974), pp. 7285–93 at p. 7287.

6 US *Hearings Documents*, 77th Session of Congress, 1st Session.
7 R. Sherwood, *Roosevelt and Hopkins* (Harper and Bros., New York, 1948), pp. 230–1; B. Rauch, *Roosevelt – From Munich to Pearl Harbor. A Study in the Creation of a Foreign Policy* (Da Capo Press, New York, 1975), pp. 301–2; M. G. Johnson, 'The Contributions of Eleanor and Franklin Roosevelt to the Development of International Protection of Human Rights' in *Human Rights Quarterly*, 9, 1987, p. 21.
8 Charles Scribner's Sons: New York, 1943
9 J. Maritain, *Human Rights and Natural Law*, p: 21.
10 Ibid. p. 47.
11 Ibid. p. 55.
12 Ibid. pp. 72–3.
13 Ibid. p. 101.
14 L. Kolakowski, 'Marxism and Human Rights' in *Daedalus – Journal of the American Academy of Arts and Sciences*, 1983, pp. 81 ff.
15 S. Lukes, 'Can a Marxist believe in Human Rights?', in *Praxis International*, 1982, pp. 334 ff.; S. Lukes, *Marxism and Morality* (OUP, Oxford, 1987), pp. 61–99.
16 J. P. Lash, *Eleanor: The Years Alone* (New American Library, New York, 1973), p. 53.
17 See General Assembly, 3rd Session, 180th Plenary Meeting (9 Dec. 1948), pp. 868–73 of the report (Ukraine); 181st Plenary Meeting (10 Dec. 1948), ibid., pp. 880–2 (Czechoslovakia); 182nd Plenary Meeting (10 Dec. 1948), ibid., pp. 903–9 (Poland).
18 See 181st Plenary Meeting (10 Dec. 1948), ibid., pp. 882–5.
19 See GAOR, IIIrd Committee Records, p. 750.
20 Ibid., p. 749. Mrs Roosevelt pointed out that 'such a provision [on the right to resist tyranny] could be interpreted as conferring a legal character on uprisings against a government which was in no way tyrannical'.
21 Cited in J. P. Lash, *Eleanor: The Years Alone*, p. 70.
22 See General Assembly, 3rd Session, 180th Plenary Meeting, p. 853 (Haiti); ibid., p. 857 (Lebanon); ibid., p. 863 (Chile); ibid., p. 864 (France); 182nd Plenary Meeting, p. 901 (Paraguay).
23 Mr Santa Cruz, General Assembly, 3rd Session, 180th Plenary Meeting, p. 863 of the report.
24 Mr Vyshinsky, 183rd Plenary Meeting, at pp. 962 and 929.
25 Mr Manuilsky, 180th Plenary Meeting, at p. 869.
26 Mr Manuilsky, 180th Plenary Meeting, at p. 873.
27 Mr Vyshinsky, 183rd Plenary Meeting, at p. 923.
28 'La Déclaration Universelle et la Mise en Oeuvre des Droits de l'Homme' in *Recueil des Cours de l'Académie de Droit International de la Haye*, vol. 79, 1951–II, pp. 242–362 at p. 278.
    (The Universal Declaration of Human Rights is contained in Appendix 1.)

29   Mr Ugon, 181st Plenary Meeting, at p. 887.
30   See UN doc. A/C.3/244/Rev.1, Corr.1.
31   See R. Cassin, 'La Déclaration Universelle et la mise en oeuvre des Droits de l'Homme', in *Recueil des Cours de l'Académie de La Haye*, vol. 79, 1951–II. p. 279 ('L'Assemblée Génerale des Nations Unies a accepté la proposition française tendant à changer l'intitulé de la Déclaration. Elle lui a conféré l'appellation de "Déclaration Universelle", car celle-ci émane de la communauté juridiquement organisée de tous les peuples du monde du genre humain et elle exprime les aspirations communes à tous les hommes').
32   In 1983, in the III Commission of the UN General Assembly the Iranian delegate (Mr Rajaie-Khorassani) stated the following:

'In his delegation's view, the concept of human rights was not limited to the Universal Declaration of Human Rights. Man was of divine origin and human dignity could not be reduced to a series of secular norms. Corruption of all kinds was widespread and must be fought. Although torture, the killing of innocent people and deprivation of freedom could not be tolerated, his delegation saw in those phenomena effects rather than causes. Only when the real causes were examined would it be possible to understand why certain concepts contained in the Universal Declaration of Human Rights needed to be revised.

Some delegations had shown sincere and honest concern at human-rights violations in the Islamic Republic of Iran. Others, through misinformation or ignorance, had levelled baseless allegations. He noted that none of the critics of his country had a 'clean slate' in the annual reports of Amnesty International. Instead of engaging in polemics, he preferred to clarify the difference between the axiological doctrine of the Islamic Republic of Iran and the socio-political values upheld in the Universal Declaration of Human Rights [. . .].

As his delegation had already stated at the thirty-sixth session of the General Assembly, conventions, declaration and resolutions or decisions of international organizations, which were contrary to Islam, had no validity in the Islamic Republic of Iran. If secular States decided, for example, to produce a convention abolishing capital punishment, his country had no objection because it would not be bound at all by such a convention. The Universal Declaration of Human Rights, which represented secular understanding of the Judaeo-Christian tradition, could not be implemented by Muslims and did not accord with the system of values recognized by the Islamic Republic of Iran; his country would therefore not hesitate to violate its provisions, since it had to choose between violating the divine law of the country and violating secular conventions. That did not mean that the allegations made against Iran were true, or that there were no elements in the Universal Declaration of Human

Rights that accorded with Islam. His country was convinced that the Declaration must be respected by all secular and non-Muslim States because the inhuman treatment and degrading practices often reported in El Salvador, Chile and South Africa could not be tolerated. Those who could not live up to the divine standards of Islam should at least meet the minimum requirements established by international organizations, if they did not wish to become centres of corruption, torture, injustice, oppression and tyranny. The Islamic Republic of Iran, which strongly condemned torture, believed that corporal punishment and the death penalty did not fall within the category of torture when carried out on the basis of Islam, in accordance with a sentence by an Islamic court.' (UN doc. A/C.3/39/SR.65, paras 91–2, 95).

33 See GAOR, A/C.3/215, p. 97.
34 See GAOR, A/C.3/215, p. 55 (Brazil); UN General Assembly, 3rd Session, 180th Plenary Meeting, p. 874 (The Netherlands).

For references to a similar proposal made in the General Assembly Third Committee by the Brazilian delegate (and the support it received from The Netherlands, Bolivia, Colombia, Argentina and Lebanon), see I. Morsink, 'The Philosophy of the Universal Declaration' in *Human Rights Quarterly*, vol. 6, 1981, p. 313 and n. 25.

35 See GAOR, A/C.3/215, p. 111.
36 182nd Plenary Meeting (10 December 1948), p. 894.
37 P. Imbert, *L'universalité des droits de l'homme* (paper submitted to the 1989 Strasbourg Colloquy on Universality of Human Rights), p. 5 of the mimeographed text.
38 See Commission on Human Rights, January 1947.
39 General Assembly, 3rd Session, 180th Plenary Meeting, p. 862.
40 H. Lauterpacht, *International Law and Human Rights* (Shoe String, Hamden, 1968, first published 1950), pp. 408–24.

CHAPTER 3 ARE HUMAN RIGHTS TRULY UNIVERSAL?

1 Report of the Commission of 25 January in *Yearbook of the European Convention of Human Rights*, vol. 19, 1976, pp. 513–949, at 792–4.
2 Judgment of 18 January 1978 *Ireland v. United Kingdom, Publications European Court of Human Rights*, Series A, vol. 25 (1978) at pp. 66–7.
3 Judgment of 17 October 1986 *Rees Case, Publications European Court of Human Rights*, Series A, vol. 106 (1987). The Commission's report of 12 December 1984 is annexed to the judgment at p. 23.
4 J. de Maistre, *Considérations sur la France* (1797), ed. P. Manent (Editions Complexe, Paris 1988), p. 87 ('La constitution de 1795, tout comme ses aînées, est fait pour l'homme. Or, il n'y a point d'*homme* dans le monde. J'ai vu, dans ma vie, des Français, des Italiens, des Russes, etc.; je sais même, grâce à Montesquieu, *qu'on peut être Persan*: mais quant à l'*homme*, je déclare ne l'avoir rencontré de ma vie; s'il existe, c'est bien à mon insu').

5   'Le Phénomène de la "Reconaissance Universelle" dans l'Experiénce Humaine' in *Le Fondement des Droits de l'Homme: Actes des Entretiens de l'Aquila 14–19 septembre 1964* (La Nuova Italia, Florence, 1966), pp. 122–5 at p. 122.

6   'De la Liberté des Anciens Comparée à celle des Modernes' in *De la Liberté Chez les Modernes*, pp. 491–515.

7   Ibid. at p. 501.

8   Ibid. at p. 506.

9   Ibid. at p. 495.

10   Ibid. at p. 502.

11   Ibid. at p. 502.

12   See note 30, chapter 2.

13   'Human Rights and Foreign Policy', address at University of Georgia School of Law, 30 April 1977, *Department of State Bulletin*, 23 May 1977, pp. 505 ff.

14   As for Iran, see note 32, chapter 2. It should be stressed that in his speech of 2 February 1990 President de Klerk emphatically stated that South Africa would live up to the general standards on human rights.

15   For the text, see *Human Rights in International Law: basic texts* (Strasbourg: Council of Europe, 1985), pp. 207–25.

16   'Islamic Universal Declaration of Human Rights' declared 19 September 1981 (UNESCO, Paris) by Mr Salem Azzam, Secretary General of the Islamic Council. For the text see *Droits de l'homme et droit des peuples*, Fondation L. Basso pour de Droit et la Libération des peuples (S. Marino, Ministero della Cultura, 1983), pp. 228–38.

17   This declaration is known as the 'Draft Charter on Human and People's Rights in the Arab World' and is reproduced in *Information Sheet No. 21* H/INF (87)1 (Strasbourg: Council of Europe, 1988), Appendix XXXX, pp. 243–61. This draft Charter represents the view of the participants of a Conference held in Syracuse, 5–12 December 1986; however it is based on a draft prepared by the General Administration for Legal Affairs of the Secretariat General of the League of Arab States.

18   It is worth mentioning in this respect the important statement made by President Gorbachev in Rome, on an official visit, on 30 November 1989. He repeatedly stressed the importance of 'eternal moral values, the simple laws of ethics and humanity', which should 'serve as reference points' for the solution of the new tasks which the world is currently facing (p. 4 of the typewritten text of his statement, kindly provided by the Soviet Embassy in Rome; see also ibid. pp. 7, 9, 18). He also stressed that 'the increasing role of the principles common to all of mankind is not obliterating but rather enriching the originality and the role of national and other characteristics' (ibid., p. 5). Another important point made by Gorbachev is that states should strive to attain a 'completely uniform [. . .] understanding and application of international law' (ibid., p. 16).

CHAPTER 4 HOW DOES THE INTERNATIONAL COMMUNITY
REACT TO GENOCIDE?

1   R. Lemkin, *Axis Rule in Occupied Europe* (Washington Carnegie
    Endowment for World Peace, 1944), pp. 75–95.
2   V. N. Dadrian, 'The Role of the Turkish Physicians in the World
    War I Genocide of Ottoman Armenians', in *Holocaust and Genocide
    Studies*, 1986, I, no. 2, pp. 169–92.
3   I. L. Horowitz, *Genocide: State Power and Mass Murder* (Transactions
    Books, New Brunswick, NJ, 1976), p. 73.
4   GA Resolution 260A (111) of 9 December 1948. The Convention
    entered into force on 12 January 1951. For the text of the Convention
    see I. Brownlie, *Basic Documents on Human Rights*, 2nd edn (Clarendon
    Press, Oxford, 1981), pp. 31–4.
5   I. L. Horowitz, *Genocide: State Power and Mass Murder*, p. 38.
6   L. Kuper, *Genocide: Its Political Use in the Twentieth Century* (London,
    Penguin, 1981) p. 101.
7   See the statement made on 19 August 1985 by the Turkish Observer
    in the UN Sub-Commission on Prevention of Discrimination and
    Protection of Minorities, in UN Doc. E/CN.4/Sub.2/1985/SR.21, p.
    5, para. 21.
8   See L. Kuper, *International Action against Genocide*, Minority Rights
    Group, Report no. 53, 1984, p. 5.
9   See N. Lewis, 'The Camp at Cecilio Baez', in R. Arens (ed.), *Genocide
    in Paraguay* (Temple University Press, Philadelphia, 1976), pp. 62–3.
10 See *International Legal Materials*, vol. 28, 1989, p. 77.
11 L. Oppenheim and H. Lauterpacht, *International Law – A Treatise*, vol.
    1, 8th edn (Longmans, London, 1955), p. 751.
12 N. Lewis, 'The Camp at Cecilio Baez', in *Genocide in Paraguay*, pp.
    62–3.
13 See the statement made on 19 August 1985 in the UN Sub-
    Commission on Prevention of Discrimination and Protection of
    Minorities by Mrs Tuckman, representative of Minority Rights
    Group in UN doc. E/CN.4/Sub.2/1985/SR.20, p. 4, para. 17.
14 UN Doc. S/4383 July 13 1960; see also B. Urquhart, *Hammarskjöld*
    (Bodley Head, London, 1972), p. 438.
15 Ibid.
16 UN Doc. S/4482, para. 12.
17 Security Council, *Official Records*, 896th meeting, 9/10 September
    1960, S/PV.896, para. 101.
18 G. Abi-Saab, *The United Nations Operations in the Congo 1960–1964*
    (OUP, Oxford, 1978), p. 58.
19 Security Council, *Official Records*, 896th meeting, 9/10 September
    1960, para. 102.
20 Ibid.
21 I understand from a reliable source that Ali Bhutto, then Prime
    Minister of Pakistan, had indicated to Bangladeshi leaders that trying

the Pakistani soldiers would have had serious psychological and political repercussions within Pakistan, endangering the attempt at restoring democracy in which Bhutto was engaged; the Bangladeshi authorities felt, after much vacillation, that it would be better to have a democratic Pakistan as interlocutor than to punish those guilty of the massacres, and therefore went along with Bhutto's request.

22   The report was discussed but not adopted at the 36th session of the Commission on Human Rights in 1980, UN Doc. E/CN.4/1335.

23   For the Vietnamese contention that their intervention was justified by the need to protect the Khmer population from genocide, see the speech by Mr Phon Hien to the General Assembly, 28 September 1979, *Official Records* 34th session, 14th plenary meeting, at p. 264, para. 203: 'Since the days when the Pol Pot regime committed genocide against its own people, it has become a renegade, and the United Front for the National Salvation of Kampuchea, which rose up to overthrow it and to save the Kampuchean people, represents revolutionary legality. Hence it is fully in keeping with international law and the United Nations Charter for Viet Nam to lend its support to this just struggle'.

24   Resolution adopted at the 539th meeting, May 27, 1977 (41st Session) reproduced in T. Buergenthal and R. Norris *Human Rights and the Inter-American System* (Oceana, Dobbs Ferry, New York, 1984), Booklet 20, p. 6.

25   GA Resolution 37/123D of 16 December 1982.

26   'Sabra and Shatila' in A. Cassese, *Violence and Law in the Modern Age* (Polity Press, Cambridge, 1988), pp. 76–87 at pp. 82 ff.

27   It is worth mentioning, as an illustration of steps taken by national authorities in cases of genocide, without any real follow-up in or by international organizations, the statement made in 1972 in Parliament by the French Foreign Minister, in reply to a question by an MP concerning the French official action, if any, taken with regard to acts of genocide in Burundi. He said the following.

'En dépit de son constant souci de ne pas s'ingérer dans les affaires intérieures des autre pays et compte tenu de la gravité particulière de la situation qui se développait au Burundi, le Gouvernement a, dès le début de la crise évoquée par l'honorable parlementaire, fait approcher par notre ambassadeur à Bujumbura le colonel Micombero, chef de l'Etat, et lui a fait marquer tout le prix que nous attachions à l'intervention d'une solution d'apaisement. Notre ambassadeur est intervenu par la suite et dans la même préoccupation, tant auprès du ministère des affaires étrangères que du commandant des forces armées burundaises. Instruction lui a été donnée d'autre part de s'associer à toutes démarches collectives entreprises par les chefs de missions diplomatiques accrédités à Usumbura. A Paris même, le ministère des affaires étrangères a fait diligence dans le même sens auprès de l'ambassadeur du Burundi. Enfin, comme le sait l'honorable parlementaire, à l'issue du conseil des ministres du 31 mai, le porte-parole du Gouvernement a fait état de la vive émotion suscitée en France par les événements survenus au Burundi. A la suite de ces démarches, nous avons reçu des autorités d'Usumbura l'assurance qu'une action pacificatrice serait entreprise en vue d'un retour rapide à une situation normale.' (*Annuaire français de droit international*, 1973, pp. 1064–5).

28 General Assembly, *Official Records*, 34th session, 14th plenary meeting at p. 270, paras. 12–13.

29 This last case was what happened in Bangladesh in 1971 (India sent in its armed forces), in Uganda in 1979 (Idi Amin's regime which had since 1971 been severely violating human rights and committing acts of genocide, among other things, was overthrown following invasion by the armed forces of Tanzania), in Cambodia (the Pol Pot regime was put to flight following invasion by the armed forces of Vietnam in 1978), and in Sri Lanka (the reciprocal massacres between Singhalese and Tamils were attenuated following conclusion of an agreement between Sri Lanka and India providing for guarantees by India in favour of the Tamil minority).

CHAPTER 5 THE SAVAGE STATES: TORTURE IN THE 1980S

1 A. Mitscherlich, *Die Idee des Friedens und die menschliche Aggressivität Vier Versuche* (Suhrkamp Verlag, Frankfurt, 1969), p. 99.

2 S. Milgram, 'Some Conditions of Obedience and Disobedience to Authority', *Human Relations* 18 (1965), p. 75.

3 C. Beccaria, *Dei delitti e delle pene* (1764), ed. G. Francioni (Mediobanca, Milano 1984), pp. 65–6.

4 Montesquieu, *Esprit des lois* ed. V. Goldschmidt, (Garnier – Flammarion, Paris, 1979), vol. I, p. 220 (Book VI, chapter XVII). See also pp. 209–10 (Book VI, chapter IX); Voltaire, 'Commentaire sur le livre des délits et des peines par un avocat de province' (1766), in *Mélanges* (Pléiade, Gallimard, Paris 1961), p. 789.

5 H. Alleg, *La Question* (Editions de Minuit, Paris, 1957).

6 A. London, *L'Aveu – Dans l'engrenage du procès de Prague* (Gallimard, Paris, 1968).

7 F. Neumann, *Behemoth: The Structure and Practice of National Socialism* (Oxford University Press, 2nd edn. Oxford, 1944), pp. 365–9. See also, by the same author, *The Democratic and Authoritarian State* (Falcon Wing Press, Glengoe, Illinois, 1957) and *The Rule of Law, Political Theory and the Legal System in Modern Society*, (Berg, Heidelberg-Dover (US), 1986) especially pp. 286–98.

8 Resolution 3452 (XXX) of 9 December 1975 adopting the Declaration on the Protection of All Persons from Being Subjected to

Torture and Other Cruel, Inhuman or Degrading Treatment or Punishment.

9   Convention against Torture .and Other Cruel, Inhuman or Degrading Treatment or Punishment. GA Resolution 39/46 of 10 December 1984, in force 26 June 1987, reproduced in *Human rights in international law – basic texts* (Council of Europe, Strasbourg, 1985) pp. 84–100.

10 Convention for the Protection of Human Rights and Fundamental Freedoms, signed in Rome 4 November 1950, in force 3 September 1953, for text see *Human rights in international law – basic texts* (Council of Europe, Strasbourg, 1985) pp. 101–39.

11 Report of the Commission of 25 January 1976, *Publications of the European Court of Human Rights*, Series B, no. 23–I, *Case of Ireland against the United Kingdom*, pp. 8–673.

12 Judgment of 25 April 1978, *Publications of the European Court of Human Rights*, Series A, vol. 25 (1978), pp. 66–7.

13 Report of the Commission of 10 July 1976. For the decision on admissibility see *Yearbook of the European Convention on Human Rights* (hereafter *Yearbook*), vol. 18, p. 82.

14 *The Greek Case*, Report of the Commission, 5 November 1969 and Resolution DH(70)1 of the Committee of Ministers, *Yearbook*, vol. 12, pp. 131–2. Note also the applications by Greece in 1956 and 1957 against the United Kingdom alleging the use of whipping and other collective punishment in Cyprus, declared admissible by the Commission, *Yearbook*, Vol. 2, pp. 182, 186.

15 See *France, Norway, Denmark, Sweden, Netherlands against Turkey*: Report of the Commission of 7 December 1985. This case ended in a friendly settlement; however, the Commission's report notes 'that the Government of Turkey have during the proceedings informed the Commission in particular of criminal prosecutions and convictions concerning cases of torture' (para. 41).

16 *Amekrane* v. *United Kingdom*, *Yearbook*, vol. 16, p. 357.

17 Report of the Commission, 14 December 1976, *Publication of the European Court of Human Rights*, Series B, vol. 24, p. 25, para. 39.

18 *Tyrer Case* Judgment of 25 April 1978, *Publications of the European Court of Human Rights*, Series A, vol. 26 (1978).

19 *Soering Case*, 7 July 1989, Series A, vol. 161, para. 111.

20 *Baader, Meins, Meinhoff and Grundmann* v. *Federal Republic of Germany*, *Yearbook*, vol. 18, p. 132.

21 *Ensslin, Baader, and Raspe* v. *Federal Republic of Germany*, *Decisions and Reports*, vol. 14, p. 64.

22 Report adopted 7 October 1981, *Decisions and Reports*, vol. 32, p. 5.

23 Report adopted 16 December 1982, *Decisions and Reports*, vol. 34, p. 24.

24 Report adopted 8 December 1982, *Decisions and Reports*, vol. 33, p. 41.

25 *R* v. *Denmark*, *Decisions and Reports*, vol. 41, p. 149.

26 *Maxine and Karen Warwick* v. *United Kingdom*, Report of the Commission, adopted 18 July 1986.
27 At para.56 of the Report.
28 At para.55 of the Report.
29 See the report of the Commission, adopted on 18 July 1986, p. 16 (paras 86–8).
30 Ibid., pp. 19–21.
31 See resolution DH(89) 5, in Council of Europe, Human Rights, *Information Sheet* no. 24, Strasbourg 1989, pp. 78–9.
32 Council of Europe Doc. H(87)4 reprinted in 27 *International Legal Materials* (1988) p. 1152. For more details see A. Cassese 'A New Approach to Human Rights: The European Convention for the Prevention of Torture' in *American Journal of International Law*, 83 (1989), p. 128ff.
33 See 672 Federal Supplement 1531 (N.D.C. 1987), p. 1535ff., in particular p. 1541 (on torture) and p. 1543 (on 'cruel, inhuman and degrading treatment'). The reasons for rejecting this last claim were twofold. First, 'Plantiffs do not cite, and the Court is not aware of, such evidence of universal consensus regarding the right to be free from "cruel, inhuman and degrading treatment" as exists, for example, with respect to official torture'. The second reason was that 'any such right poses problems of definability. The difficulties for a district court in adjudicating such a claim are manifest. Because this right lacks readily ascertainable parameters, it is unclear what behaviour falls within the proscription'. The Court so concluded: 'Lacking the requisite elements of universality and definability, this proposed tort cannot qualify as a violation of the law of nations'. This holding was confirmed by the Court in its subsequent decision on the same case, of July 25, 1988 (in 694 Federal Supplement 707 (N.D.C. 1988), pp. 711–12).
34 'Front-Line National Judges and International Law' in A. Cassese, *Violence and Law in the Modern Age* (Polity Press, Cambridge, 1988) pp. 149–71 at pp. 156–63 (Filartiga) and pp. 166–8 (Siderman).
    For the text of the two judgments see *Filartiga* v. *Peña-Irala* 630 F. 2d 876 (2d Circ. 1980) and *Siderman* v. *Republic of Argentina*, CV82–1772–RMT(MCx) (CD Cal. 7 March 1980).
35 B. Brecht, *Kalendergeschichten* (1953) (Rowohlt Verlag, Hamburg, 1988), p. 104.
36 A. Camus, *Essais* (La Pléiade, Gallimard, Paris, 1965), p. 352.

CHAPTER 6 DESCENT INTO HELL: NOTES ON APARTHEID

1 L. Kuper, *Genocide – Its Political Use in the Twentieth Century* (Yale University Press, New Haven and London, 1981), pp. 198–9.
2 Old Synagogue Court, Pretoria, 15 October to 7 November 1962. There were two counts: inciting persons to strike illegally (during the 1961 stay-at-home); and leaving the country without a valid

passport. The quotations are taken from Nelson Mandela *The Struggle is My Life* (revised edition) (International Defence and Aid Fund for Southern Africa, London, 1986).

3   *Nelson Mandela*, p. 152.
4   G. Chaliand, *Où va l'Afrique du Sud?* (Calman-Lévy, Paris, 1986), p. 27.
5   *Part of My Soul Winnie Mandela*, ed. Anne Benjamin (Penguin, Harmondsworth, 1985), pp. 102–3.
6   Resolution 418 (1977) adopted by the Security Council at its 2046th meeting on 4 November 1977. Paragraph 2 reads [the Security Council] *Decides* that all States shall cease forthwith any provision to South Africa of arms and related material of all types . . . '. Reproduced at p. 1548 of *International Legal Materials*, vol. 16.
7   GA Resolution 3068 (XXVIII) of 30 November 1973, in force 18 July 1976, for text see *International Legal Materials*, vol. 13 (1974), p. 50.
8   G. Scelle, *Manuel de droit international public* (Editions Domat – Montchrestien, Paris 1948), p. 6 ('les règles de droit [. . .] viennent [. . .] de la conjonction de l'éthique et du pouvoir').
9   Mandela chose not to give evidence in his own defence or be cross-examined, but only to make a statement. The Statement made in Pretoria Supreme Court, 20 April 1964 is quoted at pp. 161ff. of *Nelson Mandela*.
10   *Nelson Mandela*, p. 176.
11   Resolution 569 (1985) reproduced in 24 *International Legal Materials* 1985, p. 1483.
12   Declaration of 27 June 1986 reproduced in *European Political Cooperation Documentation Bulletin*, edited by the European Policy Unit at the European University Institute (Florence) and Institut für Europäische Politik (Bonn), 1986, vol. 2, no. 1 at pp. 205–6.
13   R. S. McNamara, 'South Africa Threatens to be the Middle East of the 1990s', *International Herald Tribune*, 25 October 1982, p. 5.

CHAPTER 7 THE 'FORCED DISAPPEARANCES' IN ARGENTINA: BARBARISM AND AFTER

1   Interamerican Court of Human Rights, Series C., *Decisions and Judgments*, no. 4, paras 96–108.
2   *La noche de los lapices* (Buenos Aires: Editorial Contrapunto 1986), Italian transl. by A. Riccio, *La Notte dei Lapis* (Editori Riuniti, Rome, 1987). I shall translate here from the Italian version, for I have been unable to get hold of the original text.
3   *La Notte dei Lapis*, p. 113.
4   Ibid. at p. 117.
5   Ibid. at p. 132.
6   Ibid. at p. 132.
7   Ibid. at p. 155.

8 See the English translation in *International Legal Materials*, 1987, p. 344.

9 Resolutions and Decisions adopted by the Sub-Commission at its twenty-ninth Session, 767th meeting, 30 August 1976. E/CN.4/Sub.2/378, p. 44.

10 GA Resolution 33/173 on 'Disappeared Persons' adopted 20 December 1978 at 90th Plenary Session.

11 The draft resolution was adopted by 8 votes to 1, with 8 abstentions (UN doc. E/CN.4/Sub.2/378, p. 20, para. 72). The resolution was as follows: '*The Sub-Commission on Prevention of Discrimination and Protection of Minorities.*

Deeply concerned at reports from which it appears that basic human rights and fundamental freedoms are at present in jeopardy in Argentina,

Alarmed that the situation disclosed by such reports appears to reveal in particular that in Argentina the life, liberty and security of fugitives from other countries in the region are threatened by groups over which the Government seems to have no control,

Reaffirming the importance of article 3 of the Universal Declaration of Human Rights, which states that 'everyone has the right to life, liberty and security of person',

Recalling with respect the leading role traditionally played by Latin American countries in the progressive development at the national and international level of the highest standards for the protection of human rights and fundamental freedoms, in particular the role played by Latin American countries in the development of the notion and practice of the right of asylum.

1 *Expresses the hope* that international standards on human rights will be respected for the benefit of all now deprived of their human rights and fundamental freedoms;

2 *Appeals* to Governments to offer resettlement, in conformity with the call made on 22 June 1976 by the United Nations High Commissioner for Refugees, to persons who now have refuge in Argentina;

3 *Asks* the Secretary-General to request the United Nations High Commissioner for Refugees to make his report to the General Assembly available to the Commission on Human Rights in advance of its next session, with any additional information he may have on developments relating to the matters referred to in the present resolution.'

12 See *International Legal Materials*, 1987, p. 334.

13 *Nunca Más – Informe de la Comisión Nacional Sobre la Desparición de personas*, 14 edn (Editorial Universitaria de Buenos Aires, Buenos Aires, 1986).

14   Para. 99 of the judgment. For the English translation see p. 383 of *Human Rights Law Journal*, vol. 8, no. 2–4 (1987).

15   See the whole printed text of the judgment in *El Diario del Juicio* vol. 2, nos 33–6, (January 1986). For a partial English translation, see *International Legal Materials* (1987), pp. 331–72 as well as *Human Rights Law Journal*, vol. 8, nos 2–4, (1987) at pp. 368–430.

16   *Revista de Jurisprudencia Argentina*, no. 5513, 29 April 1987. For an English translation see *Human Rights Law Journal*, nos 2–4, (1987) at pp. 430–44.

17   The record of the proceedings exceeds 20,000 pages with the Court's judgment running to over 1000 pages.

18   See the typewritten text (to the best of my knowledge, the judgment is still unpublished).

19   Law No. 14029 of 4 July 1951, *XI Anuario de Legislación Argentina* 4 (1951). Selected Articles in English can be found in *Human Rights Law Journal*, vol. 8, nos 2–4, (1987), pp. 473–4.

20   *XLIV-A Anuario de Legislación Argentina* 8 (1984). Selected Articles can be found in English in *Human Rights Law Journal*, vol. 8, nos 2–4, (1987), p. 475.

21   Law No. 23521, *Anales de Legislación y de Jurisprudencia Argentina*, no. 335, June 1987. Reproduced at p. 477 of *Human Rights Law Journal*, vol. 8, nos 2–4 (1987).

22   13 May 1987, Press release of the Presidency of the Argentinian Republic.

23   *Trial of the Major War Criminals before the International Military Tribunal*, Nuremberg, 14 November 1945–1 October 1946, *Official Documents*, vol. I (Nuremberg, 1947), p. 219.

24   See my book *Violence and Law in the Modern Age* (Polity Press, Cambridge, 1988), pp. 119ff.

25   Published in *El Derecho*, nos. 6790–4, 31 July–6 August, 1987. An abbreviated English version can be found in *Human Rights Law Journal*, vol. 8, nos 2–4 (1987), pp. 441–71.

26   'Les militaries coupables de violations des droits de l'homme sont libérés', *Le Monde*, 27 June 1987, p. 5.

CHAPTER 8 A 'CONTRIBUTION' BY THE WEST TO THE STRUGGLE AGAINST HUNGER: THE NESTLÉ AFFAIR

1   See M. Muller, *The Baby Killer*, a study sponsored by *War on Want* (London, 1974).

2   See Arbeitsgruppe Dritte Welt Bern, *Flaschenpost* (Information zum Ehrverletzungsprozess Nestlé Alimentana SA gegen Arbeitsgruppe Dritte Welt), no date, p. 4.
      For more up-to-date information see P. Harrison, *L'empire Nestlé* (Editions Favre, Paris, 1983); J. C. Buffle, *N. . . comme Nestlé* (Editions A. Moreau, Paris, 1986).

3   See   Schweizerische   Arbeitsgruppen   für   Entwicklungspolitik

(SAFEP), *Nestlé-Prozess beendet-Auseinandersetzung geht weiter*, no. 3 (Bern, December 1976), p. 6.

I should like to express my gratitude to the Swiss Justice Department for providing me with all the issues of these periodicals, as well as other documents relating to the Nestlé case.

4 See the typescript of the unpublished text, in German, of the judgment (the pagination is unclear; the text of the decision and of the reasons runs to 35 pages). The translation is mine.

I should like to thank Dr K. Schnyder, Vice-President of Nestlé, for providing me with the original text of the judgment.

On the facts surrounding the trial see also *Nestlé contre les bébés? Un dossier réuni par la Groupe de Travail Tiers Monde de Berne* (Editions F. Maspéro and Presses Universitaires de Grenoble, Paris, 1978).

5 Schweizerische Arbeitsgruppen für Entwicklungspolitik (SAFEP), *Rundbrief, Sondernummer zum Nestlé-Prozess* (Bern, August, 1976), p. 11.

6 The letter of Dr Führer is reproduced as Annex B to *Nestlé-Prozess beeendet - Auseinandersetzung geht weiter.*

7 For the information given in the text see *Nestlé-Prozess beendet – Auseinandersetzung geht weiter.*, pp. 4–5; *Solidarisme* (January, 1979), pp. 31–3; J. C. Buffle, *N. . . comme Nestlé*, pp. 87ff.

8 See E. Helsing and J. Cartwright Taylor, 'WHO and the Right to Food: Infant Nutrition Policy as a Test Case', in A. Eide, W. B. Eide, S. Goonatilake *et al.* (eds), *Food as a Human Right* (The UN Library, Tokyo 1984), pp. 223–32.

9 M. L. Bouguerra, *Les poisons du Tiers Monde* (Editions La Découverte, Paris 1985).

CHAPTER 9 THE VALUE OF HUMAN RIGHTS IN THE CONTEMPORARY WORLD

1 Voltaire, *Romans et contes*, ed. H. Bénac (Editions Garnier, Paris, 1960), p. 80.

2 G. Sorel, *Réflexions sur la violence* (1908) (Editions Ressources, Paris-Geneva, 1981). p. 149.

3 M. Robespierre, Speech of 2–11 Jan. 1792, in M. Robespierre, *Ecrits*, ed. C. Mazaurac (Messidor/Editions Sociales, Paris, 1989), p. 163 ('Personne n'aime les missionaires armés').

4 J. Hamburger, paper submitted in 1988 to the Council of Europe's Strasbourg colloquy on the Universality of Human Rights, typescript, pp. 1–3. He rightly pointed out that human rights cannot be defined 'droits naturels' in the sense that they derive from nature, for nature is inspired by principles and rules utterly contrary to the very concept of human rights: 'Le concept des droits de l'homme n'est pas inspiré par la loi naturelle de la vie, il est au contraire rébellion contre la loi naturelle' (p. 2).

5 W. Wilson proposed from the outset that admission to the League

be only granted to 'states whose government is based upon the principle of popular self-government' (see Wilson's second, third and fourth Drafts in D. H. Miller, *The Drafting of the Covenant*, vol. II (G. P. Putnam's Sons, New York-London, 1928), pp. 85, 103 and 151). The French Draft stipulated that 'no nations can be admitted to the League other than those which are constituted as States and provided with representative institutions such as will permit their being themselves considered responsible for the acts of their own Governments' (ibid., p. 239; see also p. 261). For a discussion of the French proposal and the final agreement on the formula of 'fully self-governing' states, see ibid., p. 293 (and p. 461 for the French version) and p. 303. For a Belgian proposal similar to the French one, see ibid., p. 520.

6   Cf. D. Schindler, 'Wechselwirkungen zwischen der inneren Struktur des Staates und der internationalen Ordnung' in *Festschrift für Kurt Eichenberger* (Basle, 1982), p. 78.

CHAPTER 10 THE IMPACT OF HUMAN RIGHTS ON THE INTERNATIONAL COMMUNITY

1   UN document E/600, *Report to the Economic and Social Council on the Second Session of the Commission. Held at Geneva, from 2 to 17 December 1947*, at p. 20 para. 5.

2   Council of Europe, press release no. D(86)18 (17 October 1986), p. 4.

3   The Judgment can be found in *Entscheidungen des Schweizerischen Bundesgerichts*, 1982, vol. 108, pp. 408–13. For another case see *Europäische Grundrechte Zeitschrift*, 1983, pp. 253–6.

4   *Barcelona Traction, Light and Power Co. Ltd*, in *International Court of Justice Reports, 1970*, p. 32, para. 34.

5   These various statements were made with regard to the Leticia case (in breach of a treaty with Colombia, of 1922, providing for the cession of the Leticia area to Colombia, Peruvians occupied Leticia on 1st September 1932). In the League of Nations the representative of Peru stated among other things the following: 'We say: A treaty which is immoral, and which has been drawn up in certain circumstances, may be surrounded with every sort of legal guarantee and will yet lead to war. Colombia tells you: "We cannot yield; we have a treaty". We say: "This treaty has done us an injury; it sanctioned, in time of peace, without any real compensation, the cession of a hundred thousand kilometers of Peruvian territory. Moreover, the treaty was imposed upon us by a [Peruvian] dictator" . . . Treaties must be respected if international life is to run smoothly. Peace must also be maintained. But immoral treaties disturb peace. Otherwise, the dilemma might arise: Law or peace? We say: Law and peace together; and are fully confident that you will, for this purpose, discover some form of conciliation'. (League of Nations, *Official Journal*, April 1933, pp. 504 and 506). After the criticisms of the

Colombian delegate (see ibid., p. 506), the French representative (Mr Pierre Cot) pointed out the following: 'If the Council [of the League of Nations] were to accept this theory that there are two kinds of treaties, immoral treaties and reputable treaties, where should we find ourselves next? For my part, I am afraid that people are coming a little too easily to consider that reputable treaties are those that give them satisfaction and immoral treaties are those that do not . . . [W]hat we must all understand, what we must all declare, in pursuance of the duty that devolves upon us when we sit at the table of the Council of the League, is that it is in no case possible, when a treaty exists between two States, for one of those States to release itself from the bonds of that treaty by an act of its own pure volition' (Ibid., p. 510).

6 See my book *International Law in a Divided World* (Clarendon Press, Oxford, 1986), pp. 208–11.

7 For the elimination of damage from the concept of State responsibility, see UN International Law Commission, *Yearbook 1970*, vol. II, pp. 194–5, paras, 53–4. More recently, in his report to the ILC, the new special rapporteur, Prof. G. Arangio-Ruiz has drawn a distinction between 'moral damage' that is indemnifiable by pecuniary compensation 'and "moral damage" to the State, which is more exclusively typical of international relations, and is a matter for *satisfaction* in a technical sense': International law Commission, 41st Session *Second Report on State responsibility*, UN doc. A/CN.4/425, 9 June 1989, p. 16.

8 Spinoza, *Tractatus Politicus*, ed. P. F. Moreau (Editions Réplique, Paris, 1979), p. 14 (chapter 1, para. 6).

CHAPTER 11 WHAT SHOULD WE DO?

1 Personal correspondence from Norberto Bobbio to the author.

2 'The State's Positive Role in World Affairs', *Daedalus – Journal of the American Academy of Arts and Sciences* (1979), p. 108.

3 T. Campanella, 'Politica in Aphorismos Digesta', in *Aforismi politici*, ed. by L. Firpo (G. Giappichelli, Torino, 1941), p. 177 (Cajent IX, n. 2).

4 F. Kafka, *Der Prozess* (1925) (S. Fischer Verlag, Frankfurt, 1953), p. 272; English translation by W. and E. Muir (Penguin, 1955), p. 250.

APPENDIX 1 THE UNIVERSAL DECLARATION OF HUMAN RIGHTS (1948)

1 Text reproduced from *Human Rights: A Compilation of International Instruments*, U.N., New York, 1983.

APPENDIX 2 THE MAIN INTERNATIONAL ORGANIZATIONS ACTIVE IN THE FIELD OF HUMAN RIGHTS: A PRACTICAL GUIDE

1 For more details on the structure and functions of these various organs, see E. Schwell and P. Alston, 'The Principal Institutions and other Bodies Founded under the Charter', in K. Vasak (ed.), *The Interntional Dimensions of Human Rights*, I (Greenwood Press and Unesco, Westport and Paris), 1982, pp. 245ff. For a recent assessment, see T. J. Farer, 'The UN and Human Rights: More than a Whimper, Less than a Roar', in A. Roberts and B. Kingsbury (eds), *United Nations, Divided World* (OUP, Oxford).

2 With headquarters in Geneva: Palais des Nations, CH-1211 Geneva 10; tel. 022-310211 or 346011.

3 At the time of writing every Contracting State has accepted Article 25 except Finland.

4 See Council of Europe, ECHR, *Stock-taking on the European Convention on Human Rights*, Suppl. 1987 (Strasbourg, 1988), pp. 84ff.

5 For further details about the United Kingdom and the Charter, see A. Jaspers and L. Betten (eds) *25 Years European Social Charter* (Kluwer, Deventer, 1988) pp. 27–51.

6 The English text can be found in *International Legal Materials* vol. XXI, 1982, pp. 58–68.

7 Including Algeria, Libya, Mali, Mauritania, Nigeria, Somalia, Tunisia, Uganda and Tanzania; for a complete list of Contracting States, see Council of Europe, Information Sheet no. 21 (Strasbourg, 1988), p. 120.

8 See OAU, *Rapport d'activité de la Commission Africaine des Droits de l'Homme et des Peuples*, 1988, OAU Doc. AHF/155-XXV (Annexes).

   A good description of the African Charter can be found in N. Selasini Rembe, *Africa and Regional Protection of Human Rights*, edited by the Centro per la cooperazione giuridica internazionale (Leoni editore, Rome, 1985), pp. 80ff.; in an appendix one can find various important documents, including the Charter itself on pp. 165–77, as well as a bibliography. A more complete and up-to-date work is E. G. Bello's *The African Charter on Human and Peoples' Rights. A Legal Analysis*, in Hague Academy of International Law, *Collected Courses*, 1985–V. vol. 194, pp. 21–268: this also contains the text of the Charter, on pp. 226–39.

Select Bibliography

1 GENERAL WORKS

Alston, P., 'A Third Generation of Solidarity Rights: Progressive Development or Obfuscation of International Human Rights Law', in *Netherlands International Law Review*, 1982, pp. 307ff.

Andrews, J. A. and Hines, W. D., *Keyguide to Information Sources on the International Protection of Human Rights*, Mansell Publishing, London, 1987.

Bereis, P., *Pour de nouveaux droits de l'homme*, Editions J. C. Lattès, Paris, 1985.

Bettati, M. and Kouchner, B. (eds.), *Le devoir d'ingérence*, Editions Denoel, Paris, 1987.

Cranston, M., *What are Human Rights?*, Bodley Head, London, 1973.

D'Amato, A., 'The Concept of Human Rights in International Law', in *Columbia Law Review*, 1982, pp. 1110ff.

Davies, P. (ed.), *Human Rights*, Routledge and Kegan Paul, London and New York, 1988.

Fondation L. Basso pour le Droit et la Libération des peuples, *Droits de l'homme et droits des peuples*, S. Marino, ministero della Cultura, 1983.

Hannum, H. (ed.), *Guide to International Human Rights Practice*, University of Pennsylvania Press, Philadelphia, Pa., 1984.

Henkin, L., *The Rights of Man Today*, Westview Press, Boulder, Colorado, 1978.

Henkin, L., 'Human Rights', in R. Bernhardt (ed.), *Encyclopedia of Public International Law*, vol. 8, 1985, pp. 268–74.

Hoffman, S., *Duties Beyond Borders*, Syracuse University Press, Syracuse, NY, 1981.

Hoffman, S., 'Reaching for the Most Difficult: Human Rights as a Foreign Policy Goal', in *Daedalus – Journal of the American Academy of Arts and Sciences*, 1983, pp. 19ff.

Meron, T. (ed.), *Human Rights in International Law: Legal and Policy Issues*, 2 vols, OUP, Oxford, 1984.

Meron, T., *Human Rights and Humanitarian Norms as Customary Law*, Clarendon Press, Oxford, 1989.

Ramcharan, B. G. (ed.), *Human Rights: Thirty Years after the Universal Declaration*, Nijhoff, The Hague and Boston, 1979.

Rivero, J., *Les libertés publiques*, I, 'Les Droits de l'Homme', Presses Universitaires de France, Paris, 1984, 4th edn, pp. 43–138.

Robertson, A., *Human Rights in the World*, Manchester University Press, Manchester, 1982, 2nd edn.

Sieghart, P., *The International Law of Human Rights*, OUP, Oxford, 1983.

Sieghart, P., *The Lawful Rights of Mankind*, OUP, Oxford, 1986.

Sperduti, G., 'La personne humaine et le droit international', in *Annuaire français de droit international*, 1961, pp. 141ff.

Sudre, F., *Droit international et européen des droits de l'homme*, Presses Universitaires de France, Paris, 1989.

Thierry, H., Combacau, J., Sur, S., and Vallée, C., *Droit international public*, Editions Monchréstien, Paris, 1984, 4th edn, pp. 453–89.

Vallat, F. (ed.), *An Introduction to Human Rights*, Europa, London, 1972.

Vasak, K. (ed.), *The International Dimension of Human Rights*, 2 vols, Greenwood Press, Westport (USA) and Unesco, Paris, 1982.

Weston, B. H., Lukes, R. A., and Hnatt, K. M., 'Regional Human Rights Regimes: A Comparison and Appraisal', in *Vanderbilt Journal of Transnational Law*, 1987, pp. 585–637.

2   COLLECTIONS OF DOCUMENTS

Brownlie, I., *Documents on Human Rights*, OUP, Oxford, 1983, 3rd edn.

Centre for Human Rights, Geneva, *Status of International Instruments on Human Rights*, United Nations, New York, 1987.

Council of Europe, *Human Rights in International Law. Basic Texts*, Strasbourg, 1985.

Laqueur, W. and Rubin, B. (eds), *The Human Rights Reader*, New American Library, New York, 1979.

Lillich, R. B. and Newman, F. C. (eds), *International Human Rights*, Little, Brown and Co., Boston, 1979.

Sohn, L. and Buergenthal, T. (eds), *International Protection of Human Rights*, 2 vols, Bobbs-Merrill Co., Indianapolis, Ind., 1973.

3   IDEOLOGIES, RELIGION AND HUMAN RIGHTS

General

Ebbinghaus, J., 'Le système Kantien des droits de l'homme et du citoyen dans sa signification historique et actuelle', in *Le fondement des droits de l'homme: Actes des entretiens de l'Aquila* 14–19 Septembre 1964, La Nuova Italia, Florence, 1966, pp. 49–57.

Friedmann, F. G., 'Les droits de l'homme à la lumière de l'anthropologie des civilisations', in *Cadmos*, 1983, pp. 3–14.

Hyppolite, J., 'Le phénomène de la "Reconnaissance universelle" dans l'expérience humaine', *Le fondement des droits de l'homme: Actes des entretiens de l'Aquila*, pp. 122–5.

Klein, Z., *La notion de dignité humaine dans la pensée de Kant et de Pascal*, Librairie philosophique J. Vrin, Paris, 1968.

Löwith, K., 'Human Rights in Rousseau, Hegel and Marx', *Le fondement des droits de l'homme*, pp. 58–68.

Raphael, D. D. (ed.), *Political Theory and the Rights of Man*, Macmillan, London, 1967.
Rosenbaum, A. S. (ed.), *The Philosophy of Human Rights*, Aldwych Press, London, 1981.

Religion and human rights

Aziz Said, A., 'Precept and Practice of Human Rights in Islam', in *Universal Human Rights. A Comparative and International Journal of the Social Sciences, Philosophy and Law*, I, 1979, pp. 63–79.
Dupuy, B., 'Les sources et les orientations actuelles de la réflexion chrétienne sur les droits de l'homme', in *Cadmos*, 1983, pp. 15–27.
Henkin, L., 'Judaism and Human Rights', in *Judaism: A Quarterly Journal of Jewish Life and Thought*, vol. 25, 1976, pp. 437ff.
Nawaz, M. K., 'The Concept of Human Rights in Islamic Law', in *Howard Law Journal*, 1965, pp. 325–32.
Santucci, R., *Le regard de l'Islam*, in *Cadmos*, 1983, pp. 28–42.
Various contributions, on this theme, are in Unesco, *Human Rights Teaching, Biannual Bulletin*, vol. II, 1981, no. 1, pp. 3–37.

Marxism and human rights

Bianco, L., 'Les droits de l'homme et la Chine', in *Cadmos*, 1983, pp. 43–57.
Bloch, E., *Naturrecht und menschliche Würde*, Suhrkamp Verlag, Frankfurt, 1961, (French transl.: *Droit naturel et dignité humaine*, Payot, Paris, 1976).
Cornell, D., 'Should a Marxist Believe in Rights?', *Praxis International*, 1984, pp. 45ff.
Kolakowski, L., 'Marxism and Human Rights', in *Daedalus – Journal of the American Academy of Arts and Sciences*, 1983, pp. 81ff.
Lefort, C., *L'invention démocratique: les limites de la domination totalitaire*, Fayard, Paris, 1981.
Lukes, S., 'Can a Marxist believe in Human Rights?' in *Praxis International*, 1982, pp. 334ff.
Lukes, S., *Marxism and Morality*, OUP, Oxford, 1987, pp. 61–99.
Movcham, A. P., 'The Human Rights Problem in Present-Day International Law', in G. Tunkin (ed.), *Contemporary International Law*, Progress Publishers, Moscow, 1969, pp.233–50.

4 THE PROTECTION OF HUMAN RIGHTS: THE HISTORICAL SETTING

Boutmy, E., 'La Déclaration des Droits de l'Homme et M. Jellinek', in *Annales de Sciences Politiques*, 1902, vol. XVII, pp. 415–43.
Jellinek, G., *Die Erklaerung der Menschen- und Buergerrechte*, Berlin 1902; this monograph, which is very important but difficult to find, was reprinted by R. Schnur (ed.), *Zur Geschichte der Erklaerung der Menschenrechte*,

Darmstadt, 1964, pp. 1–77. Jellinek's writing was translated into English in 1901 (H. Holt and Co., New York, 1901).

Maritain, J., *The Rights of Man and Natural Law*, Charles Scribner's Sons, New York, 1943.

Rivero, J., *Les Libertés publiques*, I, pp. 43–95.

Schnur, R. (ed.), *Zur Geschichte der Erklaerung der Menschenrechte* (see above).

5   UNIVERSALITY OF HUMAN RIGHTS

Capotorti, F., 'Human Rights: The Hard Road Towards Universality', in R. St. J. Macdonald and D. M. Johnston (eds), *The Structure and Process of International Law: Essays in Legal Philosophy, Doctrine and Theory*, M. Nijhoff, Leyden, 1983, pp. 977–1000.

Dupuy, R. J., 'L'universalité des droits de l'homme', in *Studi in onore di G. Sperduti*, Giuffré, Milan, 1984, pp. 539–56.

Graefrath, B., 'The Application of International Human Rights Standards to States with Different Economic, Social and Cultural Systems', in *Bulletin of Human Rights*, United Nations, Geneva, 1985, pp. 7–16.

Hersch, J., 'Les droits de l'homme. Un concept universel', in *Cadmos*, 1981, pp. 18–28.

Imbert, P., *'L'universalité des droits de l'homme*, unpublished paper submitted to the 1989 Strasbourg Colloquy on Universality of Human Rights, 1988.

Milne, A. J. M., *Human Rights and Human Diversity – An Essay in the Philosophy of Human Rights*, State University of New York Press, Albany, NY, 1986.

Przetacznic, F., 'The Socialist Concept of Human Rights: its Philosophical Background and Political Justification', in *Revue Belge de Droit International*, 1977, pp. 238ff.

Tomuschat, C., 'Is Universality of Human Rights Standards an Outdated and Utopian Concept?' in *Das Europa der zweiten Generation-Gedächtnisschrift für C. Sasse*, N. P. Engel Verlag, Kehl-Strasbourg, 1981, vol. II, pp. 585–609.

Tomuschat, C., 'International Standards and Cultural Diversity', in *Bulletin of Human Rights*, pp. 24–35.

Valticos, N., 'Universalité des droits de l'homme et diversité des conditions nationales', in *René Cassin Amicorum discipulorumque liber, I*, Pedone, Paris, 1969, pp. 383–403.

6   THE ROLE OF THE UN

Cassese, A., *International Law in a Divided World*, OUP, Oxford, 1986, pp. 287–316.

Meron, T. (ed.), *Human Rights in International Law*, 1984.

See also Graefrath, B., *Die Vereinten Nationen und die Menschenrechte*, VEB

Deutscher Zentralverlag, Berlin, 1956 and, by the same author, *Menschen-rechte und internationale Kooperation – 10 Jahre Praxis der Internationalen Menschenrechtskomitees*, Akademic-Verlag, Berlin, 1988.

7 THE UNIVERSAL DECLARATION

Adamishin, A. L., 'The Universal Declaration of Human Rights and past, present and future achievement in the field of human rights (the legislative function)' in *European Workshop on the Universal Declaration of Human Rights: Past, Present and Future*, United Nations, New York, 1989, pp. 23–29.

Cassin, R., 'La Déclaration universelle et la mise en oeuvre des droits de l'homme', in *Recueil des cours de l'Académie de Droit International de La Haye*, vol. 79, 1951–II, p. 237.

Graefrath, B., 'The Universal Declaration of Human Rights, 1988', in *GDR Committee for Human Rights Bulletin*, vol. 14, no. 31, 1988, pp. 167–71.

Lauterpacht, H., *International Law and Human Rights* (first published Stevens & Sons, London, 1950), Shoe String, Hamden, 1968.

Morsink, J., 'The Philosophy of the Universal Declaration', in *Human Rights Quarterly*, 1984, pp. 309–34.

See also Hareven, T., *Eleanor Roosevelt: An American Conscience*, Quadrangle Books, Chicago, 1968, pp.231–53; Lash, J. P., *Eleanor: The Years Alone*, New American Library, New York, 1973, pp. 46–72; Johnson, M. J., 'The Contributions of Eleanor and Franklin Roosevelt to the Development of International Protection for Human Rights', in *Human Rights Quarterly*, 9 (1987), pp. 35ff.

Vedel, G., 'La Déclaration universelle des droits de l'homme', in *Droit social*, 1949, pp. 372ff.

8 THE UN COVENANTS

Cohen-Jonathan, G., 'Human Rights Covenants', in R. Bernhardt (ed.), *Encyclopedia of Public International Law*, 8, 1985, pp. 297–303.

Henkin, L. (ed.), *The International Bill of Rights. The Covenant on Civil and Political Rights*, Columbia University Press, New York, 1981.

9 THE HELSINKI DECLARATION

Avangio-Ruiz, G., 'Human Rights and Non-Intervention in the Helsinki Final Act', in *Recueil des cours de l'Académie de Droit International de La Haye*, 1977–IV.

Avangio-Ruiz, G., 'Droits de l'homme et non-intervention: Helsinki, Belgrade, Madrid', in *La communità internationale*, 1980, pp. 453–507.

Buergenthal, T. (ed.), *Human Rights, International Law and the Helsinki Accord*, Allanheld, Osmun and Universe Books, Monclair and New York, 1977.

Cassese, A., 'The Approach of the Helsinki Declaration to Human Rights', in *Vanderbilt Journal of Transnational Law*, 1980, pp. 275ff.

10   THE EUROPEAN SYSTEM FOR THE PROTECTION OF HUMAN RIGHTS

The European Convention on Human Rights

van Dijk, P., *Theory and Practice of the European Convention on Human Rights*, Kluwer, Deventer, 1984.

Drzemczewski, A. and Warbrick, C., 'The European Convention on Human Rights', in *Yearbook of European Law*, 7, 1987, pp. 361ff.

Fawcett, Sir James, *The Application of the European Convention on Human Rights*, Clarendon Press, Oxford, 1987, 2nd edn.

Soyer, J. C. and de Salvia, M., 'Convention européenne des droits de l'homme', in *Jurisclasseur Procédure Pénale*, Litec, Paris, 1987, Appendix and Articles 567–621.

Matcher, F. and Petzold, H. (eds), *Protecting Human Rights: The European Dimension – Studies in honour of Gerard J. Wiarda*, C. Heymans Verlag KC, Cologne, 1988.

The European Social Charter

Harris, H., *The European Social Charter*, Virginia University Press, Charlottesville, Va., 1984.

Jaspers, A. and Betten, L. (eds), *25 Years European Social Charter*, Kluwer, Dewenter, 1988.

Strasser, W., 'The European Social Charter', in *Encyclopedia of Public International Law*, vol. 8, Amsterdam, North Holland, 1985, pp. 211–14.

Valticos, N., 'La Charte social européenne', in *Droit social*, 1963, pp. 466–82.

11   GENOCIDE

General

Dadrian, V. N., 'Factors of Anger and Aggression in Genocide', in *Journal of Human Relations*, vol. 19, 1971, pp. 394–417.

Drost, P. N., *The Crime of State*, II, 'Genocide', Sijthoff, Leyden, 1959.

Falk, R., 'Ecocide, Genocide, and the Nuremberg Tradition of Individual Responsibility', in V. Held, S. Morgenbesser and T. Nagel (eds), *Philosophy, Morality and International Affairs*, OUP, New York, 1974, pp. 123–37.

Horowitz, I. L., *Genocide: State Power and Mass Murder*, Transactions Books, New Brunswick, NJ, 1976.

Horowitz, I. L., *Taking Lives: Genocide and State Power*, Transactions Books, New Brunswick, NJ, and London, 1980.

Kuper, L., *Genocide: Its Political Use in the 20th Century*, Yale University Press, New Haven, Conn., and London, 1981.

Kuper, L., *International Action against Genocide*, Minority Rights Group, Report no. 53, London, 1984.
Kuper, L., *The Prevention of Genocide*, Yale University Press, New Haven, Conn., and London, 1985.
Porter, J. N. (ed.), *Genocide and Human Rights: a Global Anthology*, University Press of America, Washington DC, 1982.
Robinson, N., *The Genocide Convention – A Commentary*, New York, 1960.
Sartre, J. P., 'Le Génocide (1967)', in *Situation, VIII, autour de 1968*, Editions Gallimard, Paris, 1972, pp. 100–24.
Whitaker, B., *Report on Genocide*, UN doc. E/CN.4/sub.2/1985/6 (2 July 1985).

The genocide of Armenians

Bryce, J. and Toynbee, A. J., *The Treatment of Armenians in the Ottoman Empire, 1915–1916*, His Majesty's Stationery Office, London, 1916.
Dadrian, V. N., 'The Common Features of the Armenian and Jewish Cases of Genocide: A Comparative Victimological Perspective', in I. Drapkin and E. Viano (eds), *Victimology: A New Focus, vol. 4, Violence and its Victims*, Lexington Books, Lexington, Mass., 1975, pp. 99–120.
Dadrian, V. N., 'The Role of Turkish Physicians in the World War I Genocide of Ottoman Armenians', in *Holocaust and Genocide Studies*, vol. 1, no. 2, 1986, pp. 169–92.
Tribunal Permanent des peuples, *Le crime de silence – Le génocide des arméniens*, Editions Flammarion, Paris, 1984.

The genocide of the Jews

Arendt, H., *Eichmann in Jerusalem – A Report on the Banality of Evil*, Penguin Books, Harmondsworth, 1976.
Bettelheim, B., *The Informed Heart*, The Free Press, New York, 1960.
Bettelheim, B., *Surviving the Holocaust*, Fontana Paperbacks, London, 1986.
Kogon, E., *The Theory and Practice of Hell: the Concentration Camps and the System Behind Them*, Farrar-Straus, New York, 1950.
Lemkin, R., *Axis Rule in Occupied Europe*, Carnegie Endowment for International Peace, Washington DC, 1944, pp. 82–9.

12   TORTURE

Amnesty International, *Report on Torture*, Duckworth, London, 1973.
Amnesty International, *Torture in the Eighties*, Amnesty International Publications, London, 1984.
Cassese, A., 'A New Approach to Human Rights: The European Convention for the Prevention of Torture', in *American Journal of International Law*, 83, 1989, pp. 128ff.
Danelius, H., 'Torture and Cruel, Inhuman or Degrading Treatment or Punishment', in *Nordic Journal of International Law*, 1989, pp. 172ff.

Duffy, P. J., 'Article 3 of the European Convention on Human Rights', in *International and Comparative Law Quarterly*, 1983, pp. 316ff.

Klayman, B. M., 'The Definition of Torture in International Law', in *Temple Law Quarterly*, 1978, p. 449ff.

Mitscherlich, A., *Die Idee des Friedens und die menschliche Aggressivität – Vier Versuche*, Suhrkamp Verlag, Frankfurt, 1969.

Rodley, N., *The Treatment of Prisoners under International Law*, Clarendon Press, Oxford, 1987, particularly pp. 17–143.

G.P.R., 'Torture and International Crimes', in *The Review of the International Commission of Jurists*, 1976, pp. 41–50.

Spjut, R. J., 'Torture under the European Convention on Human Rights', in *American Journal of International Law*, 1979, pp. 267ff.

13 APARTHEID

Benson, M., *Nelson Mandela*, Penguin, London, 1986.

Chaliand, G., *Où va l'Afrique du Sud?*, Calman-Lévy, Paris, 1986.

Dugard, J., *Human Rights and the South African Legal Order*, Princeton University Press, Princeton, NJ, 1978.

Mandela, N., *The Struggle is My Life*, International Defence and Aid Fund for Southern Africa, London, 1986.

Raoul, M., *Déclaration universelle des droits de l'homme et réalités sud-africaines*, Unesco, Paris, 1983.

Zorgbibe, C., *Les derniers jours de l'Afrique du Sud*, Presses Universitaires de France, Paris, 1986.

14 'FORCED DISAPPEARANCES'

Egeland, J., *Humanitarian Initiative against Political 'Disappearances'*, Henry-Dunant Institute, Geneva, 1982.

Kramer, D. and Weissbrodt, D., 'The 1980 U.N. Commission on Human Rights and the Disappeared', in *Human Rights Quarterly*, 1981, pp. 18–33.

Reoch, R., '"Disappearances" and the International Protection of Human Rights', in *Yearbook of World Affairs*, 1982, pp. 166–81.

Rodley, N., *The Treatment of Prisoners under International Law*, Clarendon Press, Oxford, 1987, pp. 191–218.

United Nations, *Report of the Working Group on Enforced or Involuntary Disappearances*, UN doc. E/CN.4/1985/15 and Add. 1, and E/CN.4/1988/19 (31 Dec. 1987) and Add. 1.

15 UNDERDEVELOPMENT AND THE RIGHT TO FOOD

General

Eide, A., *Rapport sur le droit à une alimentation suffisante en tant que droit de l'homme*, UN doc. E/CN.4/Sub.2/1987/23 (7 July 1987).

Eide, A., Eide, W. B. and Goonatilake, S. (eds), *Food as a Human Right*, the UN Library, Tokyo, 1984.

International Commission of Jurists, *Human Rights and Development*, The Cedar Press, Bridgetown, Barbados, 1978.

Revue sénégalaise de droit, no. 22, December 1977 (special issue on development and human rights).

The Nestlé affair

Bouguerra, M. L., *Les poisons du Tiers Monde*, Editions La Découverte, Paris, 1985.

Buffle, J.-C., *N. . . comme Nestlé*, Editions Alain Moreau, Paris, 1986.

Harrison, P., *L'empire Nestlé*, Editions P. M. Favre, Paris, 1983.

Nestlé contre les bébés? Un dossier réuni par le Groupe de Travail Tiers Monde de Berne, Editions F. Maspéro and Presses Universitaires de Grenoble, Paris, 1978.

Index